HISTORY'S TIMELINE

CRESCENT BOOKS
New York

Editor
Fay Franklin

Authors
Jean Cooke
Ann Kramer
Theodore Rowland-Entwistle

© 1981 by Grisewood & Dempsey
Ltd. Designed and produced by
Grisewood & Dempsey Ltd.,
20-22 Great Titchfield St.,
London W1.

Published 1981 by Ward Lock
Limited, in Great Britain under the
title HISTORY FACTFINDER.
Ward Lock Limited,
47 Marylebone Lane,
London W1M 6AX,
a Pentos company.
Originally published in 1977 as
WORLD OF HISTORY.

This edition is published by
Crescent Books, distributed by
Crown Publishers, Inc.

h g f e d c

Printed in Hong Kong by South
China Printing Co.

**Library of Congress Cataloging
in Publication Data**
Main entry under title:

History's timeline.

Includes index.
1. Civilization – Chronology.
CB69.2.H57 902'.02 81-15222
ISBN 0-517-34000-3

Contents

Early Civilizations   4
The Classical World   18
The Middle Ages   46
The Renaissance   96
The Age of Kings   124
The Age of Revolution   152
Europe the Overlord   174
The Modern World   194
Reference Tables   224
Index   232

Early Civilizations

THIS FIRST PERIOD of history is the longest – and it is also the one about which we know least. It begins about 37,000 years ago, and ends with the 'Golden Age' of Amenhotep III in Egypt, nearly 3500 years ago. Even this long period is only about an eightieth part of the time that Man-like creatures have lived on the Earth – and that itself is only a fraction of Earth's own historical age. If the period that the Earth has existed were one day, then Man would have been in existence for about a minute, and all the history in this book would be compressed into half a second.

Our period begins with the arrival of modern Man in Europe, and the ending of the last Ice Age. Written records of any kind date from only about 5000 years ago, so the chronology of events in the whole of this period is largely a matter of deduction from archaeological finds. But with the aid of new scientific techniques we can build up a picture of Man's development from primitive hunter-gatherers to sophisticated city-dwellers who, even before they could write, had developed complex skills and technologies. These first civilizations grew up independent of one another in fertile river valleys in the Near East, China, and India, where rich harvests produced food surpluses and allowed Man time to think.

A wooden model boat, one of more than 1700 treasures retrieved from Tutankhamun's tomb. Statuettes of people and objects buried with a king were thought to be transformed in the next life to serve him.

Opposite: The sphinx at Giza in Egypt. The head is a portrait of the pharaoh Khafre, c. 2550 BC.
Above: This Assyrian ivory plaque was found at Nimrud, an ancient Assyrian capital. It is thought to have been made about 700 BC and is coloured with enamel and gold leaf.

5

*Below left: Neanderthal Man flourished
about 50,000 years ago.
Below right: Cro-Magnon Man was the
first truly modern man.*

EUROPE

BC		
	40,000	Last Ice Age
	30,000	Neanderthal Man dies out
	20,000	Cave painting flourishes in France and Spain
5000 BC	6000	Neolithic period
	5000	Sea divides Britain from rest of Europe
	3000	Windmill Hill culture in Britain
	2500	Knossos founded by Minoans in Crete
	2000	Bronze Age in northern Europe
	1860	Start of construction of Stonehenge
	1400	Knossos destroyed
	1050	Dorians invade Peloponnesus
1000 BC	994	Teutons move westward to Rhine
	776	First Olympic Games in Greece
	753	Rome founded (traditional)
	660	Byzantium founded
	534	Tarquinius Superbus last king of Rome
	509	Roman republic founded (traditional)
	480	Battles of Thermopylae and Salamis
	477	Athens starts rise to power

WESTERN ASIA

40,000	Cro-Magnon Man moves westward to Europe
8000	Agriculture develops in Middle East
7000	Walled settlement at Jericho
3760	Earliest date in Jewish calendar; traditional date of Creation
3000	Phoenicians settle eastern Mediterranean coast
2500	Indus valley civilization in India
2350	Sumerian empire founded
2150	Aryans invade Indus Valley
1950	End of Ur empire
1830	First dynasty of Babylonian kings
1728	Accession of Hammurabi the Great
1500	Mohenjo-Daro destroyed
1400	Iron Age in western Asia and India
1232	Israelites in Canaan
1193	Troy destroyed by Greeks
1020	Saul, King of Israel
994	David captures Jerusalem
884	Centralized government in Assyria
746	Tiglath-Pilesar III rules Assyria
732	Assyrians overthrow Damascus
722	End of kingdom of Israel
710	Assyrians destroy kingdom of Chaldea
689	Assyrians destroy Babylon
612	Nineveh destroyed
609	End of Assyrian empire
605	Nebuchadrezzar II rules Babylon
600	Windmills grind corn in Persia
563	The Buddha born
559	Cyrus the Great founds Persian Empire
521	Darius I rules Persia

ELSEWHERE

28,000	Man crosses landbridge between Asia and North America
4236	First date in Egyptian calendar
3372	First date in Mayan calendar
3100	First Egyptian dynasty
2800	Old Kingdom in Egypt
2780	First pyramid built in Egypt
2697	Huang-ti Emperor of China
2350	Yao Dynasty in China
2200	Hsia Dynasty in China
	Jomon culture in Japan
1760	Shang Dynasty in China
1730	Hyksos rule Egypt
1570	New Kingdom in Egypt
1361	Accession of Tutankhamun
1304	Accession of Rameses the Great
1122	Chou Dynasty in China
1100	First Chinese dictionary produced
814	Carthage founded by Phoenicians
770	Eastern Chou Dynasty in China
551	Birth of Confucius
500	Bantu-speaking peoples spread in East Africa

Early Civilizations

The Family of Man

Man and modern apes have a strong family resemblance. But we are not descended from the apes; we share with them common ancestors from which we branched off some 12,000,000 years ago.

The earliest 'men' yet found are known as the Australopithecines. Many skulls and other bones of these creatures have been found in Africa. They walked on two legs and made simple tools from pebbles; but we do not regard them as true men because their brains were very small. Early species of true men, belonging to the genus *Homo*, first appeared about 2 million years ago – and for a time seem to have lived alongside the last of the Australopithecines.

The most advanced of these early men is known as *Homo erectus*. Examples have been found in Africa and Asia. *Homo erectus* learned how to use fire for cooking and warmth, and to drive away wild animals. This meant that Man could begin to move into Europe, much of which was covered with ice and all of which was very cold.

Still more advanced were the early species of *Homo sapiens*, which flourished from about 200,000 years ago. One type, Neanderthal Man, was able to live in northern Europe, because his body was specially adapted to survive the intense cold. Where possible, he lived in caves. He developed many different kinds of stone tool, and also buried his dead – a very human act.

Neanderthal Man lived in Europe until about 30,000 years ago. The type of Man who lives today, *Homo sapiens sapiens*, seems to have come into Europe from the Near East. These early people, the Cro-Magnons, decorated their caves with paintings of the animals they hunted.

All these early men lived by hunting, and gathering plants. For tools they had to use stone, bone, and wood. It was not until about 8000 BC that agriculture began.

Pebbles were chipped away to make the first tools.

The First Civilizations

The first civilizations grew up when nomadic hunters and seed-gatherers began to farm the land, and so were able to form settled communities. Where the soil was rich, they could grow enough food to support non-producers like craftsmen and administrators. Probably the earliest civilization grew up in the fertile region between the rivers Tigris and Euphrates, in what is now Iraq – an area known as Mesopotamia from the Greek for 'between the rivers'.

The first people who settled here, about 5000 BC, were the Sumerians. On an agricultural economy they developed a true city life, so they must have understood the technique of specialization or division of labour. Their civilization consisted of a series of city-states, including Uruk and Lagash. These had fine buildings and public water supplies and drainage. The Sumerians devised the first known writing system; from about 3100 BC records were kept on clay tablets, thousands of which have survived. Graves contain treasures demonstrating the wealth and sophistication of the civilization and the skill of its craftsmen.

Many Sumerian traditions lie behind Bible stories. The Tower of Babel was almost certainly one of the great mounds or *ziggurats* Sumerians built for their temples. The Flood is described in the Sumerian *Epic of Gilgamesh*; archaeologists have shown that a great flood overwhelmed the area thousands of years ago.

The Sumerian civilization was gradually absorbed by the Semitic people, who migrated to Mesopotamia from Arabia around 2300 BC and founded the great empires of Assyria and Babylonia.

People of Legend

Greek legends described the magnificent civilization of King Minos of Crete. So when Arthur Evans began to excavate ruins of a hitherto unknown Cretan civilization in 1899, he named it Minoan.

The people of the island of Crete developed a civilization based on the use of bronze long before any other Europeans. Freed from the threat of war by their ships which controlled the neighbouring seas, they built no fortresses but concentrated on the comforts of life. Knossos, their capital city, was founded around 2500 BC.

The Minoan language has survived on about 200 clay tablets, but the script used, known as Linear A, has not yet been fully deciphered. About 300 years after the foundation of Knossos Greek-speakers arrived in the island. They left thousands of tablets written in another script, Linear B. This was deciphered in 1952 and found to be an early form of Greek.

Knossos was eventually destroyed by fire around 1400 BC, and Crete came under the rule of Mycenae, a city in the Peloponnesus, the southern Greek mainland.

Part of the ruins of the palace of Knossos in Crete, reconstructed by Arthur Evans.

BC
40,000 Last Ice Age; Cro-Magnon Man begins to enter Europe from Near East.
30,000 Neanderthal Man dies out.
28,000 First people cross Bering Straits landbridge from Asia to Americas.
20,000 Cave art flourishes at Lascaux, Altamira, and other sites. Man living in Australia.
10,000 Man reaches the tip of South America.
8400 First domesticated dog found in Idaho, USA.
8000 Agriculture gradually develops in Near East; sheep and cattle domesticated.
7000 Walled settlement at Jericho. Pottery develops. Man begins to learn to use metals.
5000 Rising sea level severs last landbridge between Britain and mainland Europe. First settlements in fertile river valleys of Sumer.
4236 First date in ancient Egyptian calendar.
4000 Yang-shao rice farming culture in China.
3760 First date in Jewish calendar.
3372 First date in Mayan calendar.
3100 Menes unites kingdoms of Upper and Lower Egypt, founding 1st dynasty.
3000 Bricks first used in Egyptian and Assyrian cultures.
First cities in Sumer and Egypt. Windmill Hill culture in Britain. Phoenicians settle along eastern coast of Mediterranean. Invention of wheel.
2800 Foundation of the 'Old Kingdom' of Egypt, covering IIIrd to VIth Dynasties.
2780 Zoser becomes ruler of Egypt; his physician Imhotep designs the Step Pyramid at Saqqara, the first pyramid.
2750 Gilgamesh, legendary king of Uruk, Sumeria.
2700 Khufu (Cheops) rules Egypt and builds the Great Pyramid at Giza.
2697 Huang-ti, the 'Yellow Emperor', comes to the throne in China.
2500 Early Minoan civilization in Crete: foundation of Knossos; Indus Valley civilization of India founded.
2350 Yao Dynasty in China; Sargon the Great of Akkad begins the conquest of Sumeria, founding the first great empire.
2250 Yu-shun emperor of China.
2200 Hsia Dynasty of China founded.
2100 The Empire of Ur (to 2000).
Middle Kingdom of Egypt, beginning with the VIIth Dynasty; the patriarch Abraham migrates from Ur, in Mesopotamia; Aryans begin invasion of Indus Valley.
2000 Bronze Age under way in northern Europe; Jomon culture flourishes in Japan.
1950 Sesostris I of Egypt invades Canaan; end of the empire of Ur.

The River People

One of the three oldest civilizations of the world developed in the valley of the river Indus, now in Pakistan. It was unknown until 1921, although in 1856 bricks from mounds of ruins had been used for a railway embankment. Modern research has shown that these bricks are 3500 years old; they came from the ruins of Harappa.

The cities of Harappa and Mohenjo-Daro, with some 100 smaller towns and villages, made up this ancient civilization. Harappa lies about 120 miles (193 km) south-west of Lahore, on a tributary of the Indus called the Davi. Mohenjo-Daro is on the Indus itself, about 200 miles (322 km) north-east of Karachi.

Mohenjo-Daro's buildings were laid out in a checker-board pattern. Many houses and shops have been identified among the ruins. In one corner was a heavily fortified citadel, containing a huge granary. Near it was a large ritual bath.

Artefacts found in the ruins show that the people of the Indus valley were skilled potters, and used the wheel for throwing their wares. They used stone tools, but knives and weapons of copper and bronze. A few bowls and ornamental figures in bronze have also been discovered. The people used a form of picture-writing that has not yet been deciphered.

The Indus Valley civilization was destroyed around 1500 BC by Aryan invaders from the north-west.

The Shang Dynasty

China's history goes back to a distant past where fact and legend are inextricably mixed. By the foundation of the Shang Dynasty around 1760 BC a considerable civilization had already been created. It had arisen in the valley of the Hwang-ho (Yellow River), and spread south, west, and east from that region. The graves of the Shang rulers were found at Anyang, in the province of Honan, hidden under what were known as the 'Mounds of Yin'. From this the dynasty gets its alternative name of Yin.

The Shang people lived by hunting, fishing, and farming. They made wine, and drunkenness was the downfall of some of their emperors. The silk industry was already well established, as were the arts of pottery and metal working. The Shang evolved a form of script, which has been found inscribed on thousands of pieces of bone and tortoiseshell used for divination.

This bronze vessel, called a 'ting', dates from the Shang dynasty. It was used as a container for offerings for sacrifices. Containers like this were often decorated with pictures of what they contained, so it is possible that this 'ting' may have been used in human sacrifices. However, the word for grain is also found on it, so this may have been what it held.

This Etruscan alabaster cinerary urn shows a couple in a covered wagon on their journey to the underworld. Many beautiful Etruscan artefacts survive to this day, but little is known about the people who made them.

The Etruscans

The Etruscans were a mysterious group of peoples who lived in Italy in the region south of the river Arno and north of the river Tiber, then called Etruria and roughly equivalent to modern Tuscany.

No one knows exactly when the Etruscans settled in the area, but it was probably somewhere between 1200 BC and 700 BC. In ancient times the historian Herodotus believed the Etruscans originated in Greece, but some later writers think they may have been of Italian stock. Their language, using an alphabet derived from Greek, was apparently like no other, and it has not yet been deciphered. Their religion differed from those of both Greece and Rome.

Etruria consisted of a dozen city-states. The cities were highly civilized, and they had great influence on the Romans. Indeed, the last three kings of Rome, before the creation of the republic in 509 BC, were Etruscans. There was a long struggle between Etruria and Rome, ending when the Romans conquered Etruria in the 200s BC.

1925 The Hittites conquer Babylon.
1860 Construction of Stonehenge begins in Britain.
1830 First Dynasty of Babylonian kings founded.
1760 Shang Dynasty founded in China.
1730 The Hyksos, a Semitic tribe, begin conquest of Egypt, founding XVth Dynasty.
1728 Accession of Hammurabi the Great of Babylon, author of great Code of Laws.
1570 Beginning of the New Kingdom in Egypt: Hyksos driven out; Temple of Amun at Karnak begun.
1500 Mohenjo-Daro, in Indus Valley, destroyed.
1420 Amenhotep III begins 'golden age' in Egypt.
1400 Knossos, capital of Minoan civilization in Crete, is destroyed by fire; temples at Luxor under construction; Iron Age under way in India and western Asia.
1379 Accession of Amenhotep IV in Egypt; he introduces Sun worship, abolishes all old gods, and takes name Akhenaton after Aton, the Sun-god; period of bad government.
1375 Suppiluliumas becomes king of the Hittites in Asia Minor and begins to make his kingdom into a powerful empire.
1366 Assuruballit I becomes ruler of Assyria and begins Assyrian rise to power.
1361 Boy-king Tutankhamun succeeds Akhenaton; his advisers restore the worship of the old Egyptian gods.
1319 Rameses I founds vigorous XIXth Dynasty in Egypt.
1313 Rameses' son Seti I sets out to reconquer Egyptian lands in Palestine and Syria.
1304 Accession of Rameses II, the Great, of Egypt.
1300 Construction of great rock temples of Abu Simbel begins; oppression of Israelite colony in Egypt. Sidon flourishes as great Phoenician port.
1298 Battle of Qadesh between Rameses II and the Hittites under Mutawallis; both sides claim victory.
1283 Rameses II makes peace with the Hittites.
1275 Shalmaneser I becomes ruler of Assyria, and extends its conquests.
1250 The Exodus: the Israelites under Moses leave Egypt.
1232 Israelites in Canaan: Rameses II's son Merneptah defeats them in battle.
1200 Period of the Judges begins in Israel.
1193 City of Troy is destroyed by Greek armies after a prolonged siege.
1188 Rameses III becomes ruler of Egypt; XXth Dynasty founded with capital at Tanis.
1175 Invasion of Egypt by Confederation of Sea Peoples including Philistines, Greeks, Sardinians, and Sicilians; defeated by Rameses III.

Land of the Nile

The civilization of ancient Egypt depended on the river Nile, which flooded every year, depositing rich alluvial soil along its banks. By means of irrigation canals Egyptians were able to cultivate a long, narrow strip of land on either side of the river – much the same area as the present inhabited part of modern Egypt.

By the 3000s BC the small communities in this region had become combined into two larger states: Lower Egypt, occupying the Nile delta region, and Upper Egypt, which ran south from the delta for about 500 miles (800 km) to where Aswan now stands. About 3100 BC Menes, King of Upper Egypt, conquered Lower Egypt and made the country one.

The rulers of Egypt, known as *pharaohs*, are generally grouped in families, or *dynasties*. There were 30 dynasties between Menes and 332 BC when Alexander the Great conquered the country. The most important periods of Egyptian history are the Old Kingdom (2800–2175 BC), from the IIIrd to VIth dynasties; the Middle Kingdom (2150–1800 BC), covering the XIIth dynasty; and the New Kingdom (1570–1085) from the XVIIIth to XXth dynasties. The Pyramids and the Sphinx date from the Old Kingdom, a period when Egyptian art also reached its peak.

Left: This Chinese figure comes from the Chou period. It shows a juggler balancing a bear on top of a pole. Acts such as this were very popular in China at this time. Opposite: The gold death mask of the Egyptian boy-king Tutankhamun, who died in c. 1352 BC.

The Seafarers

The Phoenicians – probably the greatest seafarers of the ancient world – lived in the Levant, the Mediterranean coastlands of what are now Lebanon, Syria, and Israel. Their principal cities, all ports, included Byblos, Sidon, Beirut, and Tyre, famous for its purple dye. Their golden age was between 1200 BC and 800 BC. During this period their hardy seamen sailed all over the Mediterranean, out into the Atlantic to the 'Tin Isles' (Britain), and even down the western coast of Africa. They founded many trading stations and colonies, of which the most famous was Carthage, near modern Tunis.

Phoenician merchants took the civilization of Babylon and the Near East to the lands bordering the Mediterranean. But the Greek armies of Alexander the Great finally overthrew Tyre and brought Phoenicia to an end in 332 BC. The greatest legacy of the Phoenicians was the alphabet which they invented in the 14th century BC or earlier, and from which the main modern alphabets derived.

1170 Growing power of newly independent Phoenician cities, especially Tyre.
1140 Phoenicians found their first North African colony at Utica, now in Tunisia.
1125 Nebuchadrezzar I, king of Babylon; he holds off renewed attacks by the Assyrians.
1122 Emperor Wu Wang founds Chou Dynasty in China, and establishes feudal system.
1116 Tiglathpileser I becomes ruler of Assyria; he fights off invasions from the north and eventually conquers Babylon.
1065 New Kingdom in Egypt ends with death of Rameses XI; Smendes, a rich merchant, becomes Pharaoh and founds the XXIst Dynasty.
1050 Philistines conquer Israel.
1045 Codron, last king of Athens is killed.
1020 Samuel, last of the Israelite judges, anoints Saul as king of Israel; Saul leads successful rebellion against the Philistines.
1000 Saul is killed at battle of Gilboa; succeeded by David, first as king of Judah, later as king of Israel; after a campaign, David captures Jerusalem and makes it his capital.
Rig Veda, religious text, compiled in India.
961 Death of David: succeeded by his son Solomon.
953 Dedication of Temple at Jerusalem, built by Solomon with help and materials from Hiram of Tyre.
935 Revival of Assyria begins with the accession of Assurdan II; by 860 he and his successors have re-established Assyria's ancient boundaries.
922 Death of Solomon; succeeded by his son, Rehoboam; rebellion against Rehoboam's rule led by Jeroboam: kingdom split into Judah in the south, under Rehoboam, and Israel in the north under Jeroboam.
854 Ahab of Israel, Ben Hadad of Damascus, and Irkhuleni of Hamath lead an allied army to halt Shalmaneser III's advance; supported by Egypt and Jehoshaphat of Judah.
842 Jehu, an Israelite soldier, leads a rebellion against Ahab's son Jehoram, founding a new dynasty in Israel.
814 The Phoenicians found Carthage (literally new town') near their North African colony of Utica.
810 Sammuramat (the Semiramis of legend) rules Assyria as regent for her son Adad-Nirari III.
800 Traditional date for the composition of Homer's epic poems The Iliad and The Odyssey.
783 Jeroboam II King of Israel (to 748); period of prosperity.
776 First definitely dated performance of the Olympic Games in Greece.
770 Eastern Chou Dynasty in China (to 256).

The Hebrews

The Hebrews were descended from nomadic Semites; one of them, Abraham, led his people from Ur on the river Euphrates to Canaan (Palestine) to found a nation dedicated to serving the one God.

In the 1500s one group, the Israelites, settled in Egypt to escape a famine. Later they became mere slaves; during the reign of Rameses II they escaped and returned to Palestine. There they came into conflict with existing settlers, the Canaanites and Philistines. Under King David the Hebrews defeated the Philistines and established their capital at Jerusalem. After the death of David's son Solomon the kingdom split in two, Israel in the north and Judah in the south. Eventually both kingdoms were overrun by the Babylonians and their populations carried off into slavery. When the Persians conquered Babylon in the 500s BC the Hebrews returned to their homeland.

Above: Legend tells that Romulus and Remus were raised by a she-wolf.

Seven Wonders of the World

These were seven large-scale constructions of the ancient world, considered to be the most marvellous sights of the time.

The *Pyramids of Egypt* are the oldest, and lie west of the Nile river. Built of stone blocks, the largest of them — that of Khufu — was 482 feet high (146 m) when built. The *Hanging Gardens of Babylon* were a massive series of roof gardens built by Nebuchadrezzar. The gold and ivory-plated *Statue of Zeus at Olympia* by Phidias stood over 30 feet (9 m) high. *The Temple of Artemis* at Ephesus was famous for its size and art. The *Mausoleum of Halicarnassus*, a monumental tomb in ancient Greek Caria, was crowned by a sculptured chariot and four horses. The *Colossus of Rhodes*, a bronze and iron statue, stood beside the harbour entrance and was over 100 feet tall (30 m). The *Pharos of Alexandria* was the most famous lighthouse of the time. It stood 440 feet high (135 m) and had a ramp leading to the fire on top.

Romulus and Remus

The earliest inhabitants of the region that is now the city of Rome were a group of tribes who occupied an area of about 700 square miles (1800 sq. km) on the southern bank of the river Tiber. They called it Latium, and are known as the Latins. The Palatine hill, near a ford over the river, became their stronghold, and round it grew up a town. The city of Rome was in existence by the 700s BC.

Many years later a legend evolved to account for the foundation of Rome, which traditionally took place in 753 BC. The story goes that twin sons were born to the war-god Mars and one of the Vestal Virgins, Rhea Sylvia. The babies were abandoned but were suckled by a she-wolf. Together they founded a city but then they quarrelled and Romulus killed Remus. The city was then named Rome, after Romulus.

Master K'ung

Confucianism, one of the traditional philosophies of China, was founded by a soldier's son descended from the ancient royal family of Shang. His name was K'ung, and he was widely known as K'ung Fu-tzu, 'Master K'ung'; Confucius is a Latinized version of this name.

K'ung began his career as a granary overseer, but at the age of 22 became a teacher. He would take anyone, however poor, as a student, providing they were keen to learn. The basis of Confucian philosophy was the attainment of goodness for its own sake. K'ung sought a position as an administrator where he could put his theories into practice, but no one would give him such a job.

Confucius is said to have compiled books of poetry, history, music, and etiquette based on traditional teachings. Until the end of the monarchy in China in 1911, Confucian teachings had a great influence on Chinese thought.

The Buddha

The founder of Buddhism, like Confucius, came from a royal family. He was Prince Siddhartha Gautama, son of the rajah of the Sakya clan, and he was born at Lumbini, now in Nepal. Until he was 29 the prince lived a life of luxury, shielded from the unpleasant sides of life. He was happily married, with a young son.

One day he saw in turn a man who was old, one who was sick, and one who was dead; and he began to ponder whether life was an unending cycle of aging, sickness, and death. Adopting a beggar's clothes and way of life, he travelled in search of truth, but found no help from the great teachers of his day. Finally, he decided he must think things out for himself. He sat down under a bo-tree to meditate, and achieved enlightenment, so becoming the *Buddha* or Enlightened One, the name by which he has been known ever since.

The Buddha spent the rest of his long life in teaching his new-found philosophy. The essence of Buddhism is to follow the Noble Eightfold Path to Enlightenment, the eight parts being the right view, motive, speech, action, pursuits, effort, mindfulness, and contemplation.

A head of Buddha, dating from the Gupta period.

753 Traditional date of the foundation of Rome by Romulus and Remus.
743 Sparta begins the First Messenian War to conquer Messenia; ends 716.
732 Assyrian armies overthrow city-state of Damascus.
722 Sargon II of Assyria captures Samaria and brings kingdom of Israel to an end.
     Ethiopian kings rule over Egypt (to 682) – the XXVth Dynasty.
710 The Assyrians destroy the kingdom of Chaldea.
705 Sennacherib King of Assyria (to 682).
701 Sennacherib establishes his capital at Nineveh.
689 Assyrians destroy Babylon and flood the site.
683 Athens ends rule of hereditary kings; replaces them with nine *archons* chosen each year from among the nobles.
682 Judah surrenders to Assyria.
669 Assurbanipal rules as king of Assyria (to 627).
663 Assurbanipal with an Assyrian army sacks Thebes in Egypt.
650 Scythian and Cimmarian raiders sweep over Syria and Palestine.
     Sparta conquers rebellious subjects in the Second Messenian War (to 630).
626 Chaldean general Nabopolassar seizes the throne of Babylon and declares the country independent from Assyria.
621 Dracon introduces Athens' first written laws, noted for their severity.
612 Medes, Babylonians, and Scythians destroy Nineveh.
609 End of the Assyrian Empire.
608 Necho of Egypt defeats and kills Josiah, King of Judah, at the battle of Megiddo.
605 Nebuchadrezzar II, the Great, King of Babylon (to 561).
     Nebuchadrezzar defeats Necho and the Egyptians at Carcemish in Syria; Judah comes under Babylonian rule.
594 Solon becomes sole Archon of Athens; introduces new, milder laws to replace those of Dracon, creates court of citizens and reforms election of magistrates.
586 Nebuchadrezzar II of Babylon sacks Jerusalem and takes the people of Judah into captivity in Babylon.
580 Nebuchadrezzar begins building the Hanging Gardens of Babylon, one of the Wonders of the World.
563 Birth of Prince Siddhartha Gautama, later the Buddah (Enlightened One) (to 483).
559 Cyrus the Great ruler of Persia (to 530); founds the Persian Empire.
551 Birth of K'ung Fu-tzu – Confucius, Chinese philosopher (to 497).

The Persian Empire

Persis – later Persia – was the name given by the Greeks to a region of southern Iran. Its people migrated there from Russia or central Asia some time before the 600s BC. First the Assyrians ruled them, then the Medes until the 500s BC. Then Cyrus persuaded the Persian tribes to unite under his leadership and to rebel against the Medes. Within three years Cyrus had not only freed Persia, but had conquered Media as well.

With a peasant army of skilful archers and cavalry, Cyrus set out on a career of conquest. By his death in battle in 530 BC, Cyrus had conquered the whole of Asia Minor, Babylonia, Syria, and Palestine, and made Persia the world's leading nation. Four years later his son Cambyses had conquered Egypt, and ruled an empire bordered by India in the east and the Mediterranean Sea in the west – an empire built up in just 25 years.

Below: Part of the great staircase at the magnificent Persian city of Persepolis. Below right: Darius III of Persia.

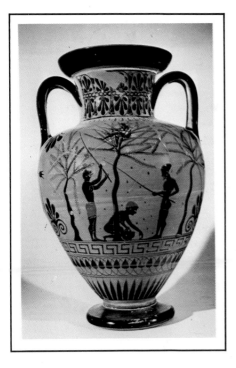

Above opposite: A 6th-century Greek vase, from Corinth, decorated with stylized beasts and birds. Above: An Athenian vase of the same period shows olive gatherers at work. In Athens, the olive tree was regarded as a gift from the goddess Athene, and sacred rites surrounded its cultivation. Below: The impression of a cylindrical Persian seal of about 500 BC, On the left it gives the name of King Darius I in three different languages. The picture shows the King hunting from his chariot.

546 Battle of Sardis; Croesus, last king of Lydia, defeated by Cyprus; Persians overrun Asia Minor.

539 Greeks defeat the Carthaginians in battle. Cyrus conquers Babylonia, and makes Judah and Phoenicia into Persian provinces.

538 Edict of Cyrus allows some Jewish exiles to return to Judah.

534 Tarquinius Superbus (Tarquin the Proud), last king of Rome (to 510).

530 Cambyses, ruler of Persia (to 521).

525 Cambyses conquers Egypt; Egypt under Persian kings until 404.

521 Darius I, ruler of Persia (to 486); Persian Empire divided into 20 satrapies (provinces), of which Egypt is one.

520 Work is resumed on the Temple in Jerusalem (completed 515).

510 Tarquinius Superbus, last king of Rome, overthrown by rebellion.

509 Traditional date for the foundation of the Roman Republic.

508 Cleisthenes reforms the constitution of Athens, and introduces democratic government. The Etruscan ruler Lars Porsena attacks Rome; heroic defence of the bridge over the river Tiber by Horatius Cocles. Rome makes treaty with Carthage.

507 Spartans under Cleomenes try to restore the aristocracy in Athens; Athenians rise and put Cleisthenes back into power.

500 About this time Bantu-speaking peoples begin spreading in East Africa.

499 Ionians rebel against their Persian rulers with Athenian support; revolt ends after Darius sacks Miletus in 494.

496 Romans defeat the Latins at Lake Regillus.

494 Plebeians in Rome revolt, and win political rights from patricians.

493 Treaty between Rome and the other countries of the Latin League, providing for mutual help throughout Latium against Etruscans.

492 Mardonius leads first Persian expedition against Athens; his fleet is shattered by a storm.

490 Second Persian expedition: Athenians defeat the Persians at the battle of Marathon.

486 Xerxes I, the Great ruler of Persia (to 465); he demands tribute from the Greek states, most of which is refused.

480 Third Persian expedition: Xerxes invades Greece with 180,000 men; Greek rearguard is wiped out defending Pass of Thermopylae; Greek fleet defeats Persians at battle of Salamis.

479 Battle of Plataea: Greek army defeats Persian army; Persian fleet is destroyed at Mycale. Athens and Piraeus fortified.

The Classical World

THE SECOND great chapter in Man's history is that of the classical civilizations of Greece and Rome to which the whole of present-day Western civilization owes its origins. Our period begins with the so-called 'Age of Pericles', in which the great Athenian leader Pericles introduced democratic ideas into the government of his city-state. Under his wise leadership the Athenians developed not only the concept of government by the people, but also the basis of all modern science and philosophy. Their writers produced some of the world's greatest plays, their sculptors some of the finest statues.

Ancient Greece gradually declined in power, torn apart by the rivalry of its warring cities, and the leadership of the western world shifted to Rome. The Romans were a harder-headed and more practical people than the Greeks, and in contrast to the independence of individual cities they introduced the concept of a strong central government. Rome ruled one of the greatest empires the world has ever seen, an empire of unified government, good communications, and strong defence. But internal quarrels weakened the empire, and by the end of our period barbarians from the north had overrun Rome, leaving only the Eastern Empire based on Constantinople to carry on the classical tradition.

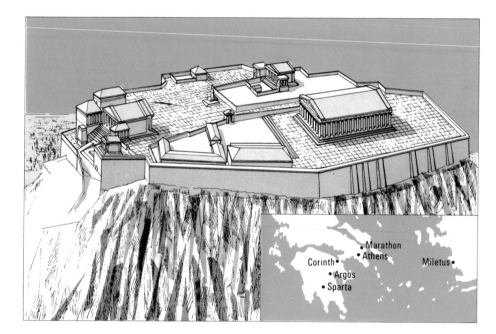

Above: A reconstruction of the Acropolis or high citadel of Athens as it probably appeared in about 400 BC. Inset: Greece and some of its city states.

EUROPE

460	Age of Pericles in Athens (to 429)
	First Peloponnesian War (to 451)
431	Second Peloponnesian War (to 421)
404	Government of the Thirty Tyrants
359	Philip II, King of Macedonia (to 336)
336	Alexander III, King of Macedonia (to 323)
264	First Punic War (to 241)
241	Sicily becomes the first Roman province
206	Scipio defeats the Carthaginians
55	Caesar unsuccessfully invades Britain
51	Caesar completes conquest of Gaul
45	Caesar becomes dictator of Rome
44	Caesar assassinated
23	Augustus resigns consulship; becomes, in effect, Emperor of Rome

AD

37	Caligula, Emperor of Rome (to 41)
54	Nero, Emperor of Rome (to 68)
77	Roman conquest of Britain (to 84)
101	Roman Empire increased to maximum extent (to 107)
212	Edict of Caracalla
250	Emperor-worship made compulsory
285	Diocletian divides Roman Empire
370	Huns from Asia invade Europe
383	Roman legions begin to leave Britain
410	Goths sack Rome
449	Jutes conquer Kent, southern Britain
451	Attila invades Gaul, and Italy (452)
476	End of Western Roman Empire

WESTERN ASIA

465	Artaxerxes I rules Persia (to 424)
445	Nehemiah rebuilds walls of Jerusalem
424	Darius II rules Persia (to 404)
400	Retreat of the Ten Thousand
387	Artaxerxes II takes Greek cities
334	Alexander begins Persian campaign
333	Alexander defeats Darius at Issus
323	Alexander dies at Babylon
305	Seleucid Dynasty founded
301	Ptolemy I rules Palestine
167	Zeus worshipped in Temple at Jerusalem; start of Jewish revolt
141	Jews liberate Jerusalem
63	Pompey captures Jerusalem; annexes Syria and Judaea
53	Battle of Carrhae
47	Antipater becomes procurator of Judaea
37	Herod the Great, King of Judaea (to 4)
5	Jesus born at Bethlehem

AD

4	Death of Herod the Great
30	Crucifixion of Jesus
45	Paul begins missionary journeys
66	Jewish revolt (to 70)
70	Titus destroys Jerusalem
73	Fall of Masada
115	Jewish revolt suppressed by Trajan
132	Bar-Kokhba revolt
135	Final Diaspora
259	Shapur I of Persia captures Valerian
267	Queen Zenobia declares independence
285	Diocletian rules Eastern Roman Empire
306	Constantine I, Emperor in the East (to 337)
313	Edict of Toleration
325	Nicaean Creed adopted
330	Constantinople capital of Roman Empire
350	Persians capture Armenia from Rome
379	Theodosius I Emperor in East (to 395)

FAR EAST

AFRICA AND ELSEWHERE

470	Hanno sails down African coast
450	Herodotus visits Egypt
c. 400	Navigation advances among Pacific islands
343	Artaxerxes III conquers Egypt
332	Alexander the Great conquers Egypt

FAR EAST

327	Alexander begins invasion of India
321	Maurya Dynasty in northern India (to 184)
304	Seleucus cedes his claim on India
300	State of Choson formed in northern Korea
247	Asoka rules Maurya Empire (to 236)
221	Ch'in Dynasty in China (to 207)
214	Construction of Great Wall of China
202	Han Dynasty in China (to AD9)
184	Sunga Dynasty in India (to 72)
140	Wu Ti rules China (to 86)
86	Disorder follows death of Wu Ti

AFRICA

305	Ptolemy I proclaimed Pharaoh
c. 300	Maya civilization in Yucatan and farther south in Central America
149	Third Punic War (to 146); Carthage ruined
51	Cleopatra VII and Ptolemy XII rule Egypt
47	Destruction of the Library at Alexandria
36	Antony marries Cleopatra
30	Antony and Cleopatra commit suicide; Egypt declared a Roman province

AD

9	Wang Mang usurps throne of China
25	Later Han Dynasty in China (to 220)
43	Ma Yuan conquers Tonkin and Annam
58	Ming Ti introduces Buddhism into China
78	Second Kushana Dynasty in India (to 96)

AD

109	Gotamiputa Sri Satakani rules Deccan (to 132)
189	Hsien Ti rules China (to 220)
220	Period of Three Kingdoms in China (to 264)
230	Sujin, first known ruler of Japan
265	Western Chin Dynasty in China (to 317)

115	Jews revolt in Egypt and North Africa; Trajan suppresses rebellion
130	Hadrian visits Egypt; new capital founded at Antinopolis
180	First African Christians martyred

317	China again divided (to 589)
320	Gupta Dynasty in northern India (to 535)
330	Samudragupta Emperor of India (to 375)
361	Empress Jingo of Japan invades Korea (to 390)
372	Buddhism introduced into Korea
407	First Mongol Empire (to 553)

396	St Augustine becomes Bishop of Hippo
c. 400	Incas established on parts of South American Pacific coast
429	Vandal kingdom in northern Africa (to 535)
439	Vandals capture Carthage

465	White Huns dominate northern India

Even before the rise of the ancient Greeks, the Olmecs had established a great civilization around the Gulf of Mexico. They laid this ceremonial pavement in the shape of a jaguar mask.

Left: A jewelled cross, symbol of Christianity, from Burgos, Spain. Christianity became widespread after recognition in the 4th century.

A street in Pompeii, preserved by the ashes of the volcanic eruption which buried the city in AD 79. More than half the city has now been excavated.

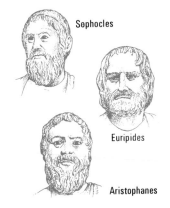

Sophocles

Euripides

Aristophanes

Father of Democracy

One of the most influential men in the history of Athens was neither a king nor a dictator. He was Pericles, a wealthy man of good family, who became the leader of 'the people's faction', a democratic political party not unlike those of today. By force of personality Pericles came to have control over the assembly of citizens, the *Ekklesia*. The only office he held was that of one of the city-state's ten generals, to which he was elected every year.

Pericles was a champion of democracy, the rule of the people by the people, and he has been described as the 'Father of Democracy'. Under his leadership the assembly took power away from the *Areopagus*, a council of aristocrats, and opened the offices of state to any citizen, no matter how poor he might be.

During the 'Age of Pericles' Athens became not only a democratic state but also one of the most beautiful cities in the world. In the 30 years in which Pericles controlled their destinies the Athenians produced their finest architecture, sculptures, and plays.

Pericles died of the plague in 429 BC, at the age of about 66.

Philosophy and Science

Philosophy and science were created by the wise men of ancient Greece, and in those days the two subjects were one and the same. It was the efforts of the philosophers to discover basic truths which led them to scientific observation.

The earliest Greek philosophers, such as Thales and Democritus, tried to decide what the nature of the universe was based on, and whether it was static or changing. The Sophists, such as Protagoras and Gorgias, questioned whether truth existed or was just a matter of personal opinion.

Socrates, probably the greatest of all Greek philosophers, argued that truth did exist, and that moral virtue was an essential for a perfect life. His teachings survive in the works of his famous pupil Plato, who believed that ideal forms exist apart from the everyday world.

Plato's chief pupil Aristotle (who was tutor to Alexander the Great) developed a system of logic, and also began the systematic study of biology. He believed in a god as the creator of all things. His works were studied in western Europe for 2000 years and his views were accepted without question. Later philosophers who founded branches of modern science included the mathematicians Euclid and Hipparchus, and the physical scientists Archimedes and Hero of Alexandria.

BC

470 The Carthaginian leader Hanno sails down the African coast as far as Cameroon.

465 Artaxerxes I rules Persia (to 424).

460 Egyptians rebel against Persian rule. 'Age of Pericles' in Athens (to 429).
First Peloponnesian War between Athens and Sparta (to 451).

450 Herodotus, first historian, visits Egypt.
The Twelve Tables: wooden tablets on which the laws of Rome are written.
Carthage begins to develop new trading centres along north and west African coasts.

449 Sacred War between Sparta and Athens over control of the oracle at Delphi (to 448).

447 Athenians begin building the Parthenon.

446 Athens and Sparta conclude the Thirty Years' Peace.

445 Nehemiah the Prophet rebuilds the walls of Jerusalem.

440 Plebeians in Rome win the right to marry patricians.

431 Second Peloponnesian War (to 421).

430 Epidemic of plague breaks out in Athens.

429 Pericles dies of the plague; the Acropolis is completed. Birth of philosopher Plato.

424 Xerxes II of Persia assassinated. Darius II ruler of Persia (to 404).

421 The Peace of Nicias ends war between Athens and Sparta.

415 War between Athens and Sparta breaks out again.

413 Athenian attack on Sicily fails.

411 Revolution in Athens: 'Government of the 5000' seizes power, but democracy is soon restored.

409 Carthage begins invasion of Sicily.

407 Alcibiades, Athenian general, quells revolt in subject states.

406 Athenian fleet defeats a Spartan fleet at the battle of Arginusae.

405 Lysander of Sparta defeats the Athenian fleet off Aegospotami.

404 Artaxerxes II ruler of Persia (to 359).
Amyrtaeus of Sais king of Egypt (to 399); the XXVIIIth Dynasty.
Spartans capture Athens; Athenian hero Alcibiades is assassinated in exile.
Short-lived Government of the Thirty Tyrants in Athens.

403 Pausanius restores democracy in Athens.

400 Greek army under Xenophon is defeated at Cunaxa in revolt against Artaxerxes II of Persia: 'Retreat of the Ten Thousand'.

399 Greek philosopher Socrates is condemned to death for heretical teaching.

Sparta and Athens

The history of ancient Greece from the 800s BC until Philip II of Macedonia conquered it in 338 BC is one of rival city-states. First one city, then another became the leading state. The chief cities included Sparta, Thebes, Athens, Olympia, Corinth, and Argos. Of these, Sparta and Athens were the most important.

Sparta, in the south-eastern part of the Peloponnesus, conquered neighbouring Messenia in the 700s BC, and by 200 years later led an association of its other neighbours, the Peloponnesian League. In the Peloponnesian War of the 400s Sparta defeated Athens, and virtually ruled all Greece. But in 371 BC the other states rose in revolt, and Sparta was overthrown, though it remained powerful for another 200 years.

Athens was Sparta's main rival for power, and led the Greek city-states in fighting off the Persian invasion in 480 BC. Even after it lost its leading position to Sparta in the 400s, Athens remained the cultural leader of Greece, a place it occupied until the Macedonian conquest and the Roman conquest which followed it.

Roman Class Warfare

Class warfare was rife in ancient Rome, and particularly in the early days of the Republic. The ruling class consisted of *patricians*, whose name comes from the Latin word for father, *pater*, because being a patrician was something inherited from one's parents. For centuries the patricians held all the high offices of state.

Their rivals were the *plebeians*, from the Latin *plebs*, the masses. The plebeians were the peasants, the workers, and the traders. For long they had no right to hold office. But by the 200s BC the plebeians had won political equality with the patricians. Eventually the *nobiles*, a new group drawn from both older classes who derived their power from their wealth, replaced the patricians as the ruling class.

A house like this might be found in any of the towns of the Roman Empire, but its open design is most suited to the warmth of the Mediterranean lands. Visitors would enter the house from the street through a passage, to be received in the inner courtyard called the atrium. This was the centre of the home; grouped around it were bedrooms, storerooms, the dining-room (triclinium) and reception-room (tablinium). The compluvium, a hole in the roof, admitted plenty of light and air, and rain – stored in the pool beneath.

1 atrium
2 tablinum
3 triclinium
4 compluvium
5 kitchen
6 peristyle

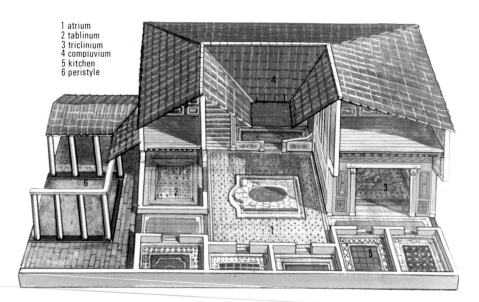

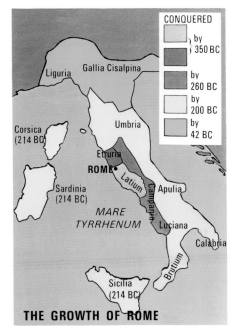

CONQUERED

▢ by
} 350 BC

▢ by
260 BC

▢ by
200 BC

▢ by
42 BC

Liguria   Gallia Cisalpina

Corsica   Umbria
(214 BC)

Etruria

ROME●

Sardinia   Latium   Apulia
(214 BC)

MARE
TYRRHENUM   Luciana   Campania

Calabria

Sicilia   Brutium
(214 BC)

THE GROWTH OF ROME

*Above: Growth of Rome as a kingdom and a
republic.*

The Latin League

The Latin League was a loose federation of
the tribes and cities of Latium – the part of
Italy just south of the river Tiber. During
the 400s BC, the members had a joint army,
and elected a dictator each year to command
it. As Rome grew in power, there were ten-
sions within the League, and in 358 BC a
treaty was signed giving Rome more say in
the elections than the others. In 340 BC the
other cities revolted. The Roman victory at
the battle of Trifanum (338 BC) ended the
war, and the League was dissolved. Rome's
domination of Italy was now assured.

395 Athens, Thebes, Corinth, and Argos form
coalition against Sparta; Lysander killed in
battle.
394 Battle of Coronae: Sparta defeats the coalition.
393 Treaty between Salamis, in Cyprus, and Egypt.
391 Romans under the dictator Marcus Furius
Camillus subjugate the Etruscans.
390 Gauls under Brennus sack Rome, but fail to
capture the Capitol.
387 Artaxerxes II of Persia captures Greek cities in
Asia Minor.
386 Spartan ruler Antalcidas negotiates peace
with Persia, and forces other Greek states to
agree to it.
380 Last native Egyptian dynasty, the XXXth (to
343).
371 The Athenian League and Sparta make peace.
370 Thebes forms the Arcadian League against
Sparta (to 362).
366 First plebeian council elected in Rome.
359 Philip II, King of Macedonia (to 336).
Artaxerxes III ruler of Persia (to 336).
355 Third Sacred War (to 346), begins when
Phocians seize Delphi and use the oracle
funds to raise an army; Macedonia fights
against Athens. Alexander the Great born.
351 Persian invasion of Egypt fails.
350 Jewish revolt against the Persians fails.
346 Peace of Philocrates: Athenian statesman
Philocrates leads a delegation to sue for peace
from Macedonia.
343 Artaxerxes III of Persia leads an army into
Egypt and conquers it.
Persian rule in Egypt. The XXXIst Dynasty (to
332).
339 The Fourth Sacred War (to 338): Philip of
Macedonia conquers Greece.
338 Darius III, ruler of Persia (to 330).
336 Assassination of Philip of Macedonia.
Alexander III (the Great), son of Philip and
Olympias, king of Macedonia (to 323).
Alexander crushes a revolt by Athens, Thebes,
and other Greek cities.
334 Alexander begins campaign against Persia;
defeats Darius III at the river Granicus in Asia
Minor.
333 Alexander defeats Darius again at the battle of
Issus, capturing the Persian queen and her
children; Alexander refuses Darius's offer of
ransom and part of his empire. Alexander
captures Tyre; end of Phoenician empire.
332 Alexander invades and conquers Egypt; foundation of Alexandria.
331 Renewal of the Persian campaign: Alexander
defeats Darius at Arbela; end of the Persian
Empire.

The Classical World

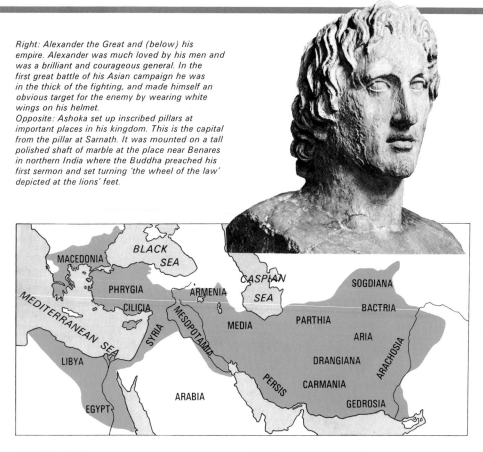

Right: Alexander the Great and (below) his empire. Alexander was much loved by his men and was a brilliant and courageous general. In the first great battle of his Asian campaign he was in the thick of the fighting, and made himself an obvious target for the enemy by wearing white wings on his helmet.

Opposite: Ashoka set up inscribed pillars at important places in his kingdom. This is the capital from the pillar at Sarnath. It was mounted on a tall polished shaft of marble at the place near Benares in northern India where the Buddha preached his first sermon and set turning 'the wheel of the law' depicted at the lions' feet.

The World Conqueror

Alexander the Great was the remarkable child of remarkable parents. His father, Philip II of Macedonia, was an athletic, impulsive, hard-drinking man; his mother, Olympias, was a mystic and an ardent worshipper of the god Dionysus.

Alexander became king at the age of 20. Quelling a rebellion by other Greek city-states under Macedonian rule, he set out to conquer Persia. His first campaign against the Persians, in 334 BC, gave him control of Asia Minor (modern Turkey). The following year he routed the Persian King Darius III. In the next year he conquered Egypt, and 331 BC saw him completing the conquest of Persia.

For a year or two Alexander was busy in a series of short, swift campaigns consolidating his new empire, but in 327 he led his armies over the Hindu Kush mountains into the valley of the river Indus to conquer India. At this his war-weary troops struck, and Alexander had to return to Babylon, which he had made his capital. There he died of malaria, aged not quite 33, and his great empire was soon divided between his generals.

An Empire in India

The first great empire in India was founded in 321 BC by a shadowy warrior, Chandragupta Maurya. He was commander-in-chief of the army of Magadha, or South Bihar, then under the rule of the Nanda dynasty. Chandragupta led a revolt which failed, and fled to take refuge and counsel with Alexander the Great, then in north-western India. He then made another attack on the Nanda king (possibly with Greek support), killed him, and ascended the throne.

Chandragupta united northern India, and his empire extended from Bengal to the Hindu Kush on the borders of Afghanistan. In 305 BC he repelled an attempted invasion by Seleucus Nicator, one of Alexander's generals who had taken over the eastern part of the Macedonian empire.

The most notable of the Maurya emperors was Chandragupta's grandson, Asoka, who reigned from 247 BC to 236 BC. Asoka became a Buddhist, and did a great deal to spread Buddhism by means of missionaries.

330 Darius is murdered; Alexander in complete control of Persia.

327 Alexander begins invasion of India.

326 Alexander wins battle of the Hydaspes; but his soldiers refuse to go any farther east, and he has to retreat.

323 Alexander dies at Babylon; his generals divide his empire among themselves.
Ptolemy satrap (governor) of Egypt.
Birth of Euclid.

321 Chandragupta founds the Maurya Dynasty in northern India; it lasts until 184.

320 Ptolemy captures Jerusalem; Libya becomes an Egyptian province.
Birth of Theocrites.

316 Olympias, mother of Alexander the Great, murdered in revenge for killings she had ordered.

312 Seleucus, one of Alexander's generals, begins to take control in Syria.
The Roman censor Appius Claudius begins building the Appian Way from Rome to Capua.

310 The Etruscans join the Samnites in an attack on Rome, but are defeated at Lake Vadimo.

307 Two of Alexander's generals ruling in Greece, Antigonus I and Demetrius I, take the title of king; the other governors follow suit.

306 Trade treaty between Rome and Carthage.

305 Ptolemy I takes the title of king in Egypt, and is soon proclaimed pharaoh; Seleucus I becomes king of Babylon, founding the Seleucid dynasty.
Agathocles, tyrant of Syracuse in Sicily, makes peace with Carthage after a heavy defeat and is allowed to take the title of king.

304 Seleucus cedes his claim on India to Chandragupta in exchange for 500 elephants.
Rome makes peace with the Samnites and its other enemies; gains area around Naples.

301 Antigonus I is killed in battle of Issus against Seleucus I and his allies; Seleucus rules Syria and Ptolemy I rules Palestine.

300 State of Choson is formed in northern Korea.
Treaty between Rome and Carthage.

298 Third Samnite War ends in 290 in Roman victory in central Italy.

285 Ptolemy II Philadelphus rules Egypt (to 247).

276 Ptolemy II marries his sister Arsinoe.
Antigonus II Gonatus rules Greece (to 239).

272 Antigonus defeats invasion by Pyrrhus of Epirus.

264 First Punic War between Rome and Carthage (ends 241).

254 Rome takes Panormus in Sicily from Carthage.

250 Hebrew scriptures translated into Greek.

247 Ptolemy III rules Egypt (to 221).

The Ch'in

China, the name by which that country is known by other nations, comes from a dynasty which ruled the land for only 14 years. The state of Ch'in in the north-west of the country was the most powerful in China in the 200s BC. Six other states opposed it, but the rulers of Ch'in and their diplomats were both wily and treacherous. They divided the other states by promises, which were not kept, and threats, which were, so that the Ch'in received territory as peace offerings.

Above: A Chinese gilt bronze leopard with garnet eyes, made during the Han dynasty (late 2nd century BC), a period noted for its art.

There is an old Chinese proverb: 'To give away land to appease the Ch'in is like putting out a fire by piling wood on it.' By 221 BC the Ch'in had conquered all their rivals, and their ruler, Shih Huang Ti, became emperor. He styled himself 'the first emperor', and indeed he was the first to rule over a united empire. He reorganized the government, sweeping away the feudal system of his predecessors and bringing everything under his personal rule. He standardized everything he could, from the Chinese script to weights and measures and the gauge of wagon wheels. He had all books and records burned that did not relate to Ch'in achievements, and killed scholars who opposed him. Finally, he had the Great Wall of China constructed to safeguard the country against invasion from the north.

Shih Huang Ti dreamed of a dynasty that would last 10,000 generations. But when he died after nine years his throne was inherited by a weakling, Tsu Ying. Unable to continue his father's tyranny, he died in a bloody rebellion, and the Ch'in dynasty perished with him.

The figure of a woman from the Ch'in dynasty (221–207 BC). The Ch'in dynasty marked a turning point in Chinese history.

This coin, struck by the Carthaginians in Spain, shows an elephant and its keeper. Hannibal took 37 elephants from Spain, across the Pyrenees and Alps, into Italy.

Hannibal

Hannibal (247–183 BC), one of the greatest generals in history, was the son of another famous Carthaginian general, Hamilcar Barca. When the Second Punic War broke out in 218 BC Hannibal decided to take the fighting into Italy. Braving incredible difficulties and hardships, he led an army of almost 60,000 men, together with 37 elephants, across the Pyrenees, over the river Rhône by a pontoon bridge, and through the Little St Bernard Pass into Italy. In two years he won three major victories over the Romans. But lack of reinforcements left him with gradually weakening forces, while the Romans turned their attention to attacks on Carthage itself.

In 204 BC Hannibal was recalled, and in 202 was defeated by Scipio Africanus at Zama near Carthage. Under Roman pressure the Carthaginians banished him, and he fled to Crete. There the Romans pursued him, and rather than become their prisoner he took his own life.

247   Asoka rules the Maurya Empire in India (to 236), and becomes a Buddhist.
Devanampiya Tissa rules Sri Lanka (to 207) and adopts Buddhism under Asoka's influence.

241   Peace between Rome and Carthage: Carthage surrenders Sicily, which becomes the first Roman province.

240   Revolt of Carthaginian mercenaries; crushed by Hamilcar Barca in 238

238   Carthaginians begin conquest of Spain.

225   Romans defeat Celts at Telamon in Italy.

223   Antiochus III, the Great, ruler of Babylonian empire (to 187).

221   Ch'in Dynasty in China (to 207), from which the country takes its name.
Ptolemy IV Philopater rules Egypt (to 203).
Philip V rules Macedonia (to 179).

218   Second Punic War between Rome and Carthage (ends 201). Carthaginian general Hannibal leads army from Spain over the Alps to invade Italy, defeating Publius Cornelius Scipio at river Ticinus, and Sempronius Longus at river Trebia.

217   Hannibal annihilates a Roman army at Lake Trasimene.

216   Hannibal wins another great victory at Cannae.

215   First Macedonian War: Philip of Macedonia attacks Rome in support of Carthage; ends in Peace of Phoenice in 205.
Roman general Marcus Claudius Marcellus defeats Hannibal at Nola.

214   Construction of Great Wall of China begins.
Marcellus begins conquest of Sicily from the Carthaginians; completed 210.

206   Publius Cornelius Scipio the Younger defeats the Carthaginians in Spain.

203   Ptolemy V Epiphanes rules Egypt (to 181); Rosetta Stone recording his accession carved.

202   Han Dynasty in China (to AD 9), founded by Liu Pang.

200   Second Macedonian War (ends 196): Greeks with Roman support rebel against Macedonian rule; Philip is forced to surrender Greece.

192   Syrian War (to 189): Antiochus III defeated in war with Rome.

184   Sunga Dynasty in India founded by Pushayanitra.

183   Hannibal commits suicide to avoid being handed over to the Romans.

181   Ptolemy VI Philomator rules Egypt (to 145).

179   Perseus, son of Philip V, King of Macedonia; continues the war with Rome until 167.

175   Antiochus IV Epiphanes, King of the Seleucid Empire (to 163).

171   Third Macedonian War (to 167): Macedonians under Perseus again attack Rome.

The Punic Wars

The Punic Wars were three contests between Rome and Carthage, the great North African city founded by the Phoenicians. Their name comes from *Punus*, a Latin word meaning a Carthaginian. The cause of the wars was commercial rivalry in the Mediterranean Sea.

The First Punic War (264–241 BC) was a quarrel for control over Sicily. The Romans won and made Sicily Rome's first province.

The Second Punic War (218–201 BC) arose because Rome resented Carthaginian expansion in Spain, and was angry at the destruction of Saguntum (a town allied to Rome) by the Carthaginian general Hannibal. Hannibal met the Roman challenge by invading Italy, where he remained until 204 BC. While he was still there the Roman general Publius Cornelius Scipio invaded Spain and drove the Carthaginians out of the country. The war ended after the destruction of the Carthaginian army at the battle of Zama in North Africa.

The Third Punic War (149–146 BC) flared up when Carthage attacked Rome's ally, King Massinissa of Eastern Numidia (now eastern Algeria). A Roman army invaded Africa and besieged Carthage for two years. Finally the Romans stormed the city and destroyed it utterly.

Opposite: Julius Caesar (100–44 BC) rose to power as a general and eventually became dictator of the Roman Empire. His many victories, and moves such as almost doubling army pay, made him extremely popular with his armies who supported his growing power.

Below: A Roman army camp. The camps of the frontier legions gradually became more permanent until real towns grew up around them.

The Roman Army

The might of Rome was based on its army, a superb, well-drilled fighting force whose discipline and weapons proved superior to those of most of their foes.

The basis of the army was the legion, a body varying in size but consisting at the time of Augustus of about 6000 men, all Roman citizen volunteers serving for 20 years. Sub-divisions of the legion were the maniple, of which there were 30, and the century – 2 to a maniple. The main officers were the centurions, each in charge of 100 men – hence the name *century*. But the size of the century varied in later years; under Diocletian in the AD 200s the strength of a legion was as low as 2000 men.

Each legion was supported by an auxiliary force of conscripted non-Romans, of about the same strength. The total strength of the army varied, but was 28 legions under Augustus. The legions were moved from place to place according to the needs of defence. Legions tended to be loyal to their own generals, and this support gave popular generals such as Julius Caesar great power.

170 Antiochus IV invades Egypt and captures Ptolemy VI; Egyptians proclaim his younger brother Ptolemy VIII Euergetes king; Antiochus withdraws and the brothers reign jointly.
168 Battle of Pydna: Romans defeat and capture Perseus.
167 Antiochus IV begins persecution of the Jews: worship of Zeus in the Temple at Jerusalem. Jews under Judas Maccabaeus revolt against Antiochus until 164; Jewish worship restored.
160 Judas Maccabaeus killed in battle against the Syrians. Jonathan Maccabaeus, younger brother of Judas, leader of the Jews (to 143).
157 Judaea becomes an independent principality.
149 Fourth Macedonian War until 148: Macedonia becomes a Roman province.
Third Punic War (ends 146): Romans destroy Carthage.
145 Ptolemy VII Neos Philopator, ruler of Egypt, under regency of his mother, Cleopatra II. Ptolemy VIII Euergetes seizes the throne (to 116), marrying first Cleopatra II and then her daughter, Cleopatra III.
143 Simon Maccabaeus, elder brother of Judas and Jonathan, leader of the Jews (to 134).
141 Jerusalem liberated by the Jews: Judaea is proclaimed an independent kingdom.
140 Wu Ti, 'Martial Emperor', of China (to 86).
135 First Servile War (to 132): revolt of Roman slaves in Sicily crushed.
134 John Hyrcanus, son of Simon Maccabaeus, ruler of Judaea (to 104).
116 Ptolemaic empire is split up under will of Ptolemy VIII: years of strife follow.
111 War begins between Rome and Jugurtha, King of Numidia in northern Africa.
106 Gaius Marius elected consul; sent to Africa.
108 Emperor Wu Ti of China conquers Choson. Celtic Cimbri ravages Gaul.
105 Marius and Lucius Cornelius Sulla defeat Jugurtha of Numidia, who is taken to Rome and killed.
104 Aristobulus I, King of Judaea (to 103).
103 Alexander Jannaeus, King of Judaea (to 76). Second Servile War in Rome (ends 99).
91 War between Rome and Italian cities; civil war in Rome; Sulla defeats Marius.
90 Revolt of Pharisees in Judaea.
89 Roman army under Sulla regains control of Italy: all Italians granted Roman citizenship.
88 First Mithridatic War (to 84): Rome against Mithridates IV Eupator, King of Pontus. Civil war in Rome (to 82): Sulla victorious.
87 Sulla defeats Mithridates and takes Athens. Death of Emperor Wu Ti leads to period of disorder in China.

Cleopatra

The last member of the Ptolemaic Dynasty to rule Egypt was the most remarkable: Cleopatra VII, daughter of Ptolemy XII. A highly intelligent woman of enormous charm and few morals, she was of Greek and Macedonian descent.

Cleopatra was 18 when she became queen, marrying – according to Egyptian custom – her younger brother, the ten-year-old Ptolemy XIII. A quarrel between the two was settled in 47 BC by the arrival in Egypt of the Roman general Julius Caesar, who killed Ptolemy in battle. Cleopatra became Caesar's mistress and went to Rome with him, though nominally she married an even younger brother, Ptolemy XIV.

After Caesar was murdered in 44 BC, Cleopatra went back to Egypt. Ptolemy XIV died and Cleopatra ruled jointly with Ptolemy XV, her son by Caesar, often known as Cesarion.

Three years later Caesar's friend and fellow general Marcus Antonius (Mark Antony) encountered Cleopatra and fell under her spell; they had twin children, Alexander Helios and Cleopatra Selene. In 36 BC he married her to gain the Egyptian throne – though he already had a wife, the sister of Caesar's heir Gaius Octavius (Octavian). Octavius revenged her by defeating the fleet of Antony and Cleopatra at Actium. Antony committed suicide. Octavius, as the new ruler, was also prepared to marry Cleopatra, but she preferred to kill herself. Octavius had Cesarion and Alexander Helios killed. Cleopatra Selene married the king of Numidia; their son Ptolemy, last of the line, was killed by Caligula.

The 'Aqueducts of Paradise' in Smyrna, Turkey, built during the Roman occupation. Romans were superb engineers and builders of public works like this, and the spread of the Empire (along their sturdy roads) resulted in Roman structures being found in every Mediterranean country.

The Triumvirates

A triumvirate is a group of three people in power or authority, and there were two such triumvirates in Roman history.

The First Triumvirate was formed by three distinguished Roman generals, Marcus Licinius Crassus, Gnaeus Pompeius (Pompey), and Julius Caesar. The three agreed to rule Rome together, though at the time the triumvirate was formed only Caesar held the key post of consul. The

coalition ended in civil war in which Caesar defeated Pompey, Crassus having died in a previous battle.

The Second Triumvirate was formed in 43 BC after Caesar's assassination. Its members were Caesar's friend Marcus Antonius (Mark Antony), his great-nephew and heir Gaius Octavius (Octavian), and Marcus Lepidus. This triumvirate also ended in civil war, in which Octavius defeated Marcus Antonius at the battle of Actium in 31 BC.

83 Second Mithridatic War (to 81): the Romans successfully invade Pontus.
82 Sulla becomes dictator of Rome.
78 Death of Sulla: revolt of Marcus Aemilius Lepidus, who is defeated by Gnaeus Pompeius (Pompey the Great).
76 Salome Alexandra rules Judaea (to 67).
74 Third Mithridatic War (to 61): Mithridates annexes Bithnyia, which Rome claims.
73 Lucius Licinius Lucullus with a Roman army defeats Mithridates and occupies Pontus.
Third Servile War (to 71): Spartacus leads a revolt of slaves and gladiators, which is crushed by the consuls Pompey and Marcus Licinius Crassus.
67 Hyrcanus II rules Judaea; civil war with brother Aristobulus II.
65 Pompey with a Roman army invades Syria and conquers Palestine.
63 Pompey captures Jerusalem, annexes Syria. Death of Aristobulus II, King of Judaea; Pompey annexes Judaea.
Mithridates VI of Syria commits suicide.
Hyrcanus II high priest of Judaea (to 40).
61 Gaius Julius Caesar, nephew of Marius and governor of Spain, wins first major victories.
60 First Triumvirate formed to rule Rome: Pompey, Crassus, and Caesar.
58 Caesar appointed governor of Gaul.
55 Caesar conquers northern Gaul, and unsuccessfully attempts to invade Britain.
54 Second invasion of Britain by Romans under Caesar: Cassivellaunus, powerful British leader, agrees to pay tribute to Rome.
53 Battle of Carrhae: Crassus is killed fighting the Parthians.
52 Pompey appointed sole consul in Rome.
Vercingetorix leads the Gauls in revolt; is crushed by Caesar.
51 Cleopatra VII and her brother Ptolemy XIII become joint rulers of Egypt.
Caesar completes the conquest of Gaul, and writes *De Bello Gallico*.
50 Political manoeuvring between Caesar and Pompey; Pompey's supporters attempt to thwart Caesar's return to the consulship.
49 The Senate orders Caesar to give up his command in Gaul; Caesar crosses the river Rubicon into Italy, a gesture of defiance starting a civil war; Pompey flees to Greece.
48 Caesar defeats Pompey at Pharsalia in Greece.
47 Cleopatra orders Pompey to be murdered; Caesar conquers Cleopatra's enemies and makes her his mistress.
Antipater becomes procurator of Judaea, and his son Herod governor of Galilee.

Far left: The first Roman emperor, Caesar Augustus (2 BC–AD 14).
Left: The Roman orator Marcus Tullius Cicero (106–43 BC). A statesman and lawyer, he was famous for his eloquence and administrative ability. He made a series of speeches in which he tried to warn the Roman public about the ambitious Mark Antony. Eventually, Mark Antony had him killed.

The Birth of Christianity

Jesus Christ was born in Bethlehem in the Roman vassal kingdom of Palestine in the reign of Herod the Great. Since Herod died in 4 BC, Jesus must have been born before that date – probably in 5 BC. (Our date for his birth, *Anno Domini* or AD 0, comes from the rough calculations of a 6th-century Roman monk.) Herod's intention to massacre all infants in the area of Bethlehem led his mother Mary and her husband Joseph to take Jesus to Egypt; after Herod's death they returned to Nazareth in Galilee. Jesus's childhood is not recorded, except for his visit to the Temple of Jerusalem at the age of 12.

When Jesus was about 30 he began his journeys through Palestine, preaching his message of love and tolerance. But he was looked on with suspicion by strict Jews. In about AD 30 he was arrested in Jerusalem, and his claim to be the Messiah, which constituted blasphemy, enabled his accusers to recommend the death penalty. This had to be backed by the Roman governor who, rather than risk riots, allowed him to be crucified. Three days later his tomb was found empty, and for several weeks after Jesus appeared to his disciples.

After Jesus finally left his disciples they began to preach his teachings and were soon charged with blasphemy. Among their persecutors was Saul of Tarsus, but he was himself converted and became the greatest of the apostles. Under his influence Gentiles (non-Jews) all over the Mediterranean were converted to Christianity.

A 15th-century stained glass window from Ulm, Germany, showing the birth of Christ. Such windows helped to tell the Bible story to people who could not read or write.

The First Roman Emperor

After the death of Julius Caesar his great-nephew and heir, Gaius Octavius, ruled the western part of the Roman empire, and Marcus Antonius the east, holding office as consuls. On Antony's death Octavius, at the age of 33, became undisputed master of the whole empire.

At first Octavius ruled as consul, being re-elected every year. But in 27 BC he was granted supreme power by the Senate and the title of *Augustus*, 'exalted'. Eventually he was made consul for life.

Octavius used the title *Imperator Caesar Augustus*; 'Imperator' indicating his possession of 'imperium', absolute power. He claimed to have restored the Roman Republic, but in reality, the new Augustus held the reins of power, ruling very effectively and giving Rome a much needed period of peace after civil war.

The Herods

Several rulers named Herod appear in the pages of the *New Testament*.

Herod the Great was king of Judaea from 37 to 4 BC, under Roman appointment. He placated the Jews by rebuilding the Temple in Jerusalem. But he was a ruthless man and had killed all male infants under the age of one year in Bethlehem because it was prophesied that a king of the Jews had been born there.

Two of his sons, *Herod Antipas* and *Philip the Tetrarch*, governed Galilee and Ituraea respectively. Antipas had John the Baptist killed. *Herod Agrippa I*, a grandson of Herod the Great, also became king of Judaea, from AD 37 to 44. He had the apostle James put to death. His son *Herod Agrippa II* was king of Chalcis, in Lebanon. Another of Herod the Great's sons, Archaelaus, succeeded him as ruler of Judaea. He is known as *Herod Archaelaus*.

46	Caesar returns to Rome with Cleopatra, and crushes a mutiny by the Tenth Legion; Caesar defeats Pompey's son Sextus in Africa, which becomes a Roman province.
45	Caesar becomes virtual dictator of Rome; introduces the Julian Calendar; again defeats Sextus, in Spain; adopts his nephew Gaius Octavius (Octavian) as his heir.
44	Caesar is assassinated by a group of conspirators headed by Junius Brutus and Cassius Longinus; Marcus Antonius (Mark Antony), Caesar's master of the horse, seizes power; rivalry between Antony and Octavian.
43	Second Triumvirate formed by Octavian, Antony, and Marcus Lepidus.
	Birth of Ovid.
	Antony orders murder of Cicero, the orator.
42	Caesar deified: temple to him is erected in the Forum, where he was murdered.
	Battle of Philippi: the Triumvirate defeats Brutus and Cassius, who commit suicide.
40	Antony marries Octavian's sister Octavia.
37	Triumvirate is renewed for five years.
	Herod the Great, King of Judaea (to 4).
	Antony, still married to Octavia, marries Cleopatra in Egypt.
36	Octavian's fleet defeats Pompey's fleet; death of Pompey.
32	Antony formally divorces Octavia; Octavian declares war on Antony and Cleopatra.
31	Battle of Actium: Octavian's fleet defeats the combined fleets of Antony and Cleopatra.
30	Antony and Cleopatra commit suicide, Octavian declares Egypt a Roman province.
29	Octavian, back in Rome, holds three triumphs and proclaims peace.
27	Octavian is given supreme power by the Senate, with the title of Augustus; but the republic nominally continues.
	Augustus begins two-year campaign in Spain to subdue rebellious tribes.
23	Augustus resigns the consulship but gains other privileges; adopts the unofficial title of *princeps* – chief of the republic.
15	Roman empire extended to the upper Danube.
12	Revolt in Pannonia (now northern Yugoslavia), quelled after three years by Augustus's stepson, Tiberius Claudius Nero Caesar.
8	Death of the Roman poets Virgil and Horace.
5	Probable year of birth of Jesus of Nazareth at Bethlehem.
4	Death of Herod the Great: kingdom is partitioned among his sons: Herod Archaelaus, ethnarch of Samaria and Judaea; Herod Antipas, tetrarch of Galilee; Philip, tetrarch of Ituraea.

Opposite: Two of the four Evangelists (Gospel writers), St Matthew and St Luke, are portrayed here in a 15th-century fresco in Cyprus.

Below: This beautiful Celtic bronze shield was found in the river Thames in London. The design in the centre includes four owl faces, simplified into a pattern.

Above: This altar, found in the remains of a Roman fort in London, was dedicated to the god Mithras. It shows him sacrificing a bull. Mithras was the Indo-Iranian god of light whose cult reached the Roman Empire in the late 1st century AD. The cult became especially popular with the soldiers of the Roman army.

The Gods of Rome

The earliest gods of ancient Rome symbolized the powers of nature, particularly growth (the goddess Ceres). Thousands of minor gods had special interests like the winds, the forests, or harvesting. There were also personal household gods, *Lares* (ancestral spirits) and *Penates* (spirits of the larder). The head of the household embodied a family god, the *Genius*.

Later, the Romans adopted many Greek gods, and identified them with some of their own gods – for example Venus (the Greek Aphrodite), or Mercury (Hermes). In the days of the first emperors many Romans turned to oriental religions, but in 380 Rome adopted Christianity.

The Gospels

The stories of Jesus's life and teachings were at first told by word of mouth, by those who had witnessed them. But as these men grew old it became necessary to write them down. Four accounts of Jesus's life have come down to us, known as the Gospels of Matthew, Mark, Luke, and John.

The first three are known as the Synoptic Gospels, which means they give a united view of the story. Many scholars now believe *Mark* was written first, probably based on the memories Simon Peter had told to John Mark (who had himself met Jesus as a young man). *Matthew* and *Luke* were both based partly on *Mark*, and partly on other sources now lost. *Matthew* is traditionally attributed to the apostle Matthew, while the author of *Luke* is thought to have been a doctor, who accompanied Paul on many of his journeys and who wrote the *Acts of the Apostles*.

The Gospel of *John* is a very different narrative, and was written later than the other three. It was possibly written by the Apostle John, son of Zebedee, or by someone recording his memories. One of the three *Epistles of John* may also be the work of the apostle. All the Gospels were written in Greek which was the common language of scholars of the time.

AD

5	Rome acknowledges Cymbeline, King of the Catuvellauni, as king of Britain.
6	Romans depose Herod Archaelaus and appoint procurators to govern Judaea.
9	Usurper Wang Mang becomes Emperor of China (to AD 23) – the Hsin Dynasty.
14	Death of Augustus. Tiberius, Emperor of Rome (to 37).
18	Death of poet Ovid. Caiaphas, high priest in Jerusalem (to 36).
25	Later Han Dynasty in China (to 220).
26	Tiberius retires to Capri; continues to govern in absence. Pontius Pilate, procurator of Judaea (to 36).
27	Baptism of Jesus by John the Baptist.
28	John the Baptist is executed on Herod's orders.
30	Pilate orders the crucifixion of Jesus.
31	Martyrdom of Stephen.
32	Conversion to Christianity of Saul (Paul) of Tarsus.
34	Paul's first visit to Jerusalem.
37	Herod Agrippa, King of northern Palestine (to 44). Gaius Claudius Caesar ('Caligula', meaning 'little boot'), Emperor of Rome (to 41).
41	Caligula's irrational conduct leads to his assassination. Claudius Drusus, Roman emperor (to 54). Claudius makes Agrippa king of Judaea.
43	Romans under Aulus Plautius invade Britain; London is founded.
44	Judaea under procurators again.
45	Paul begins his missionary journeys.
48	Claudius's wife Messalina executed; he marries his niece Agrippina.
51	Caractacus, British general, is captured and taken to Rome.
54	Claudius is murdered, possibly by Agrippina. Nero Drusus, Agrippina's son, Emperor (to 68).
58	Emperor Ming-Ti of China introduces Buddhism into his country. Paul the Apostle is imprisoned in Caesarea.
59	Nero murders his mother, Agrippina.
60	Paul, brought to trial before Festus, procurator of Judaea, appeals to Rome.
61	Boudicca, Queen of the Iceni, leads a rebellion in Britain; defeated and killed by the Roman governor, Suetonius Paulinus.
62	Nero divorces and exiles his wife, Octavia, then has her murdered; he marries Poppaea Sabina, wife of his friend Otho.
64	Fire destroys most of Rome; Nero orders the persecution of Christians as scapegoats; probable date of Apostle Peter's martyrdom.

The Emperor Trajan (top right) sets out with the
fleet from Ancona in north-east Italy. This scene is
one of many carved on Trajan's Column in Rome,
showing his achievements.

The Destruction of Pompeii

Vesuvius, the volcano near Naples, lay dormant for many centuries. In AD 63, this peaceful scene was shattered by a violent earthquake; for six years further tremors were felt until on August 24, AD 79 Vesuvius exploded. The nearby towns of Pompeii and Stabiae were buried under a hail of ashes and lava fragments, while a sea of mud overwhelmed Herculaneum.

The excavation of Pompeii began in 1748, and more than half the town has now been uncovered, as have parts of Herculaneum and Stabiae. Items from everyday life have been found preserved intact.

Now people may walk through the streets of Pompeii as its citizens did, seeing the chariot wheel ruts in the stone roads, looking at shops with their signs, and viewing the well-preserved murals and mosaics in the houses – one floor mosaic of a fierce hound bears the legend *cave canem*, beware of the dog. In the museum food jars, lamps, jugs, kitchen scales, and even a bathtub are on display.

Persecution of Christians

The Romans persecuted the early Christians for a variety of reasons. Probably the most important was that not to conform with the state religion was treason. Ugly rumours were also circulated about the Christians, perhaps because they met in secret to take part in strange rites.

Upper-class Christians were beheaded; the rest were burned or eaten by wild beasts as a public entertainment. Begun in AD 64 by the Emperor Nero, seeking a scapegoat for the fire which had destroyed half of Rome, persecution was ended by the Emperors Constantine, a Christian, and Licinius in 313.

65	Philosopher Seneca commits suicide on Nero's orders. *The Gospel according to Mark* is written about this time.
66	Revolt of the Jews against misgovernment by Roman procurators (to 70).
67	Roman general Vespasian is sent to Judaea to suppress revolt. Probable date of the martyrdom of Paul.
68	Rebellion against Nero, who commits suicide. Galba, legate of Hispania Tarraconensis, Emperor of Rome (to 69).
69	Otho has Galba murdered and becomes emperor; is defeated by Vitellius, who then becomes emperor; Vespasian, recalled from Judaea, defeats and kills Vitellius. Vespasian, Emperor of Rome (to 79).
70	Vespasian's son Titus captures and destroys Jerusalem and suppresses the Jewish revolt. *The Gospel according to Matthew* is written about this time.
73	Fall of Masada, last stronghold of the Jewish Zealots in Palestine. Vespasian begins extending the Empire in Germany (until 74).
75	*The Gospel according to Luke* is written about this time.
77	The Roman conquest of Britain; Julius Agricola is imperial governor (to 84).
78	Kamishka rules as Great King in northern India (to 96), founding the Second Kushana Dynasty.
79	Titus, Emperor of Rome (to 81). Vesuvius erupts, burying the cities of Pompeii, Herculaneum, and Stabiae.
80	Another fire in Rome; the Colosseum and the Baths of Titus are completed.
81	Domitian, younger brother of Titus, Roman Emperor (to 96). Domitian begins building defence lines on German frontier of the Empire.
95	Probable time of the writing of *The Gospel according to John* and *The Book of Revelation*.
96	Assassination of Domitian; Nerva Emperor of Rome (to 98).
98	Trajan, general commanding in lower Germany, Emperor of Rome (to 117).
101	The Dacian Wars (end 107): Trajan increases the Empire to its greatest extent; commemorated by Trajan's Column, in Rome.
115	The Jews in Egypt, North Africa, Palestine, and Cyprus rebel against Roman rule; repressed with great severity by Trajan.
116	Trajan makes the river Tigris the Empire's eastern boundary, forming new provinces in Mesopotamia and Assyria.

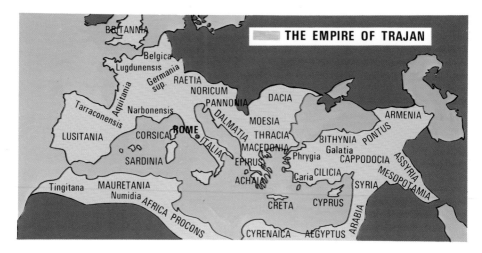

THE EMPIRE OF TRAJAN

After the Romans had conquered most of the Mediterranean lands, they turned north to conquer Gaul (France) and then Britain. Their empire also included Spain and parts of North Africa. The Roman Empire lasted in Europe until AD 476, when barbarians from the north-east invaded Rome and deposed the last Emperor in the West, but survived in the east until the Turkish conquest of Constantinople in 1453.

Below left: A coin of the emperor Hadrian.
Below: This wall was built by Hadrian across the north of England as a defence against the fierce northern tribes. Many fortified walls such as this protected the frontiers of the Roman Empire. Hadrian's Wall is about 70 miles (112 kilometres) long.

Israel's First President

The Jews revolted against Roman rule twice. The first revolt, in AD 66–70, ended in the destruction of Jerusalem. The second uprising occurred in 132, when well-organized guerrilla forces led by Shimeon Bar-Kockba drove the Romans from Jerusalem and occupied it.

Bar-Kockba proclaimed 'Year One of the Redemption of Israel'. From one document discovered in 1960 it appears that the leader described himself as 'President over Israel'.

Independence lasted only three years; and in a final battle Bar-Kockba was killed.

The Decline of Rome

Attacks by barbarian tribes from Germany began to menace the Roman Empire in the 200s. It became difficult for one emperor to defend and rule the whole vast area, so in 285 the Emperor Diocletian divided it into west and east. He ruled the east, having his capital at Nicomedia in Asia Minor; in the west a co-emperor, the general Maximian, ruled from Milan.

The Empire was reunited in 324 by Constantine, but split again in 364. From 394 to 395 it was again united, under Theodosius I, but then split for the last time.

A succession of weak emperors ruled the west, the first, Honorius, under the influence of a Vandal general, Stilicho. Menaced by continual attacks from the Visigoths and other barbarians, the Romans began to abandon the outlying parts of the Empire, starting with Britain, which they evacuated in 407. Three years later the Visigoths under their leader Alaric sacked Rome. The Romans regained control, and in 451 fought off Attila and the Huns at the battle of Châlons-sur-Marne. But in 455 a Vandal horde sacked Rome, and from then on more and more barbarians settled in Italy. The last emperor in the west, Romulus Augustus, was deposed in 476.

117	Hadrian, legate of Syria and cousin of Trajan, Roman Emperor (to 138).
122	Hadrian visits Britain and begins construction of wall and fortifications between northern England and Scotland.
124	The Pantheon in Rome is completed.
130	Hadrian visits Egypt: new capital city is begun at Antinopolis.
132	Jews led by Shimeon Bar-Kokhba and Rabbi Akiba Ben-Joseph rebel against Roman rule; they capture Jerusalem and set up an independent state of Israel.
133	Julius Severus, governor of Britain, is sent to Palestine to crush the revolt.
135	End of the Jewish revolt: death of Bar-Kokhba and Akiba Ben-Joseph. Final Diaspora (dispersion) of the Jews.
138	Antoninus Pius, Emperor of Rome (to 161).
150	Claudius Ptolemy completes his *Geographia*.
161	Marcus Aurelius, Roman Emperor (to 180).
166	The Emperor Huan Ti receives gifts from Marcus Aurelius. Serious outbreak of plague in the Empire until 167.
180	First African Christians are martyred at Scillium. Commodus, son of Marcus Aurelius, Emperor of Rome (to 192).
189	Reign of Hsien-Ti, last of the Han emperors (to 220); government is in the hands of military dictators.
193	Pertinax chosen emperor, but is murdered by the Praetorian Guard, who choose Didius Julian instead. Septimus Severus becomes emperor of Rome (to 211), seizes Rome, and ends Julian's reign after two months; Julian is executed.
197	Clodius Albinus, governor of Britain, another claimant to the Imperial throne, is killed by Severus at the battle of Lyon.
208	Severus goes to defend Britain, and repairs Hadrian's Wall.
211	Caracalla, Severus's eldest son, Emperor of Rome (to 217).
212	Caracalla murders his brother and rival, Geta. Edict of Caracalla extends citizenship to almost all freemen in the empire.
217	Macrinus, Emperor of Rome (to 218).
218	Elagabalus, Emperor of Rome (to 222); his mother, Julia Maesa, actually rules.
220	Period of the Three Kingdoms in China (until 265).
222	Alexander Severus, Emperor of Rome (to 235).
227	Ardashir founds new Persian empire.
230	Emperor Sujin, first known ruler of Japan.
235	Maximinus, Emperor of Rome (to 238).
238	Gordian III, Emperor of Rome (to 244).

Left: A medallion of the emperor Diocletian. He was an efficient ruler, carrying out a great census of population and land use. He also simplified the tax system, but his attempt to fix wages and prices throughout the empire met with failure.

A detail from a fresco of the Gupta period in the caves of Ajanta, showing the child Buddha being taught by other children. The 30 caves in central India were used as Buddhist temples until the 7th century AD.

The Gupta Dynasty

The Gupta dynasty of northern India was founded in the year 320 by Chandragupta I, who was originally a petty chief in Bihar. By marriage and conquest he extended his territory, and assumed the title of king. He also assumed the name Chandragupta, which was borne by the founder of the Maurya Empire 600 years earlier. His successors all added the termination -*gupta*, 'protected', to their names.

Chandragupta I was succeeded by Samudragupta, his son, whose reign lasted 45 years until 375. Samudragupta embarked on a policy of conquest which greatly extended his empire to include most of Bengal. His son, Chandragupta II, extended the empire still farther until it covered most of northern India. The Guptas held this vast land until the invasion of the White Huns in the late 400s.

Under the Guptas life was remarkably free from bureaucratic restrictions, and fines were the punishment for most offences. Most of the people were vegetarians. The Gupta period was one of great art and literature, among the writers being Kalidasa, regarded as India's finest poet. Many beautiful cities were built during this time.

Constantine the Great

Constantine I, known as the Great, was the son of the Emperor Constantius I, who ruled the Western Empire. Constantius died while on a visit to Britain, and Constantine was at once hailed as emperor by the troops there. He ruled Britain and Gaul for six years while another claimant, Maxentius, ruled in Rome.

In 312 Constantine defeated and killed Maxentius at the battle of the Milvian Bridge. Just before the battle he saw an outline of a cross superimposed on a cloud, and this converted him to Christianity; he at

The centre of the Great Dish of the Mildenhall treasure, a magnificent hoard of Roman artefacts dating from the 4th century AD.

once introduced religious toleration, ending the persecution of Christians. In 324 he defeated Licinius, Emperor of the East, and ruled the whole Roman Empire. A year later he called the first world council of the Christian Church to meet at Nicaea (now Iznik, Turkey).

In 330 Constantine moved the Empire's capital away from pagan Rome to a new city, Constantinople, built on the site of the village of Byzantium (now Istanbul).

244	Philip the Arabian, Emperor of Rome (to 249).
249	Decius, Emperor of Rome (to 251).
250	Decius orders persecution of the Christians; emperor-worship is made compulsory.
251	Gallus, Emperor of Rome (to 253); following Decius's death in battle with the Goths.
253	Valerian, Emperor of Rome (to 259), with his son Gallienus as co-Emperor.
259	Shapur I of Persia captures Valerian in battle; Valerian dies in captivity. Gallienus, Emperor of Rome (to 268): period of the Thirty Tyrants (pretenders to the throne).
265	China reunited under Western Chin Dynasty until 317.
268	Goths sack Athens, Corinth, and Sparta. Claudius II, Emperor of Rome (to 270).
270	Aurelianus, Emperor of Rome (to 275).
275	Tacitus, Emperor of Rome; is killed by his troops in 276.
276	Probus, Emperor of Rome; is killed in 282 by soldiers who object to doing peaceful work.
282	Carus, Emperor of Rome; is killed in battle in 283 by his own troops.
284	Diocletian, Emperor of Rome (to 305).
286	Diocletian divides the Empire: he rules the East and Maximian the West.
287	Revolt by Carausius, commander of the Roman British fleet, who rules Britain as emperor until murdered by Allectus, a fellow rebel, in 293.
303	Diocletian orders a general persecution of the Christians.
305	Diocletian and Maximian abdicate: a power struggle follows.
306	Constantine I, the Great, Emperor in the East (to 337).
308	Maxentius, son of Maximian, Emperor in the West (to 312).
312	Constantine defeats and kills Maxentius at battle of Milvian Bridge; Constantine is converted to Christianity.
313	Edict of Toleration proclaimed at Milan: Constantine allows Christianity in the Empire.
320	Chandragupta I, ruler in northern India (to 330); foundation of the Gupta Dynasty.
324	Constantine reunites the Roman Empire.
330	Constantine inaugurates new city of Constantinople, on the site of Byzantium, as capital of the Roman Empire.
337	Constantine is baptized a Christian on his deathbed. Joint rule of Constantine's three sons: Constantine II (to 340); Constans (to 350); Constantius (to 361).
350	Christianity reaches Ethiopia.
351	Constantius reunites the Roman Empire.

Above: A beautiful silver bowl, decorated with patterns of human and animal figures. It was discovered in Gundestrop in Denmark. The barbarians were skilled metalworkers, and produced many such objects.

Opposite: This brooch would have been worn by a barbarian to fasten his cloak at the shoulder. Each tribe had a characteristic brooch shape. Clay moulds were used to cast bronze, silver or gold into the desired form.

Attila the Hun

The Huns were a nomadic Mongol tribe who established an empire in eastern Europe from the Caspian Sea north to the Baltic. In 433 two brothers, Bleda and Attila, became joint rulers on the death of their uncle. By a campaign of bloodshed and destruction Attila forced the Eastern Roman Empire to pay the Huns an annual tribute in gold. In 445 he killed his brother and became sole ruler.

In 450 Honoria, sister of the Western Emperor Valentinian III, asked Attila to help her escape from an unwelcome marriage. Attila immediately claimed her as his bride, together with the western half of the Empire, and invaded Gaul. A combined Roman and Visigoth army repulsed him.

Attila switched his attack to Italy, but was prevented from ravaging Rome by an outbreak of plague and famine. He died peacefully two years later.

351 Julian attempts to reintroduce paganism instead of Christianity.
363 Jovianus, Emperor of Rome (to 364); he surrenders Mesopotamia to the Persians.
364 Valentine, Emperor of Rome (to 375). Valens, Emperor in the East (to 378).
369 Roman general Theodosius drives the Picts and Scots out of Roman Britain.
370 Huns from Asia invade Europe.
372 Buddhism is introduced into Korea.
375 Gratian, Emperor of Rome (to 383). Chandragupta II, Emperor of the Gupta Empire in northern India (to 415).
378 Valens, Emperor in the East, is defeated and killed by the Goths at Adrianople.
379 Theodosius the Great, Roman Emperor in the East (to 395).
383 Magnus Maximus, Emperor in the West (to 388); he conquers Spain and Gaul. Roman legions begin to leave Britain.
388 Theodosius captures Magnus Maximus and executes him.
394 Theodosius briefly reunites the Roman Empire.
395 Honorius, Emperor in the West (to 423); his brother Arcadius Emperor in the East (to 408). Stilicho, Vandal leader of the Roman forces (to 397), drives the Visigoths out of Greece.
401 Innocent I, Pope (to 417): he claims universal jurisdiction over the Roman Church.
406 Vandals and other barbarians overrun Gaul.
407 The first Mongol Empire, founded by the Avars (until 553). Last Roman troops withdraw from Britain; Romano-Britons are left to fend for themselves.
410 The Goths under Alaric sack Rome.
425 Valentinian III, Emperor in the West (to 455). Raids by Angles, Saxons, and Jutes on Britain.
429 Vandal kingdom in northern Africa until 535.
432 St Patrick begins mission to Ireland.
433 Attila, ruler of the Huns (to 453).
439 Vandals under Gaiseric capture Carthage.
440 Leo the Great, Pope (to 461).
449 The Jutes under Hengest and Horsa conquer Kent, in southern Britain.
451 Attila invades Gaul: repulsed by Franks, Alemanni, and Romans at battle of Châlons.
452 Attila invades northern Italy.
455 Gaiseric and the Vandals sack Rome.
465 White Huns dominate northern India.
471 Theodoric the Great, King of the Ostrogoths (to 526).
475 Romulus Augustus, last Roman Emperor in the West (to 476).
476 Goths under Odovacar depose Romulus Augustus; end of the Western Empire.

The Barbarians

The term *Barbarians* was used by the Romans to describe the uncivilized peoples outside their empire. The word is particularly used of those northern tribes which overran the Roman Empire.

The *Huns* were nomadic Mongols from Asia, who arrived in Europe about AD 370.

The *Goths* were Germanic people, originally from Scandinavia. In the 200s they split into the *Ostrogoths* (East Goths) living between the Don and Dniester rivers, and the *Visigoths* (Valiant or Western Goths) living in what is now Ukraine.

The *Vandals*, a Germanic people, lived between the Oder and Vistula rivers.

The Middle Ages

THE PERIOD of history which lies between ancient times and modern times, from the fall of the Western Roman Empire to the fall of Constantinople and the end of the Eastern Roman Empire, is generally known as the Middle Ages. It was a period when the removal of the strong, central government of Rome left Europe in chaos. The mighty empire was fragmented into small kingdoms, and in many places rule was by local lords, each of whom exercised power only in the immediate vicinity of his own castle. This was a time, too, of poverty and hardship; with the lack of wealth and consequently of people able to act as patrons, there was a decline in learning. In the Near East, however, learning flourished while the religion of Islam was to prove a unifying force, while in Asia and in the Americas complex independent civilizations flourished.

But the European picture did not remain dark. Gradually there was a growth of nationalist feeling, and strong kings began to make countries out of their lands. The introduction of the feudal system gave a structure on which government could be based. Finally, the steadily growing power and wealth of the Church provided another unifying force, and gave some men leisure to pursue lives of scholarship and study.

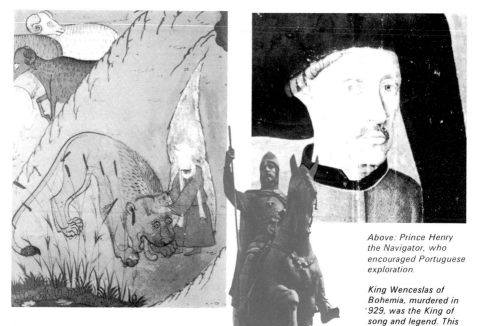

Above: Prince Henry the Navigator, who encouraged Portuguese exploration.

King Wenceslas of Bohemia, murdered in '929, was the King of song and legend. This statue of Wenceslas is in the square named after him in Prague.

Above: Muhammad taming the lion – one of several legends told about the prophet. Islam forbids the portrayal of Muhammad's face.

EUROPE

493	Theodoric, King of Ostrogoths becomes king of all Italy
584	Kingdom of Mercia founded in England
590	Gregory I, the Great, Pope (to 604)
597	St Augustine lands in England
620	Vikings begin invading Ireland
664	Synod of Whitby
669	Theodore of Tarsus sent to England
732	Charles Martel defeats Moors at Tours
756	Papal States founded in Italy
771	Charlemagne, King of the Franks (to 814)
787	First Danish invasion of Britain
861	Vikings discover Iceland
871	Alfred the Great, King of Wessex (to 899)
911	Hrolf the Ganger granted Normandy
936	Otto I, the Great, King of Germany (to 973)
962	Revival of Holy Roman Empire in West
1016	Danes rule England (to 1042)
1066	Battle of Hastings
1075	Dispute over appointment of bishops (to 1122)
1152	Frederick I, Holy Roman Emperor (to 1190)
1170	Thomas à Becket murdered
1171	Henry II annexes Ireland
1215	Magna Carta
1240	Battle of the Neva
1241	Mongols withdraw from Europe
1254	Great Interregnum in Germany (to 1273)
1265	De Montfort's Parliament
1273	Rudolf I, Holy Roman Emperor (to 1291)
1295	Model Parliament of Edward I
1305	Papal See removed to Avignon (to 1378)
1306	Robert the Bruce, King of Scotland (to 1329)
1338	Hundred Years' War (to 1453)
1348	Black Death ravages Europe (to 1351)
1377	The Great Schism (to 1417)
1431	Jeanne d'Arc burned as a witch
1453	End of Hundred Years' War

ASIA

527	Justinian, Byzantine Emperor (to 565)
552	Buddhism introduced into Japan
562	End of Japanese power in Korea
570	Muhammad born at Mecca
589	Wen Ti reunites China
625	Muhammad begins dictating the Koran
632	Death of Muhammad
635	Muslims begin conquest of Syria and Persia
661	Omayyad Dynasty in Islam
663	Japanese finally withdraw from Korea
674	Arab conquest reaches Indus River
712	Muslim establish state in Sind
751	Arabs defeat Chinese at Samarkand
787	Harun al-Raschid, Caliph at Baghdad (to 809)
907	Civil war in China
939	Civil wars break out in Japan
960	Sung Dynasty in China
995	Golden age of the arts in Japan (to 1028)
998	Mahmud founds empire in India
1021	Caliph al-Hakim founds Druse sect
1054	Eastern Church independent of Rome
1071	Seljuks conquer most of Asia Minor
1096	First Crusade
1156	Civil wars ravage Japan
1161	Explosives used in battle in China
1189	Third Crusade (to 1192)
1190	Mongol Empire grows in eastern Asia
1202	Fourth Crusade (to 1204)
1206	Temujin proclaimed Genghis Khan
1210	Mongols begin invasion of China
1260	Kublai elected Khan
1271	Marco Polo visits Kublai Khan (stays to 1295)
1274	First Mongol invasion of Japan
1291	Saracens capture Acre from Christians
1294	Death of Kublai Khan
1301	Osman defeats Byzantines
1363	Tamerlane begins conquest of Asia
1368	Ming Dynasty in China (to 1644)
1390	Turks conquer all of Asia Minor
1402	Tamerlane takes most of Ottoman Empire
1451	Mohammed II, Sultan of Turkey
1453	Fall of Constantinople

AFRICA	ELSEWHERE
477 Huneric, Vandal King of North Africa (to 484)	
484 Gunthamund, King of North Africa (to 496)	
496 Thrasamund, King of North Africa (to 523)	
523 Hilderic, King of North Africa (to 530)	
530 Gelimer, King of North Africa (to 534)	
534 Belisarius conquers North African Vandals	
554 Justinian reforms Egypt's administration	
639 Muslim conquest of Egypt (to 642)	
697 Arabs destroy Carthage	
700 Arabs capture Tunis	
702 Arabic made official language of Egypt	
725 Copts in Egypt rebel	
850 Acropolis of Zimbabwe built	
	900 Mayas emigrate to Yucatán Peninsula
920 Golden Age of Ghana Empire (to 1050)	
922 Fatimid Dynasty seizes Morocco	
980 Arabs settle east coast of Africa	981 Eric the Red settles in Greenland
999 Bagauda, first King of Kano	1002 Leif Ericsson explores North American coast
1077 Almoravid Dynasty in Ghana (to 1087)	
1130 Almohad Dynasty in Morocco (to 1169)	1100 Polynesian islands colonized
1167 Amalric captures Cairo	1151 End of Toltec Empire in Mexico
1168 Arabs recapture Cairo	
1196 Marimid Dynasty in Morocco (to 1464)	1189 Last known Norse visit to North America
1200 Jews in Morocco given privileges	1200 Hunac Ceel revolts against Maya
1217 Fifth Crusade, against Egypt (to 1222) fails	
1235 Sundiata Keita, King of Mali (to 1255)	
1240 End of Empire of Ghana	
1307 Kankan Mansa Musa, King of Mali (to 1332)	
1316 Search for Prester John in Ethiopia	1325 Aztecs found Tenochtitlán
1341 Sulaiman, King of Mali (to 1360)	
	1438 Inca Empire established in Peru

A T'ang dynasty horse. At first the Chinese only had ponies, but in the 2nd century BC *large horses such as this pottery figure depicts were brought back from Central Asia. They became status symbols for rich men and officials. During the T'ang dynasty, pottery figures and animals became very lifelike and beautiful. The pottery of China had such an influence on the world that today the word 'china has come to mean all sorts of pottery and porcelain.*

A monk copies out a manuscript in a scriptorium
(writing room). In the Middle Ages few people
outside the Church could read and write and those
who could had usually been educated by the
monks. The monastery libraries preserved much
classical learning but books disapproved of by the
Church were kept hidden away or destroyed.

The Monks

The great monasteries found throughout Europe during the Middle Ages were centres of learning, a source of relief for the poor and sick, and often wealthy landowners. In many regions they were the most forceful reminder of the spiritual and political power of the Church.

But the way of life called monasticism – living apart from the world in order to devote oneself to God – grew up in Asia long before the time of Christ. The first Christians to adopt it lived as solitary hermits. In the 300s, an Egyptian hermit, St Anthony of Thebes, formed a community by bringing several hermits together.

Soon other religious communities, of monks and nuns, formed in imitation of this first one. Several communities were linked by following the same 'rule' – a guide to how the community should live drawn up by a monastic leader. The greatest rule was that of St Benedict of Nursia, who founded the monastery of Monte Cassino in Italy about 529. Benedict directed that a monk's life should be one of prayer and manual labour. But under the guidance of Pope Gregory VII, some monks became scholars and teachers. At a time when few laymen could read or write, they preserved much classical learning which would otherwise have been lost. Monks prayed for the souls of the dead, and had practical duties such as caring for the sick and feeding the poor. The religious houses – both male and female – provided almost all the medical skill available then.

As important community centres in Europe during the Middle Ages, monasteries also provided shelter for travellers, becoming in effect the first modern guest houses. The large Benedictine abbey of Cluny in France once entertained the royal court of Louis IX of France and the papal court of Innocent IV at the same time, but smaller monasteries cared for wayfarers.

477	Huneric, Vandal King of North Africa (to 484). Budhagupta, last important Gupta Emperor in northern India (to 495).
481	Clovis, King of the Franks (to 511).
484	Gunthamund, Vandal King of North Africa (to 496).
493	Theodoric the Great, King of all Italy.
496	Thrasamund, Vandal King of North Africa (to 523). Clovis is converted to Christianity.
503	Britons under war leader Arthur defeat Saxons at Mount Badon. War between Byzantine Empire and Persia (ends 505).
507	Franks conquer the Visigoths in southern France.
511	Death of Clovis; the Frankish Empire is divided among his four sons.
523	Hilderic, Vandal King in North Africa (to 530).
524	War between Byzantine Empire and Persia (ends 531).
527	Justinian, Byzantine Emperor (to 565).
529	Justinian has all the Empire's laws codified in three volumes; finished in 565.
530	Gelimer, Vandal King in North Africa (to 534).
533	So-called 'Eternal Peace' is signed between Byzantine Empire and Persia.
534	The Byzantine general Belisarius conquers the Vandal kingdom of North Africa. The Franks conquer Burgundy.
535	Byzantine forces begin to reconquer Italy, which takes until 554.
540	New war breaks out between the Byzantine Empire and Persia; lasts until 562.
542	Epidemic of plague in the Empire (ends 546).
550	St David takes Christianity to Wales.
552	Buddhism is introduced into Japan.
553	Justinian reforms the administration of Egypt.
554	Byzantine armies conquer south-eastern Spain.
562	End of effective Japanese power in Korea.
563	Irish monk St Columba founds a monastery on island of Iona and begins conversion of the Picts to Christianity.
565	Justin II, nephew of Justinian, Byzantine Emperor (to 578).
568	Lombards conquer northern Italy; kingdom is founded by Alcuin.
570	Muhammad, founder of Islam, born at Mecca.
572	Persians dominate Arabia (until 628). War between Byzantium and Persia (ends 591).
581	Wen Ti, formerly chief minister of the Chou, founds the Sui Dynasty in China.
584	Foundation of the Anglo-Saxon kingdom of Mercia in England.
587	Visigoths in Spain are converted to Christianity.

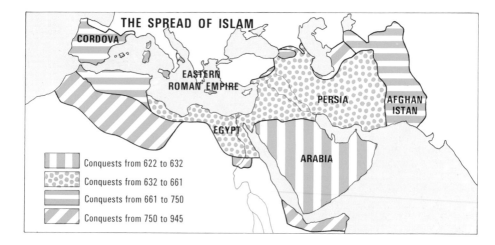

THE SPREAD OF ISLAM

CORDOVA

EASTERN ROMAN EMPIRE

PERSIA

AFGHANISTAN

EGYPT

ARABIA

Conquests from 622 to 632
Conquests from 632 to 661
Conquests from 661 to 750
Conquests from 750 to 945

A pottery camel from the T'ang dynasty period in China (618–907), a time of expansion and great artistic achievement.

The Prophet

Muhammad, the founder of Islam, was born in Mecca in Arabia and was brought up by his uncle, chief of a small tribe. He spent his boyhood tending sheep and camels, and then entered the service of a wealthy widow, Khadija, whom he later married.

When he was about 40 Muhammad had a vision that he was commanded by the Archangel Gabriel to proclaim the one true God, Allah. He began preaching in Mecca, and drew on himself such persecution that in 622 he had to flee to a nearby city now known as Medina, 'city of the prophet'. This event, the *Hegira*, marks the beginning of the Muslim calendar.

In Medina Muhammad's following grew rapidly, and in 630 he recaptured Mecca. There he forbade the worship of idols, and ordered that non-believers should never enter the city again. To this day, only Muslims are allowed to go there.

Muhammad dictated the tenets of his faith to his followers, and they were written down to form the *Koran*, the holy book of Islam. But he insisted that they were not his teachings, but the word of God, whose prophet and mouthpiece he was.

In addition to being a great religion, Islam was also a nationalistic movement; by the time Muhammad died in 632 it controlled all Arabia, and has since spread its influence through Africa and Asia.

Left: This Islamic painting shows the Ka'aba, the sacred building in Mecca which is the sanctuary of Islam. The Ka'aba contains the Black Stone which, according to ancient tradition, fell from heaven. Arab conquests in the Middle Ages spread the influence of Islam throughout the Near East and into parts of Europe. The map above shows the swiftness and extent of this spread. The Muslims spread not only their religion but also their way of life, and goods and ideas were freely exchanged throughout the vast empire.

589	Arabs, Khazars, and Turks invade Persia, but are defeated. Wen Ti conquers the southern Ch'en and reunites China.
590	Gregory I, the Great, Pope (to 604).
593	Suiko, Empress of Japan (to 628).
597	St Augustine lands in England and converts the kingdom of Kent to Christianity.
605	Grand Canal built in China (finished 610).
606	Harsha, Emperor in northern India (to 647).
610	Vision of Muhammad.
618	T'ang Dynasty in China (to 907), founded by T'ai Tsu; murder of Yang Ti 'The Shady', last of the Sui emperors.
620	Vikings begin invading Ireland.
622	The Hegira: Muhammad flees from Mecca to Yathrib (now Medina).
624	Muhammad marries Aisha. Buddhism becomes the established religion of Japan.
625	Persian attack on Constantinople fails. Muhammad begins dictating the *Koran*.
626	Emperor Heraclius I of Byzantium expels the Persians from Egypt.
627	Heraclius defeats the Persians at Nineveh. T'ai Tsung, The Great, Emperor of China (to 649); period of military conquest and patronage of arts and letters.
630	Muhammad captures Mecca, and sets out the principles of Islam.
632	Death of Muhammad; is succeeded as leader of Islam by his father-in-law, Abu Bekr, first Caliph (to 634).
633	Mercians under Penda defeat Northumbrians.
634	Omar I, Caliph at Mecca (to 644): beginning of Islamic Holy War against Persians.
635	Muslims begin conquest of Syria (to 641) and Persia (to 642).
638	Muslims capture Jerusalem.
639	Muslims begin conquest of Egypt (to 642).
642	Mercians under Penda again defeat the Northumbrians.
644	Othman, Caliph of Islam (to 656), following the assassination of Omar.
645	Byzantine forces recapture Alexandria, whose people rise against the Arabs. The Taikwa edict of reform nationalizes land in Japan and reorganizes the government; period of imitation of Chinese way of life.
646	The Arabs recapture Alexandria.
649	The Arabs conquer Cyprus.
655	Battle of the Masts: Arab fleet defeats Byzantine fleet off Alexandria — first major Arab naval victory. Oswy, king of Northumbria, defeats and kills Penda of Mercia.

Saxons and Danes

The Romans finally abandoned Britain in AD 407. From then on, the country was raided by Picts from Scotland, Angles and Saxons from Germany, and Jutes from Jutland in Denmark. The Jutes settled in Kent, and the Isle of Wight. By soon after 600, most of the rest of England was under Anglo-Saxon rule.

England was divided into seven kingdoms, called by historians the *Heptarchy*, from a Greek word meaning 'rule of seven'. The kingdoms were Kent, Sussex, and Wessex in the south and west; Mercia, East Anglia, and Essex in the midlands and east, and Northumbria.

In the late 700s Vikings, or *Northmen*, began raiding Britain. The Vikings who attacked England were mostly from Denmark. In the 850s these Danish invaders began to settle in England, and by 870 they had overrun all the kingdoms but Wessex. From 839 Wessex was ruled by Ethelwulf, whose father, Egbert, was the first king claiming to rule all England. Ethelwulf died in 858 and was succeeded in turn by his sons Ethelbald, Ethelbert, and Ethelred I. In 871 the youngest son, Alfred, came to the throne. Wessex was under constant Danish attack, and in 871 alone Alfred fought nine battles. The Danes overran Wessex in the winter of 877–878, but in the spring Alfred defeated them decisively and restored peace to his land. By the Treaty of Wedmore the Danes ruled the north and east of England – the *Danelaw* – and Alfred ruled the south and west.

The Danelaw lasted for less than a hundred years. Early in the 10th century East Anglia and the Danish midlands were taken by the king of Wessex. The Danish settlers in Northumbria were attacked by invaders from Norway whose leaders made themselves kings of York until Alfred's grandson Eadred expelled the last of them in 954.

The Byzantine Empire

When Constantine the Great transferred the capital of the Roman Empire from Rome to his new city of Constantinople in 330, he not only moved the centre of power farther east, but also paved the way for the continuation of the Roman Empire after the fall of Rome in 476.

Because Constantinople was built on the site of ancient Greek Byzantium, historians often call the Eastern Roman Empire the Byzantine Empire. It reached its height during the reign of Justinian I, from 527 to 565. His great generals Narses and Belisarius extended it to include Asia Minor, the Balkan Peninsula, Palestine, Egypt, northern Africa, southern Spain, and part of Italy. In the years after Justinian's death the Byzantine Empire gradually shrank till it included little more than Greece and the Balkan territories.

The Empire had its own form of Christianity, preserved as the Eastern Orthodox Church. It was also a rich centre of culture, art, and scholarship, whose influence spread westwards into southern Europe. It was eventually overthrown by the Turks in 1453, a date which marks the end of the Middle Ages.

Hagia Sophia in Istanbul was built as a Christian church in the 500s. Its name means Church of Holy Wisdom. It was built by the emperor Justinian as a centre for the religious life of Constantinople, and over 10,000 people worked on it. Justinian considered it a triumph, declaring 'Solomon, I have outdone thee'. It was converted to a mosque by the Turks after the fall of Constantinople in 1453, and today it is a museum.

656	Ali, Caliph of Islam (to 661) following the assassination of Othman.
661	Omayyad Dynasty in Islam (lasts until 750) is founded by Muawiya, Caliph to 680.
663	Japanese finally withdraw from Korea.
664	Synod of Whitby: Oswy abandons the Celtic Christian Church and accepts the faith of Rome; decline of the Celtic Church.
668	Korea is reunited under the kingdom of Silla; the Silla Period (to 935).
669	The Greek monk Theodore of Tarsus is sent to England as Archbishop of Canterbury to reorganize the Church in England.
673	Arabs besiege Constantinople until 678 without success.
674	Arab eastward conquest reaches the river Indus, in modern Pakistan.
675	Bulgars begin settling south of the river Danube, founding their first empire.
680	Civil war among the Arabs.
685	Abdalmalik, Caliph of Islam (to 705); he sets up new administration in the Arab empire.
687	Pepin the Younger, mayor of the palace, unites the Frankish kingdom by a victory at Tertry. The Arabs destroy Carthage.
700	The Arabs capture Tunis: Christianity in North Africa is almost exterminated. Thuringia becomes part of the Frankish kingdom. The Psalms are translated into Anglo-Saxon; production of the Lindisfarne Gospels.
702	Ethiopians attack Arab ships in Red Sea: Arabs occupy Ethiopian ports. Arabic is declared official language of Egypt.
707	Muslims capture Tangier.
709	Muslims capture Ceuta.
710	Justinian II confirms papal privileges. Roderic, last Visigothic king in Spain (to 711)
711	The Moors (Arabs and Berbers from Morocco) invade Spain: Roderic is defeated and the Visigothic monarchy ends.
712	Muslims establish a state in Sind, now in Pakistan.
716	Second Arab siege of Constantinople (until 717); it fails.
718	Visigothic prince, Pelayo, founds kingdom of the Asturias in Spanish mountains; the Moors now hold most of the rest of Spain and Portugal, and advance northwards. Christians defeat Moors in Spain at battle of Covadonga.
726	Byzantine Emperor Leo III begins the Iconoclast Movement – opposition to images; Pope Gregory II opposes him. King Ine of Wessex first levies 'Peter's Pence', tax to support a college in Rome.

Above: Charlemagne revived the idea of a Roman Empire in the West. A religious and civilized man, he reformed administration in his empire. He founded the Carolingian dynasty and was canonised as a saint in the 12th century.

Right: When Charlemagne died, his only living son, Louis the Pious, inherited all his lands. When Louis died, however, he had three sons who were already squabbling over his lands. Eventually, agreement was reached, and Charlemagne's empire was divided between them as shown.

Charlemagne

Probably the greatest warrior-king of the Dark Ages was Charles, son of Pepin the Short; he became king of the Franks from 768. His power and his exploits earned him the title of *Carolus Magnus* – Charles the Great, or Charlemagne in Old French.

At first Charlemagne shared his throne with his brother Carloman, who died in 771. Charlemagne fought many campaigns to make his kingdom safe from attack by German tribes; at the request of the Pope he subdued Lombardy, in northern Italy, and he also conquered part of northern Spain to prevent the Moors there from coming farther north. On Christmas Day in the year 800, Pope Leo III crowned Charlemagne as 'Emperor of the West' in St Peter's Basilica, Rome. In this way Charles attempted to revive the glories of the Roman Empire; he founded what later came to be known as the Holy Roman Empire, covering a large part of Europe.

A tall, tawny-haired man of enormous energy, Charles was also a great patron of the arts and scholarship. He founded an academy at Aachen, his capital.

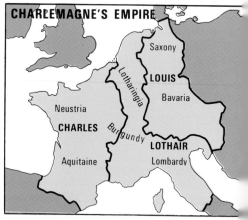

CHARLEMAGNE'S EMPIRE

Saxony

Lotharingia

LOUIS

Bavaria

Neustria

CHARLES

Burgundy

LOTHAIR

Aquitaine

Lombardy

Ancient Ghana

The modern country of Ghana, formerly the Gold Coast, takes its name from an ancient empire which dominated West Africa during the Dark Ages. Ancient Ghana lay many miles north of the present country, between the Sahara desert and the Niger and Senegal rivers.

Ghana was probably founded some time in the AD 300s. From then until about 770 its rulers were the Maga dynasty, a Berber family, though the people were Negroes of the Soninke tribes. In 770 the Maga were ousted by the Soninke, and the empire expanded greatly under the rule of Kaya Maghan Sisse, who was king around 790.

At this time Ghana began to acquire a reputation as a land of gold. It rose to its greatest glory in the 900s, and so again attracted the attention of the Arabs. After many years of warfare the Berber Almoravid dynasty seized power, though they did not hold it long. The empire declined and in 1240 was overrun by the people of Mali.

Harun al-Raschid

Harun al-Raschid (766–809) succeeded his brother, al-Hadi, as caliph of Baghdad in 786. The title *caliph* meant deputy to Muhammad, the founder of Islam. At first Harun ruled with the aid of the wealthy Persian family of Barmecide, but in 803 he suddenly turned against them and imprisoned the whole family. After that he ruled alone. From 791 Harun was engaged in war with the Byzantine Empire, and he also had to quell a series of rebellions in his own far-flung territories.

Harun encouraged the arts and scholarship, and his court at Baghdad was a centre of culture. It is described, with some exaggerations, in the legends of *The Thousand and One Nights*.

730	Pope Gregory II excommunicates Leo III.
731	Venerable Bede, British monk, completes his history of the Church in England.
732	Charles Martel, mayor of the palace and real ruler of the Franks, defeats the Moors at Tours, halting northward advance.
733	Leo III withdraws Byzantine provinces of southern Italy from papal jurisdiction.
735	Death of the Venerable Bede.
737	Charles Martel again defeats the Moors at Narbonne.
739	Another Coptic rebellion in Egypt.
741	Pepin the Short succeeds his father, Charles Martel, as mayor of the palace.
746	Greeks retake Cyprus from the Arabs.
751	Pepin the Short is crowned King of the Franks, founding the Carolingian Dynasty.
	Arabs defeat the Chinese at Samarkand.
	Lombards under Aistulf capture Ravenna from the Byzantine Empire.
756	Abd-al-Rahman ibn Mu'awiya establishes the Omayyad Dynasty at Córdoba, Spain.
	Pepin leads an army to protect Pope Stephen III from the Lombards: formation of the Papal States in Italy.
757	Offa, King of Mercia (to 796): he builds Offa's Dyke to keep out the Welsh.
767	Another Coptic revolt in Egypt, (ends 772).
771	Charlemagne (Charles the Great), son of Pepin, sole King of the Franks (to 814).
772	Charlemagne subdues Saxony and converts it to Christianity.
773	Charlemagne annexes the Lombard kingdom.
778	Moors and Basques defeat the Franks at Roncesvalles, in the Pyrenees.
779	Offa, King of Mercia, becomes King of all England.
780	Constantine VI, Byzantine Emperor (to 797): a child under the influence of his mother, Irene.
782	Charlemagne summons the monk and scholar Alcuin of York to head the palace school at Aachen: revival of learning in Europe.
786	Harun al-Raschid, Caliph at Baghdad (to 809).
787	Council of Nicaea orders resumed worship of images in the Church.
	Danes invade Britain for the first time.
788	Charlemagne annexes Bavaria.
791	Constantine imprisons his mother because of her cruelty and assumes power.
796	Death of Offa: end of Mercian supremacy in England.
797	Irene, Empress of Byzantium (to 802) has her son blinded; she is eventually deposed.
800	Pope Leo III crowns Charlemagne in Rome as Holy Roman Emperor of the West.
	Vikings invade Germany.

The Northmen

For centuries, whenever Scandinavia became too overcrowded and inadequate to support their primitive way of life, the Scandinavians, or Vikings, took to the sea and colonized other places.

The Northmen, as they were also known, were called Vikings from an ancient word for 'camp', since they set up camps during their raids. They were ruthless raiders, and people used to pray: 'From the fury of the Northmen, good Lord deliver us'. Their reckless bravery led them over the unknown seas to colonize Iceland and then Greenland, while in 1002 one Viking, Leif Ericsson, led an expedition across the north Atlantic to the shores of North America, where colonies persisted for many years.

Under the name of Danes, the Vikings conquered much of northern England and Ireland; they settled in northern France, where they became known as Normans; they penetrated into the Mediterranean Sea; and one tribe, the Russ, established a colony around Kiev and gave their name to Russia around the AD 800s.

Above: A stone carving showing Viking raiders in their ship.
Below: A map showing the extent of the Viking voyages during their great period of expansion from 790 to 1080.

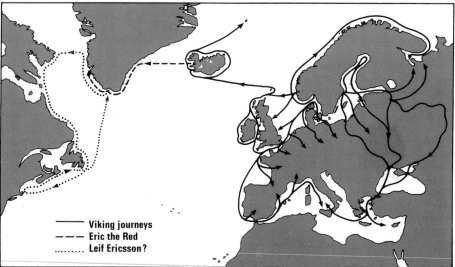

——— Viking journeys
– – – Eric the Red
········· Leif Ericsson?

Scotland: One Nation

The early history of Scotland is confused and obscure. Among the earliest settlers appear to have been the Picts. Scots from Ireland formed the Christian kingdom of Dalriada to the north and west of the river Clyde; Britons colonized the south-west, Strathclyde, and Anglo-Saxons settled in the south-east, Bernicia.

Around 850 Kenneth MacAlpine, King of the Scots, annexed the Pictish lands, and in the 980s Kenneth II took over Bernicia. Malcolm II (1005–1034) gained Strathclyde, and was the first king to unite most of present-day Scotland. His son, Duncan, was killed by the usurper Macbeth, a provincial chief in turn killed in battle by Duncan's son, Malcolm III.

Malcolm III married a Saxon princess, and acknowledged William I of England as his overlord. But he set the pattern for the frequent border raids which were a feature of Anglo-Scottish relationships for the next 500 years.

802	Egbert, King of Wessex (to 839).
803	Harun al-Raschid suddenly ends power of the Barmecide family in Baghdad.
814	Louis the Pious, son of Charlemagne, Emperor and King of the Franks (to 840).
	The Arabs adopt Indian numerals (0–9).
828	Egbert of Wessex is recognized as overlord of other English kings.
838	Louis the Pious divides his empire among his sons Lothair, Louis the German, and Charles the Bald.
839	Ethelwulf, son of Egbert, King of Wessex (to 858).
840	Lothair I, Emperor (to 855); his brothers are allied against him.
	Mojmir forms a confederation of Slav tribes in Bohemia, Moravia, Slovakia, Hungary, and Transylvania.
843	Treaty of Verdun redivides the Frankish Empire: Louis the German rules east of the Rhine, Charles the Bald rules France, Lothair rules Italy, Provence, Burgundy, Lorraine.
844	Kenneth MacAlpine, King of the Scots, conquers the Picts; founds a unified Scotland.
850	Acropolis of Zimbabwe in Rhodesia is built.
855	Louis II, son of Lothair, Emperor (to 875); Lothair's lands are again divided.
856	Main tide of Viking assaults on England until 875.
858	Ethelbald, eldest son of Ethelwulf, King of Wessex (to 860).
860	Ethelbert, second son of Ethelwulf, King of Wessex (to 865).
861	Vikings discover Iceland.
862	Rurik with the Viking tribe of Russ seizes power in northern Russia, founding Novgorod.
865	Ethelred I, third son of Ethelwulf, King of Wessex (to 871).
	Russian Vikings attack Constantinople.
	Major Viking force invades England, conquering Northumbria, East Anglia, and Mercia.
867	The Photian Schism: the Byzantine Church under Photius, Patriarch of Constantinople, challenges the authority of the Pope.
869	The Arabs capture Malta.
871	The Danes attack Wessex; are defeated by Ethelred at Ashdown.
	Alfred the Great, last son of Ethelwulf, King of Wessex (to 891).
874	Vikings settle in Iceland.
875	Charles the Bald, Emperor (to 877); anarchy follows his death.
878	Alfred decisively defeats the Danes at Edington; by the Treaty of Wedmore England is divided between Wessex in the south and the Danes in the north – the Danelaw.

EUROPE IN THE MIDDLE AGES

Above: Europe at the height of the Middle Ages looks very different from the Europe we know today. The Holy Roman Empire dominates much of modern France, Italy and Germany. Elsewhere countries like Spain are made up of small independent states.

The Holy Roman Empire

The Holy Roman Empire was a loose federation of states in central Europe. It was basically the area covered by modern Germany, Austria, Switzerland, and northern Italy, though its boundaries varied greatly over the centuries.

It was founded by the German King Otto I, the Great, who came to the throne in 936. It was his ambition to revive the glories of the old Roman Empire, which had been briefly renewed by Charlemagne in 800. In 962, Otto had himself crowned as 'Emperor Augustus', founding a line of emperors which endured until Napoleon I abolished the Empire in 1806. The title 'Holy Roman Emperor' was assumed by Frederick Barbarossa in 1157.

All the emperors after Otto were elected by the princes of the Empire; from 1356 seven of these princes held the right to vote and were called *electors*, and later two more were added to their numbers.

Only under the very strongest rulers did the Empire have any cohesion or real power, and by the 1700s it fully justified the French writer Voltaire's quip that it was 'neither holy, nor Roman, nor an empire'.

Bohemian Martyrs

The most famous ruler of Bohemia – the western part of present day Czechoslovakia – was Wenceslas, who became prince of Bohemia in 921 at the age of 14. He was at first brought up by his grandmother Ludmilla, a convert to Christianity; but Wenceslas's mother Drahomira had Ludmilla murdered and then acted as regent until he came of age. Wenceslas did his best to convert his people to Christianity, but he was opposed by a faction led by his younger brother Boleslav. In 929 Boleslav waylaid Wenceslas on his way to Mass and killed him. Acclaimed as martyrs, Wenceslas and Ludmilla were both canonized.

The Maya

About 1000 BC a strange civilization emerged in the lowland jungles of Central America. The people who created it – the Maya – were not city-dwellers like most early civilized peoples but lived in small farming villages. But they built great ceremonial centres – complexes of pyramid-like temples and palaces which were the focus of their religion and their political life. There were four main centres (each ruling a quarter of the country) and many smaller ones.

The Maya had a system of picture writing and an accurate calendar. Their astronomers could predict eclipses of the Sun. Maya artists excelled in carving jade and stone. But in about AD 900 the Maya deserted their centres and the old stable way of life collapsed; the Spaniards who came in the 1500s met little resistance from the decadent remnant, weakened by fighting among themselves.

880	Byzantine Emperor Basil recovers Italy from the Arabs.
881	Charles III, the Fat, Emperor and King of Germany, becomes King of the Franks, re-uniting Charlemagne's empire.
886	Alfred captures London from the Danes.
891	Alfred founds the Anglo-Saxon Chronicle, history of England.
893	Charles the Simple, King of France (to 929).
899	Edward the Elder, King of Wessex (to 924). Magyars from the East invade Moravia.
900	Alfonso III, the Great of Castile begins to reconquer Spain from the Moors. Mayas emigrate to the Yucatán peninsula of Mexico. Hausa kingdom of Daura founded in Nigeria. Bulgars accept the Eastern Orthodox religion.
901	Edward the Elder takes the title 'King of the Angles and Saxons'.
906	Magyars begin invading Germany.
907	End of T'ang Dynasty in China is followed by civil war until 960. Mongols begin their capture of Inner Mongolia and parts of northern China (completed 1123).
910	Abbey of Cluny founded in France.
911	Viking Rollo (Hrolf the Ganger) granted Normandy by the Franks, who are unable to dislodge him from France.
912	Rollo baptized a Christian as Robert.
913	Edward the Elder recaptures Essex from the Danes.
918	State of Korgo founded in Korea.
919	Henry I, the Fowler, King of Germany (to 936).
920	Golden Age of the Empire of Ghana begins.
922	Fatimid Dynasty seize Morocco.
924	Athelstan, son of Edward the Elder, becomes king of Wessex and effective ruler of most of England (to 939).
926	Athelstan annexes Northumbria, and forces the kings of Wales, Strathclyde, the Picts, and the Scots to submit to him.
929	Murder of King Wenceslas of Bohemia.
932	Wood-block printing adopted in China for mass-producing classical books.
935	Koryo Period in Korea (to 1392): country under the control of state of Koryo.
936	Otto I, the Great, son of Henry the Fowler, King of Germany (to 973).
937	Battle of Brunanburh: Athelstan defeats alliance of Scots, Celts, Danes, and Vikings, and takes the title of 'King of all Britain'.
939	Edmund, brother of Athelstan, King of England (to 946). First of a series of civil wars breaks out in Japan.

fighting force. But the reforms were not properly carried out, and the way was paved for the Mongol take-over by Genghis Khan.

The arts of China during the Sung period reflect the malaise which afflicted the country. Poets and painters were backward-looking, imitating or remembering past glories and achievements. Artists were preoccupied with human emotions, and poetry became overloaded with imagery, literary allusions, and other devices which make it difficult for later generations to understand or enjoy. But about this time professional story-tellers made their appearance, wandering about like the minstrels of western Europe, entertaining anyone they could persuade to listen in return for a few coins, and they led in time to the development of the Chinese novel.

Left: A 10th-century Chinese prayer sheet reproduced by wood-block printing.

Below right: Robert II 'the Pious', son of Hugh Capet, composing Church music.

The Sung Dynasty

The Sung Dynasty which ruled China from 960 to 1275 owed its existence to a young officer who thought he saw a vision. It meant, he declared, that a new emperor was about to take over China from the young Chou Emperor Kung Ti. His brother officers thought this must mean their highly successful general, Chao K'uang-yin. Arousing him from his sleep, they hailed him as their new ruler, Sung T'ai Tsu.

T'ai Tsu and his successors did their best to pull China together after more than 50 years of civil war, but the task was beyond them. In 1068 Wang An-shih, who was prime minister under Emperor Sung Shen Tsung, carried out radical reforms of government, simplifying the tax system and pruning the huge army down to a reasonable

The Magyars

The Magyars who created the kingdom of Hungary came from the steppes of Russia, between the river Volga and the Ural mountains. By the beginning of the 9th century they were living round the mouth of the river Don, but they migrated to the Middle Danube area in the late 9th century.

Although the Magyars numbered only some 25,000 they easily subjected the inhabitants and defeated a German force. For a time they raided the surrounding countries for slaves and booty but after the Emperor Otto I defeated them at Lechfeld in 955 they realized the need to make peace with their neighbours. They were baptized Christians; under Stephen I the state was organized into 46 counties and 10 dioceses, and his rule was one of prosperity and peace.

The Capetians

The royal family which ruled France for more than 800 years owed its name to the nickname of its founder, Hugh, Duke of Francia. Hugh was called *Capet* from the short cape he wore as lay abbot of St Martin de Tours. As the most powerful vassal of Louis V, King of France, Hugh contrived to have himself elected king on Louis's death in 987.

Hugh Capet's position was not a strong one. He ruled directly over a large part of northern France, with his capital at Paris; but many of his vassals, such as the dukes of Normandy, Burgundy, and Aquitaine, were almost as powerful. However, no single vassal was strong enough to overthrow Hugh, and they were all sufficiently jealous of one another to avoid making an alliance which could seize the throne.

Having himself been elected, Hugh made sure of the succession by having his son crowned in his own lifetime, a practice which lasted for two centuries and contributed greatly to the stability of France.

942	Malcolm I, King of Scots (to 953).
945	Dunstan becomes abbot of Glastonbury.
	The Scots annex Cumberland and Westmorland from the English.
946	Edred, younger brother of Edmund, King of England (to 955); Dunstan his chief minister.
950	Otto I conquers Bohemia.
	Kupe, great Maori (Polynesian) navigator, discovers New Zealand on canoe voyage.
951	Otto campaigns in Italy.
955	Battle of the Lechfeld: Otto defeats the Magyars and ends their westward advance.
	Edwy, son of Edmund, King of England (to 959).
956	Edwy sends Dunstan into exile.
957	Mercians and Northumbrians rebel against Edwy.
959	Edgar the Peaceful, younger brother of Edwy, King of England (to 975).
	Dunstan recalled from exile: becomes Archbishop of Canterbury.
960	Sung Dynasty in China (to 1275).
	Mieszko I, first ruler of Poland (to 992).
961	Otto I undertakes a second expedition to Italy to protect Pope John XII (ends 964).
962	Pope John XII crowns Otto as Emperor in Rome: revival of the Empire in the West.
	St Bernard's Hospice founded in Switzerland.
966	Otto's third expedition to Italy (to 972): his son, Otto II, crowned as future Emperor.
971	Kenneth II, King of Scots (to 995).
973	Otto II, King and Emperor (to 983).
975	Edward the Martyr, son of Edgar, King of England (to 978).
978	The Chinese begin compiling an encyclcpedia of 1000 volumes.
	Edward the Martyr murdered at Corfe Castle.
	Ethelred II, the Redeless (ill-counselled), younger brother of Edward the Martyr, King of England (to 1016).
980	Arabs begin settling along the eastern coast of Africa.
	The Danes renew their raids on England, attacking Chester and Southampton.
981	Viking explorer Eric the Red, exiled from Iceland, settles in a land he names Greenland to attract other colonists.
985	Sweyn Forkbeard, King of Denmark (to 1014).
987	Hugh Capet elected King of France (to 996); foundation of the Capetian Dynasty.
988	Vladimir of Kiev introduces Eastern Orthodox religion into his lands.
991	Battle of Maldon: Byrhtnoth of Essex defeated by Danish invaders.
	Ethelred II buys off the Danes with 10,000 pounds of silver.

This picture from a 15th-century book,
'Les Très Riches Heures du duc de Berry',
shows peasants at work in the fields
before their Lord's castle. Under the feudal
system the relation between lord and
peasant was the basis of everyday life.

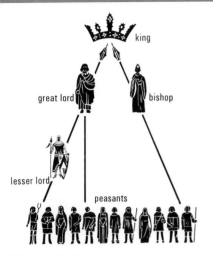

king

great lord

bishop

lesser lord

peasants

The Feudal System

The feudal system was the principal way of life and government in most of western Europe during medieval times. It developed under the Franks during the 800s, and gradually spread to Germany, Scandinavia, Spain, Italy, and the British Isles. It was particularly strong in England under the rule of the Normans.

The basis of the feudal system was the granting of land by a powerful person to a less powerful man in return for service. The system began at the top with the king and passed down through his great barons to lesser nobles and finally to the serfs.

The service rendered by the nobles to their immediate superiors was mainly military: they had to fight on their overlord's behalf. At the other end of the scale a serf might be virtually a slave, while freemen held land of their own but had to work for several days a week on their lord's land. In return, the strength of the overlord protected those who were dependent on him.

As a result of the system, life for most people centred on the castles or manors of the various lords. The villages round these were largely self-supporting.

992	Ethelred makes a truce with Duke Richard I of Normandy.
	Boleslaw the Brave, son of Mieszko, King of Poland (to 1025).
993	Olaf Skutkonung, first Christian King of Sweden (to 1024).
994	Danes under Sweyn and Norwegians under Olaf Trygvesson sail up river Thames and besiege London; bought off by Ethelred.
995	Japanese literary and artistic golden age under the rule of Fujiwara Michinaga (to 1028).
	Olaf Trygvesson returns to Norway, deposes Haakon the Great, and makes himself king.
996	Richard II, Duke of Normandy (to 1027).
	Robert II, the Pious, son of Hugh Capet, King of France (to 1031).
998	Mahmud, Turkish ruler of Ghazni (to 1030), founds empire in northern India and eastern Afghanistan.
	Stephen I (St Stephen), first King of Hungary (to 1038).
999	Bagauda, first King of Kano, in northern Nigeria.
	The Poles conquer Silesia.
1000	The Viking Biarni Heriulfsson, blown off course, sights coast of North America.
	Battle of Svolder: Sweyn kills Olaf of Norway and annexes Norway to Denmark.
	Ethelred II ravages Cumberland.
	Gunpowder perfected by Chinese about now.
1002	Leif Ericsson, son of Eric the Red, leads an expedition to the west: journeys down coast of North America possibly as far as Maryland.
	Ethelred marries Emma, sister of Duke Richard of Normandy.
	Massacre of St Brice's Day: Ethelred ordered the slaughter of all Danish settlers and mercenaries in southern England.
1003	Sweyn and an army of Norsemen land in England and wreak a terrible vengeance.
1007	Ethelred buys two years' peace from the Danes for 36,000 pounds of silver.
1012	The Danes sack Canterbury: bought off for 48,000 pounds of silver.
1013	Sweyn lands in England and is proclaimed king; Ethelred flees to Normandy.
1014	The English recall Ethelred II as King on the death of Sweyn; Canute retreats to Denmark.
1015	Canute again invades England; war between Danes and Saxons.
1016	Edmund Ironside, son of Ethelred II, King of England: he and Canute divide the kingdom, Canute holds the north and Edmund Wessex; Edmund is assassinated.
	Canute, King of England (to 1035).
	Olaf II, King of Norway (to 1028).

The Seljuk Turks

The Seljuk Turks were a tribe of nomads, led by a chief named Seljuk, who settled near Bokhara (now in Uzbekistan, in the Soviet Union), in the late 900s. Some of these restless warriors then set out to conquer fresh lands farther west.

In 1071 Alp Arslan, 'the Lion Hero', led his men into Armenia, where he was attacked by a Byzantine army under the Emperor Romanus IV Diogenes. This was to prove fatal for the Byzantines. The Turks feigned flight, then rounded on their foes and defeated them, capturing the Emperor who was eventually released for ransom.

The battle ended Byzantine power in Asia Minor, and the Seljuk Turks were able to move in and found what was to become the Turkish Empire. Under Alp Arslan's son Malik Shah (1055–1092) the Seljuk Empire reached its zenith.

Map of the Holy Roman Empire. The boundaries were continually changing, but in general encompassed lands held by the rulers of Germany and northern Italy. The Empire was officially ended by Napoleon in 1806.

Pope v Emperor

During the Middle Ages Europe was torn by a power struggle between the emperors of the Holy Roman Empire and the popes. The popes claimed complete spiritual authority over Christian Europe; the emperors – with whose support most popes were elected – claimed control over the Church's activities within their territories, and the right to confirm the election of popes.

Matters came to a head in 1075 when Pope Gregory VII forbade the Emperor Henry IV to control the election of bishops in Germany. Henry declared Gregory deposed, whereupon Gregory excommunicated Henry – that is, banned him from the Church. Many German princes refused to support Henry, who had to submit. In 1077, he went to see Gregory at Canossa in northern Italy, and after waiting three days in the snow declared himself penitent. But in 1080 Henry deposed Gregory.

The Jews

After the destruction of Jerusalem in AD 70 most Jews were exiles from their homeland. The *Diaspora* (dispersion) took Jews all over Europe and northern Africa, where they formed small communities in various cities. There they preserved their traditions of religion, learning, skill in many trades, and skill in business. Their religion allowed them to be moneylenders – a trade forbidden to Christians – which made them unpopular. The main centres were in Spain, where the Jews were known as *Sephardim*, and Germany, where they were called *Ashkenasim* and spoke *Yiddish* or Judeo-German.

At the time of the crusades the Christians began to see the Jews as directly responsible for the martyrdom of Jesus; persecuting the Jews became a highly commendable religious act. Jews were forced to live in ghettos, and were attacked and massacred at the least provocation. In the 1100s even the Moors in Spain, who had tolerated Jewish communities, turned against them. The first country to expel the Jews entirely was England, in 1290.

Opposite: Otto III is crowned Holy Roman Emperor at the age of 15. He was involved in several disputes between various popes, and eventually set his friend Gerbert of Aurillac on the papal throne as Sylvester II. His plan was to renew the Roman Empire on the lines of that of Constantine the Great and Charlemagne, with Rome as his capital. He revived Roman and Byzantine titles and ceremonies, and began to build a palace. However, the Romans expelled him, and he died trying to recover the city, aged only 21. Such attempts by emperors to place the person of their choice on the papal throne were not uncommon, often for reasons far more selfish than those of Otto. This contributed to the mutual hostility between Church and emperor which was to continue throughout the Middle Ages.

1017 Canute divides England into four earldoms.
1018 Mahmud of Ghazni pillages the sacred city of Muttra, in India.
1019 Canute marries Emma of Normandy, widow of Ethelred II.
1021 Caliph al-Hakim proclaims himself divine, and founds the Druse sect.
1024 Conrad II, German King and Holy Roman Emperor (to 1039).
1027 Robert le Diable, Duke of Normandy (to 1035).
1028 Zoë, Empress of Byzantine Empire (to 1050). Canute conquers Norway; his son Sweyn becomes King of that country.
1030 Olaf tries to regain throne of Norway: is killed at battle of Stiklestad.
1031 Henry I, King of France (to 1060).
1034 Duncan becomes King of Scots (to 1040).
1035 Death of Canute: his possessions are divided. William, bastard son of Robert, becomes Duke of Normandy (to 1087). Harold I, Harefoot, King of England (to 1040). Hardicanute, King of Denmark (to 1042).
1039 Henry III, the Black, Holy Roman Emperor (to 1056).
1040 Hardicanute, King of England (to 1042); he dies of drink. Macbeth, Mormaer of Moray, kills Duncan in battle at Elgin. Macbeth, King of Scots (to 1057).
1042 Edward the Confessor, son of Ethelred II, King of England (to 1066); power is in the hands of Earl Godwin and his sons. Magnus the Good, son of Olaf II, King of Denmark (to 1047).
1046 Harald Haardraada, King of Norway (to 1066).
1047 Sweyn II, Canute's nephew, King of Denmark (to 1076).
1051 Earl Godwin exiled (until 1052): he returns with a fleet and wins back his power.
1052 Edward the Confessor founds Westminster Abbey, near London.
1053 Death of Godwin: his son Harold succeeds him as Earl of Wessex.
1054 Abdallah ben Yassim begins the Muslim conquest of West Africa. Final break between the Byzantine Empire and the Roman Church; Eastern Church is now completely independent.
1055 Harold's brother Tostig becomes Earl of Northumbria.
1056 Henry IV, Holy Roman Emperor (to 1106); his mother, Agnes, acts as regent until 1065.
1057 Battle of Lumphanan: Malcolm Canmore ('Big head'), son of Duncan, defeats and kills Macbeth. Lulach, stepson of Macbeth, King of Scots (to 1058).

The Norman Conquest

When King Edward the Confessor of England died in 1066 he left no children. Who was to succeed him? The chief English claimant was his brother-in-law, Harold Godwinsson; another powerful contender was his cousin Duke William of Normandy. Edward may have promised him the throne in 1051; and William had strengthened his claim by persuading Harold (possibly by a trick) to swear loyalty to him.

On Edward's death, the English Witan (council) elected Harold king. For some months Harold kept his army ready to repel a Norman invasion. But then he had to go north to beat off an attack by his brother Tostig and King Harald Haardraada of Norway, whom he defeated at Stamford Bridge. Immediately after the battle, he heard that William had landed in Sussex. He and his bodyguard hastened south and raised fresh,

Harold pulls an arrow from his eye during the battle of Hastings: a scene from the Bayeux tapestry.

inexperienced troops. They met the Normans at Senlac, near Hastings; Harold was killed and his army defeated. On Christmas Day 1066 William 'the Conqueror' was crowned in Westminster Abbey.

William now carried out a systematic campaign to subdue the rebellious Saxons. He confiscated large estates and bestowed them on his followers – taking care to give them small areas scattered over the kingdom to prevent them from becoming too powerful. All landowners, great and small, swore loyalty directly to him. We have a minutely detailed record of England after the Conquest in the Domesday Survey of 1086, which William commissioned to help in tax assessment.

1058 Boleslav II, the Bold, King of Poland (to 1079); conqueror of Upper Slovakia.
Malcolm Canmore, King of Scots (to 1093), having killed Lulach in battle.
1060 Philip I, King of France (to 1108).
1061 Muslim Almoravid Dynasty in North Africa; later conquers Spain.
Malcolm Canmore invades Northumbria.
1062 Yusuf ben Tashfin founds Marrakesh, in Morocco.
1063 Harold and Tostig subdue Wales.
1064 Harold is shipwrecked in Normandy, and swears a solemn oath to support William of Normandy's claim to England.
1065 Northumbria rebels against Tostig, who is exiled.
1066 Harold II is crowned king the day after Edward the Confessor dies.
Tostig and Harold Haardraada of Norway invade England: Harold defeats them at the battle of Stamford Bridge, killing both.
Battle of Hastings, 19 days after battle of Stamford Bridge: William of Normandy with a motley invasion force defeats and kills Harold II.
William I, the Conqueror, first Norman King of England (to 1087).
1067 Work is begun on building the Tower of London, and rebuilding Monte Cassino monastery, Italy.
1068 Shen Tsung, Emperor of China (to 1085): radical reforms are carried through by his minister Wang An-shih.
The Norman Conquest continues until 1069: William subdues the north of England (the 'Harrying of the North'): the region is laid waste.
1069 Famine in Egypt (until 1072).
1070 Hereward the Wake begins a Saxon revolt in the Fens of eastern England.
1071 Battle of Manzikert: the Seljuk leader Alp Arslan defeats the Byzantines and conquers most of Asia Minor.
1072 William invades Scotland, and also receives the submission of Hereward the Wake.
The Norman conquest of Sicily ends 1091.
Alfonso VI, King of Castile (to 1109).
1073 Gregory VII (Hildebrand of Soana), Pope (to 1085).
1075 Seljuk leader Malik Shah conquers Syria and Palestine.
Dispute between pope and emperor over who should appoint bishops.
1076 Synod of Worms: bishops declare Pope Gregory deposed.
Gregory excommunicates Henry IV.

This 12th-century ambulatory at Peterborough Cathedral in eastern England is typical of the Romanesque style of architecture introduced into England by the Normans. The rounded arches and sturdy pillars have become a familiar feature of the church design of the years which followed.

The Crusades

In an age where religion was the mainspring of daily life, the occupation of Palestine, scene of Jesus's life, by the 'infidel' Muslims filled many Christians with horror. Interference by the Seljuk Turks with the bands of Christian pilgrims going to Jerusalem inspired Pope Urban II to call for a Crusade to free the Holy Land from the Saracens, as the Muslims were known.

There were eight crusades: the first captured much of Palestine from the Saracens, but after nearly 90 years the Saracens recaptured Jerusalem. Later crusades were less successful and in the fourth the crusaders, unable to pay the Venetians for shipping, were persuaded to sack the Christian city of Constantinople instead. The first crusade lasted from 1096 to 1099; the last was in 1270.

In the Children's Crusade of 1212, 50,000 children from France and Germany set off for the Holy Land. The German contingent was turned back; the others were sold into slavery from Marseille, a tragedy that is said to be the origin of the story of the Pied Piper.

1077 Henry, fearful for his throne, does penance to Gregory at Canossa.
Civil war in the Holy Roman Empire (ends 1080).
Almoravid Dynasty in Ghana (until 1087).
1080 Canute IV, King of Denmark (to 1086).
Gregory again excommunicates Henry IV and declares him deposed.
1081 Alexius I Comnenus, Byzantine Emperor (to 1118).
1083 Henry IV storms Rome.
1084 Robert Guiscard, Duke of Paulia, forces Henry to retreat to Germany.
1085 Alfonso VI captures Toledo from the Moors.
1086 Canute IV of Denmark is assassinated: Danish threat to England is lifted.
Domesday Book is completed in England.
1087 William II, Rufus, King of England (to 1100); his elder brother Robert is Duke of Normandy.
1088 Urban II, Pope (to 1099).
1090 Hasan ibn al-Sabbah, first 'Old Man of the Mountain', founds the Assassin sect in Persia.
1093 Donald Bane, King of Scots (to 1097), following the death of his brother, Malcolm III, in battle against the English.
1096 First Crusade begins, following an appeal by Pope Urban II to free the Holy Places.
1097 Edgar, second son of Malcolm Canmore, King of Scotland (to 1107); he defeats Donald Bane with the assistance of William II of England.
1098 St Robert founds the first Cistercian monastery at Cîteaux, France.
Crusaders defeat the Saracens (Muslims) at Antioch.
1099 Crusaders capture Jerusalem; Godfrey of Bouillon is elected King of Jerusalem.
1100 Henry I, youngest son of William the Conqueror, King of England (to 1135), following assassination of William Rufus.
Baldwin of Bouillon, Count of Edessa; Raymond of Toulouse, Count of Tripoli; Bohemund of Otranto, Prince of Antioch.
Colonization of Polynesian islands under way.
1104 Crusaders capture Acre.
1106 Henry V, Holy Roman Emperor (to 1125).
Henry I defeats his brother Robert, Duke of Normandy, at battle of Tinchebrai: Robert remains captive for life.
1107 Alexander I, younger brother of Edgar, King of Scotland (to 1124). ·
1108 Louis VI, King of France (to 1137).
1109 War between England and France (until 1113).
1111 Emperor Henry V forces Pope Paschal II to acknowledge power of the emperor.
1113 Founding of the Order of St John is formally acknowledged by the papacy.

Art and Literature

The Middle Ages produced much fine craftsmanship, mostly dedicated to the glory of God.

In *architecture* a style called *Romanesque* developed about 1000; buildings were massive, with sturdy pillars and rounded arches. During the 1100s a lighter style evolved, now known as *Gothic*. Pointed arches and slender pillars in cathedrals gave an appearance of grace and elaborate decoration.

Painters of the period aimed at realistic figures, and used bright colours under the influence of Byzantine (eastern European) art. Monks produced illuminated (illustrated) manuscripts. But artists had not yet fully mastered the technique of perspective.

In *music*, the plainsong or Church chant dominated the simple melodic music of the time, but gradually composers began to put two or more melodies together, producing *polyphonic* (many-voiced) music. Such composers included John Dunstable of England and Guillaume de Marchaut of France; their style was known as *Ars Nova*, the 'New Art'.

Literature was dominated at first by stories in verse, the *sagas* of the Vikings and the *romances* of knighthood and chivalry such as the legends of King Arthur and Charlemagne. Shorter *lyric* poetry grew up in the later Middle Ages, with Italy's Dante Alighieri and Petrarch. In England, Geoffrey Chaucer combined stories in verse with shrewd commentaries on life and the people around him.

Medieval writers: from left Dante, Petrarch, and Chaucer.

The Crusading Orders of Knighthood

The Crusades which began in 1096 and lasted until nearly 1300 gave a great opportunity to the idealistic knights of Christian Europe. For many, the legends of romance and chivalry could come true in battle against the Saracens (Muslims). A number of special orders of knights were founded, pledged to liberate the Holy Land (Palestine) from the infidels (followers of Islam), and to protect Christian pilgrims.

The first was the Order of the Hospital of St John, founded in Italy in 1080 and approved by the pope in 1113. The Knights Hospitallers, as they were called, were dedicated to guarding a pilgrim hospital, or hostel, in Jerusalem. The Order of Knights Templars, founded in Jerusalem in 1119, was formed especially to fight in the Crusades. Its name came from the fact that the knights had their headquarters on the site of Solomon's Temple.

An illuminated 'B' in the Winchester Bible (1100s).

St Bernard, who founded the Cistercian monastery at Clairvaux in France, shown with his monks in a 15th-century stained-glass window. Many monastic orders reached the height of their powers in the Middle Ages.

1114 Matilda (Maud), daughter of Henry I of England, marries Emperor Henry V.
1115 Stephen II, King of Hungary (to 1131).
St Bernard founds the Abbey of Clairvaux, France, and becomes its first abbot.
1118 John II Comnenus, Byzantine Emperor (to 1143).
1119 Hugues de Payens founds the Order of Knights Templars.
1120 William, heir of Henry I of England, is drowned in wreck of the 'White Ship'.
1122 Concordat of Worms: conference of German princes ends the dispute between pope and emperor over appointing bishops.
1123 Death of Omar Khayyám, Persian poet.
1124 David I, younger brother of Alexander I, King of Scotland (to 1153).
1125 Lothair of Saxony elected Holy Roman Emperor (to 1137).
1126 Alfonso VII, King of Castile, Spain (to 1157).
1128 Alfonso Henriques, Count of Portugal; makes Portugal independent of Spain by 1143.
1129 Empress Matilda, widow of Henry V, marries Geoffrey the Handsome, Count of Anjou, nicknamed 'Plantagenet'.
1130 Almohad Dynasty, founded by the preacher Ibn Tumart, comes to power in Morocco (until 1169).
1135 Stephen of Boulogne seizes the English crown on the death of his uncle, Henry I; civil war breaks out.
1137 Louis VII, King of France (to 1180).
1138 Conrad III, Holy Roman Emperor (to 1152).
Battle of the Standard: defeat of David I of Scotland, fighting on behalf of Matilda in English civil war.
1139 Matilda lands in England.
The Second Lateran Council ends a schism in the Church following the illegal election of Anacletus II as rival to Innocent II.
1141 Matilda captures Stephen at the battle of Lincoln, and reigns disastrously as queen; she is driven out by a popular rising, and Stephen restored.
1143 Alfonso becomes King of Portugal (to 1185).
1145 The Almohades begin conquest of Moorish Spain which continues until 1150.
1147 The Second Crusade, following an appeal by St Bernard of Clairvaux (ends 1149).
1148 The Crusaders fail to capture Damascus.
Matilda leaves England for the last time.
1151 Toltec Empire in Mexico comes to an end.
Death of Geoffrey of Anjou.
1152 Marriage of Louis VII of France and Eleanor of Aquitaine is annulled on grounds of blood relationship.

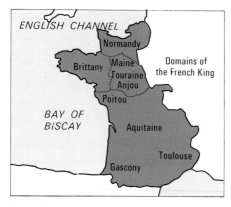

England's French possessions in the 1100s.

Henry of Anjou

The death of Henry I, William the Conqueror's youngest son, in 1135 plunged England into civil war, because he left no son to succeed him. Henry bequeathed the throne to his daughter, Matilda, but it was seized by his nephew, Stephen of Blois. Matilda, who was married to Geoffrey of Anjou, failed to gain control of England, but she did retain Normandy. In 1153 her son, Henry, invaded England and forced Stephen to make him his heir.

Henry II, who became king when Stephen died in 1154, was the ruler of a vast empire. He had inherited Normandy from his mother, and Anjou, Touraine, and Maine from his father. In 1152 he married Eleanor, divorced wife of the French King Louis VII. She brought him as her dowry the rich duchy of Aquitaine, so that Henry then ruled more than half of France.

The dynasty founded by Henry is properly known as *Angevin*, from the family estate of Anjou, but its popular name is *Plantagenet*. This name comes from a nickname applied to Henry's father who wore a sprig of broom, *planta genista*, in his cap as a badge.

The Island City

The city of Venice was founded in the 500s by refugees from the Huns and the Lombards. Settling on islands among the lagoons along Italy's north Adriatic coast, they gradually established trade based on salt and salted fish. Venetian merchants built fleets in which they sailed to the ports of the Levant – the eastern Mediterranean – where they traded their own wares for goods from eastern Asia – spices from the Indies, gold and jewels from India, silk from China. The spice trade was particularly valuable since spices were a means of preserving and flavouring food in the winter.

Venetian merchants had a hand in the first three crusades, and so won trading rights in ports like Sidon and Tyre. In the fourth crusade of 1204, in exchange for ships, the crusaders recaptured Zara (in Yugoslavia) for Venice and sacked Constantinople which Venice partly acquired. In the late Middle Ages the area from the Aegean Sea to Rhodes and Crete was dominated by the Venetians, and in the 14th and 15th centuries Venice was the richest trading city in Europe.

Thomas the Martyr

As a young man of education, Thomas à Becket entered the service of Theobald, Archbishop of Canterbury, who rewarded him for his work with the archdeaconry of Canterbury. In 1155 Becket was chosen by Henry II to be the royal chancellor, a post he held for seven years as a close and loyal servant to the King.

Then Henry rewarded Becket by making him Archbishop of Canterbury in succession to Theobald. At once his whole character changed: Becket lived a life of simplicity and poverty, and though he had helped Henry to curb the power of the bishops, he now actively asserted the Church's rights.

Violent quarrels with Henry and a long period of exile followed. After being reconciled, the two men disputed once more; Henry asked who would rid him of 'this turbulent priest'. Four knights heard, and killed Becket on the altar steps at Canterbury. Becket was canonized in 1173 and Canterbury became a pilgrim shrine.

Thomas à Becket, Archbishop of Canterbury, is murdered in his own cathedral by the four knights Richard Brito, Hugh de Morville, William Tracy, and Reginald Fitzurse.

1152 Eleanor marries Henry of Anjou, allying Aquitaine to his lands of Anjou and Normandy, two months after her divorce.
Frederick I Barbarossa, Holy Roman Emperor (to 1190).

1153 Malcolm IV, 'The Maiden', grandson of David I, King of Scotland (to 1165).
Henry of Anjou, son of Matilda, invades England and forces Stephen to make him heir to the English throne.

1154 Henry II, King of England (to 1189); he also rules more than half of France.
Pope Adrian IV (to 1159) (Nicholas Breakspear, the only English pope).

1155 Henry II appoints the Archdeacon of Canterbury, Thomas à Becket, as Chancellor.
Adrian IV grants Henry II the right to rule Ireland.

1156 Civil wars ravage Japan (until 1185).

1158 Alfonso VIII, King of Castile (to 1214).

1159 Alexander III, Pope (to 1181).
Henry II levies scutage – payment in cash instead of military service.

1161 Explosives are used in China at the battle of Ts'ai-shih.

1162 Becket is appointed Archbishop of Canterbury and at once quarrels with Henry II over the Church's rights.

1164 Constitutions of Clarendon: restatement of laws governing trial of ecclesiastics in England; Becket is forced to flee to France.

1165 William the Lion, younger brother of Malcolm IV, King of Scotland (to 1214).

1167 Amalric, King of Jerusalem, captures Cairo.

1168 Arabs recapture Cairo.

1169 Saladin (Salah-al-Din Yusuf ibn-Ayyub), vizier of Egypt (to 1193); sultan from 1174.

1170 Becket is reconciled with Henry II, returns to Canterbury; is murdered by four knights after Henry's hasty words against him.

1171 Henry II formally annexes Ireland.

1173 Rebellion of Henry's eldest sons, Henry, Richard, and Geoffrey, supported by their mother, Eleanor of Aquitaine.
Thomas à Becket canonized.

1174 Saladin conquers Syria.

1177 Baldwin IV of Jerusalem defeats Saladin at Montgisard.

1179 Grand Assize of Windsor, increasing power of royal courts in England.
Saladin besieges Tyre.

1180 Truce between Baldwin IV and Saladin.
Philip II, King of France (to 1223).
Alexius II Comnenus, Byzantine Emperor (to 1183).

1182 Philip II banishes the Jews from France.

The Middle Ages

Opposite: The armour of a Japanese samurai was not only efficient but also very beautiful. Made of enamelled metal links, it was tough as well as light and flexible. The samurai were a powerful warrior class who played an important part in Japan's political struggles.

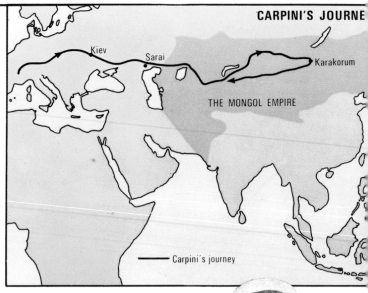

CARPINI'S JOURNE

Kiev
Sarai
Karakorum

THE MONGOL EMPIRE

—— Carpini's journey

The Franciscan friar John of Plano Carpini crossed Asia to contact the Mongols on behalf of the pope. Carpini wrote of the discipline, speed, and skill of the mounted Mongol warriors.

The Mongols

In the early Middle Ages the Mongols were a group of nomadic tribes living in Mongolia, in central Asia. They were herdsmen and fierce warriors. In the 1190s one tribal chief, Temujin – later called Genghis Khan – united the tribes and set out to extend Mongol rule through northern China, Siberia, and Persia.

His grandson, Kublai Khan, completed the conquest of China and founded the Yuan dynasty there. Mongol warriors under Batu swept into eastern Europe in 1237, and a year later set up the Mongol kingdom known as the Golden Horde on the lower reaches of the Volga River. Later empires were set up by Tamerlane in western and central Asia in the late 1300s, and by Babar in India in 1526. This kingdom was known as the Mughal empire, from a Persian version of the word Mongol. It lasted into the 1700s.

Genghis Khan had an empire stretching from Korea to the Black Sea, and was attacking China when he died in 1227, aged 65.

The Shoguns

Although Japan can claim that records of its emperors date from 660 BC, the emperors have had very little power in the country since the Middle Ages. From 1192 to 1867, power was exercised by the *shoguns*, a title meaning supreme commanders.

The first shoguns were appointed to subdue the Ainu of northern Japan about 720 and the post remained. In 1192 Minamoto Yoritomo was given the title of shogun with authority over all Japan's military families. As the power of such families grew, so did those of the shogun. In effect, the shogunate was a military dictatorship – but one that was hereditary.

The post of shogun was inherited by members of the Minamoto family until the 1300s, when the Ashikaga family took over. This family ruled until the 1600s, when the Tokugawa family assumed the shogunate. In 1868 the last Tokugawa shogun was forced by a court revolution to hand his powers back to the emperor.

1183 Andronicus I, Byzantine Emperor (to 1185).
1185 Sancho I, King of Portugal (to 1211).
Kamakura period in Japan (until 1333).
Isaac II, Byzantine Emperor (to 1195).
1187 Saladin captures Jerusalem.
1189 Richard I, Coeur de Lion, eldest surviving son of Henry II, King of England (to 1199).
Last recorded Norse visit to North America.
Third Crusade (ended 1192): leaders, Frederick Barbarossa, Philip of France, Richard of England.
1190 Mongol leader Temujin begins to create an empire in eastern Asia.
Frederick Barbarossa is drowned on his way to Palestine.
Henry VI, Holy Roman Emperor (to 1197).
Lalibela, Emperor of Ethiopia (to 1225).
1191 Richard I conquers Cyprus and captures the city of Acre.
1192 Richard I captures Jaffa, makes peace with Saladin; on the way home he is captured by his enemy, Duke Leopold of Austria.
Minamoto Yoritomo, Shogun of Japan.
1193 Death of Saladin.
Leopold hands Richard over to Emperor Henry VI, who demands a ransom.
Muslims capture Bihar and Bengal.
Al-Aziz Imad al-Din, successor to Saladin (to 1198).
1194 Henry VI conquers Sicily.
Richard is ransomed and returned to England.
1195 Alexius III, Byzantine Emperor (to 1203).
1196 Marimid Dynasty in Morocco (lasts until 1464); founded at Fez.
Pedro II, King of Aragon (to 1213).
1197 Ottakar I, King of Bohemia (to 1230).
Civil war follows the death of Henry VI in Germany.
1198 Otto IV, Holy Roman Emperor (to 1212).
Innocent III, Pope (to 1216).
1199 John Lackland, youngest son of Henry II, King of England (to 1216).
1200 Hunac Ceel revolts against the Maya of Chichén Itzá and sets up a new capital at Mayapán.
Jews are given special privileges in Morocco.
1202 Famine in Egypt (until 1204).
Fourth Crusade (ends 1204): crusaders, unable to pay Venice for transport, agree to conquer on its behalf.
1203 John of England orders the murder of his nephew Arthur, Duke of Brittany.
1204 Crusaders capture Constantinople and sack it, installing a Latin ruler.
1206 Temujin is proclaimed Genghis Khan, 'Emperor within the Seas'.

Trade

In the Middle Ages roads were bad and much of the trade was carried out by sea and river. In Northern Europe the countries around the Baltic produced grain, timber, fish and furs, while wool and cloth were particularly important in England. Many of the goods were taken to the great markets at Bruges and Antwerp in the Netherlands. Here too came galleys from Venice bringing wine, olives, fruit and salt from the warm Mediterranean countries. They also brought luxuries from the east including silks, jewels, and spices used for preserving food.

Trade routes overland in Europe followed the old Roman roads, though these were now usually just gravel and mud. Traffic was heavy. Merchants loaded their goods on to pack animals and travelled in convoys for safety. No one travelled at night for fear of robbers. Trade fairs grew where the main routes crossed. The region of Champagne in eastern France became famous for the fairs held there every year, the most important of which lasted 49 days.

The Cloth Hall at Ypres in Belgium, built in the 13th century. A magnificent example of Gothic architecture, the hall reflects the wealth and international importance of the Flemish clothing trade at the time. It was destroyed during World War I but later rebuilt.

Above: The seal of King John upon the Magna Carta was a major step for democracy away from the absolute power of the Crown.

The Great Charter

King John of England abused his power and privilege, taxing his subjects harshly and seizing Church lands. Barons and Church leaders banded together, and assembled to meet John at Runnymede, by the river Thames, on June 15, 1215. There they drew up a document to which the King had to append his seal.

The barons designed the document, later to be known as the Magna Carta – the Great Charter – to protect their interests and to gain power at the expense of the Crown. But it is regarded as one of the foundations of modern democracy since it guaranteed tax collection only by legal means, justice to all men without fear or favour, and no imprisonment without trial. Many legal systems are based on this charter.

1206 Dynasty of slave kings in India (until 1290).
1207 Pope Innocent III appoints Stephen Langton Archbishop of Canterbury; John refuses to let him take office.
1208 Innocent III lays England under interdict. Crusade against Albigensians, heretical sect in France (until 1213).
1209 Cambridge University is founded in England. Innocent excommunicates John for attacks on Church property.
1210 Innocent excommunicates Emperor Otto IV. Francis of Assisi founds the Franciscan Order. Mongols led by Genghis Khan begin invasion of China.
1211 Alfonso II, King of Portugal (to 1223).
1212 Frederick II, Holy Roman Emperor (to 1250). Children's Crusade: 30,000 children from France and Germany set off for Palestine – probable origin of 'Pied Piper' legend; thousands are sold into slavery.
1213 Innocent declares John deposed; John hurriedly makes peace. James I, the Conqueror, King of Aragon (to 1276).
1215 Magna Carta: English barons force John to agree to a statement of their rights. St Dominic founds the Dominican Order, a body of preaching friars, at Toulouse.
1216 Henry III becomes king of England at age nine (to 1272). Honorius III, Pope (to 1227).
1217 Fifth Crusade (ends 1222): it fails to capture Egypt.
1218 Genghis Khan conquers Persia.
1219 Mongols conquer Bokhara. Hojo clan rules Japan (until 1333), following the end of the Minamoto family.
1223 Louis VIII, King of France (to 1226). Mongols invade Russia.
1224 War between France and England (ends 1227).
1226 Louis IX (St Louis), King of France (to 1270).
1227 Gregory IX, Pope (to 1241). Henry III begins personal rule in England. Genghis Khan dies, and his empire is divided among his sons.
1228 Sixth Crusade, led by Emperor Frederick II (ends 1229); Crusaders recapture Jerusalem. Teutonic Knights begin conquering Prussia.
1229 Ogadai, son of Genghis, is elected khan (to 1241).
1232 Earliest known use of rockets in war between Mongols and Chinese.
1234 Mongols annex the Chin Empire.
1235 Sundiata Keita; King of Mali (to 1255).
1236 Alexander Nevski, Prince of Novgorod (to 1263).

Father of the Commons

The development of the English Parliament owes a great deal to a French-born nobleman, Simon de Montfort, Earl of Leicester (c. 1208–1265). He was married to Eleanor, sister of the King, Henry III.

Henry was a dictatorial ruler, influenced by foreign advisers whom he made his favourites. His actions aroused the anger of the barons – the nobles of England.

De Montfort, a clever and strong-minded man, became the leader of the barons. In 1258 he forced Henry to agree to the *Provisions of Oxford*, a programme of reforms. One reform was that a council of 15 barons was to advise Henry how to rule. But in 1261

Henry went back on his word and cancelled all the reforms. Civil war broke out early in 1264, and within a few weeks de Montfort captured Henry and his heir, Prince Edward, at the battle of Lewes.

De Montfort ruled England for more than a year. In 1264 and 1265 he called a Parliament in Henry's name, in which for the first time burgesses – leading citizens from the main towns – were summoned to take part. They were the first commoners to become members of Parliament. This act has earned de Montfort the title 'Father of the House of Commons'. But soon afterwards Prince Edward escaped, raised an army, and killed de Montfort at the battle of Evesham.

The Habsburgs

For more than 600 years European politics was dominated by members of the Habsburg family. During this period they provided nearly all the Holy Roman emperors; they ruled the Austrian Empire until World War I; and during the 1500s became kings of Spain. The family name comes from their castle, called Habichtsburg, 'Hawk's castle', in Switzerland.

Rudolf IV of Habsburg was elected 'king of Germany' in 1273. He was effectively the family's first Holy Roman emperor but could not be crowned because of intrigues at the papal court. He then added Austria and Styria to his hereditary possessions. The Spanish Crown came when Philip the Fair married the heiress of Castile and Aragon. But intermarriage weakened the line, and the Spanish Habsburgs died out in 1700.

The interior of Sainte-Chapelle, Paris, a Gothic masterpiece built by Louis IX to house relics brought back from the Holy Land.

Opposite: Rudolf of Habsburg receives news of his election as German king in 1273. Though effectively Holy Roman Emperor, he was never crowned.

King and Saint

Louis IX of France was a great soldier, a wise and just ruler, and an outstandingly good and holy man. He succeeded to the throne when he was only 12 but his mother, Madame Blanche, held the kingdom together against the threat of discontented nobles. When Louis took over power he proved a strong king, anxious to maintain feudal relationships and live at peace with neighbouring kingdoms. He was sought as an arbitrator from far and wide, and devoted as he was to the Church he never allowed it to influence him unduly. He died of plague on the Eighth Crusade, and was canonized in 1297.

1240 End of the Empire of Ghana: it is incorporated into the Kingdom of Mali.
Mongols capture Moscow.
Mongols destroy Kiev.
Battle of Neva: Alexander Nevski defeats the Swedes.

1241 Mongols withdraw from Europe following the death of Ogadai Khan.

1242 Batu establishes Mongol kingdom of 'The Golden Horde' on lower Volga River.

1243 Innocent IV, Pope (to 1254).
Egyptians capture Jerusalem from the Christians.

1245 Innocent IV calls the Synod of Lyon, which declares Frederick II deposed.

1247 Bitter war in Italy between Frederick and papal allies (ends 1250).

1248 Seventh Crusade, led by Louis IX of France (ends 1270).

1250 Conrad IV, Holy Roman Emperor (to 1254).
Saracens capture Louis IX in Egypt; he is ransomed.

1253 Ottokar II, the Great, King of Bohemia (to 1278).

1254 The Great Interregnum; bitter struggle for the Imperial crown (to 1273).

1256 Pope Alexander IV founds the Augustinian Order from several groups of hermits.
Prince Llewellyn sweeps English from Wales.

1260 Kublai, Mongol leader, is elected khan by his army at Shan-tu, in China.
Yüan (Mongol) Dynasty in China (until 1368).

1261 Urban IV, Pope (to 1264).

1263 Norway gives up the Hebrides to the Scots.

1264 Simon de Montfort and other English barons defeat Henry III at battle of Lewes.

1265 De Montfort's Parliament: burgesses from major towns summoned to Parliament for the first time.
Henry III's son Edward defeats and kills Simon de Montfort at battle of Evesham.
Clement IV, Pope (to 1268).

1268 Muslims from Egypt capture Antioch, held by the Christians.
Papacy vacant until 1271.

1270 Death of Louis IX of France on Seventh Crusade.
Philip III, the Bold, King of France (to 1285).

1271 Marco Polo, his father, and his uncle set off to visit the court of Kublai Khan; return 1295.
Gregory X, Pope (to 1276).

1272 Edward I, King of England (to 1307).

1273 Rudolf I, Holy Roman Emperor (to 1291).

1274 Synod of Lyons, called by Pope Gregory X, recommends that conclaves should be secret to avoid corruption.

Merchants of Venice

The traders of Venice travelled far and wide in their search for merchandise and customers, but few so far as the brothers Nicolò and Maffeo Polo, and Nicolò's son Marco. In 1260 the brothers set out on a venture which took them to the court of the Mongol Emperor Kublai Khan in China. It was so successful that when they returned to Venice in 1269 they decided to go back to China, taking Marco.

When the Polos returned in 1295 they were laden with rubies and emeralds. They had spent altogether 17 years at Kublai Khan's court, and Marco had become a travelling envoy for the Great Khan.

Three years after his return Marco was taken prisoner in a sea battle with the Genoans. In captivity, he dictated the story of his adventures, *The Book of Marco Polo*. His contemporaries dismissed many of his tales as imaginary, but research has confirmed a number of them.

Right: The Emperor Kublai Khan, for whom Marco Polo became a travelling envoy. Top right: Part of Kublai Khan's capital of Cambaluc, now called Peking.

Opposite: The great seal of John Balliol, King of Scotland.

Left: The caravan of the Venetian explorer Marco Polo, from an old Catalan manuscript. Marco, his father, Nicolò Polo, and his uncle Maffeo Polo, travelled to Cathay (China) from 1271 to 1275. They stayed there in the service of Kublai Khan until 1292, when they set out for home. They reached Venice again in 1295.

Balliol and Bruce

When Alexander III of Scotland died in 1286 his heir was a three-year-old granddaughter, Margaret, known as 'The Maid of Norway' because her mother was queen of Norway. But the little girl died in 1290, and 13 men at once laid claim to the throne of Scotland. The Scottish lords asked Edward I of England to arbitrate, and he chose John Balliol, a descendant of the Scottish royal house. But Balliol rebelled, so Edward deposed him and ruled Scotland himself for 10 years.

An abortive rebellion by a patriotic knight, William Wallace, in 1297–1298 was crushed with great severity, and Wallace was executed in 1305. But the following year a new champion appeared: Robert Bruce, a distant cousin of Balliol. Edward died on his way to Scotland to fight Bruce, and the Scots cleared the English from their land. In 1314 Edward's feeble son, Edward II, led a fresh army to crush Bruce, but was overwhelmingly defeated at the battle of Bannockburn. War continued until 1328, when the English recognized Scottish independence with Robert Bruce as king.

1274 First Mongol invasion of Japan at orders of Kublai Khan; Mongols fail to gain a foothold.
1275 Marco Polo enters the service of Kublai Khan.
1276 Innocent V, first Dominican to become pope, dies five months after election.
Adrian V dies five weeks after being elected pope, but revokes conclave rules.
Pope John XXI (to 1277), who dies after eight months in office.
1277 English Franciscan philosopher Roger Bacon is exiled for heresy (until 1292).
Nicholas III, Pope (to 1280).
1278 Rudolf I defeats and kills Ottokar of Bohemia at battle of the Marchfeld.
1279 Rudolf I surrenders claims to Sicily and the Papal States.
1280 Death of Albertus Magnus, German philosopher and scientist.
1281 Second Mongol invasion of Japan ends in disaster.
Martin IV, Pope (to 1285).
1283 Edward I defeats and kills Llewellyn, Prince of Wales, and executes Llewellyn's brother David; conquest of Wales complete.
1285 Philip IV, the Fair, King of France (to 1314).
Honorius IV, Pope (to 1287).
1286 Margaret, the Maid of Norway, child Queen of Scotland, in succession to her grandfather Alexander III (to 1290).
1288 Nicholas IV, Pope (to 1292).
1289 Friar John of Montecorvino becomes the first archbishop of Peking.
1290 Struggle for the succession in Scotland follows the death of Margaret, the Maid of Norway: 13 people claim the throne.
Turkish leader Firuz founds the Khalji Dynasty (until 1320) in Delhi.
Edward I expels all Jews from England.
1291 Saracens (Muslims) capture Acre, last Christian stronghold in Palestine. End of the crusades.
Scots acknowledge Edward I of England as suzerain; he arbitrates in succession dispute.
1292 John Balliol, King of Scotland on the nomination of Edward I (to 1296).
Adolf, Count of Nassau, Holy Roman Emperor (to 1298).
1294 Death of Kublai Khan.
Celestine V (the hermit Peter of Morrone), Pope; he resigns after five months.
Boniface VIII, Pope, lawyer, diplomat, and practiser of magic arts (to 1303).
1295 Temur Oljaitu (Ch'eng Tsung), grandson of Kublai Khan, Emperor of China (to 1307).
Model Parliament of Edward I: knights and burgesses from English shires and towns summoned. First representative parliament.

The Friars

The first Christian religious orders consisted of men or women who withdrew from the world the better to worship God in the great monasteries which spread over Europe in the Middle Ages. But the growth of towns, and of poor communities of people in them who had no contact with religion, brought a need for an order of teachers. These were the friars, a term which comes from the Latin word *frater*, brother, by which they addressed one another.

The first friars were the Franciscans, the 'little brothers' or Friars Minor founded by St Francis of Assisi in 1210. Six years later St Dominic founded the Dominican Order. Members of both orders were dedicated to lives of poverty and simplicity, spending their time preaching and teaching, and earning their livelihood by the work of their hands. In time the friars became too busy with their religious duties to do other work, and had to live by begging; for this reason friars of the teaching orders are called mendicants. Other important orders are the Carmelites, who came from Palestine to Europe in the mid-13th century, and the Austin Friars or Friars Hermit who developed in the 12th century.

The 'Babylonian Captivity'

The last great attempt to assert the temporal power of the papacy was made by Boniface VIII, who was elected pope in 1294. His rude and domineering ways, and his attempts to feather the nest of his own family, led to an attempt to force his resignation. His successor, Benedict XI, died almost immediately, possibly poisoned. The next pope was a Frenchman, Clement V, who removed the papal court from Rome to Avignon, in southern France, to escape the political turmoil which was raging in Italy.

The papacy remained at Avignon during the reign of seven popes, from 1305 to 1377, when Pope Gregory XI transferred the papal court back to Rome. This period of papal history is often called the 'Babylonian Captivity', an allusion to the time when the Jews were held captive in Babylon.

The Sankore Mosque in Timbuktu, built in 1469, a sign of Muslim influence in the Mali Empire.

Left: This fresco (wall painting) by the artist Giotto shows St Francis preaching to the birds. St Francis founded the first order of friars, called Franciscans after him.

The Mali Empire

The ancient kingdom of Ghana, in western Africa, collapsed in 1076, and in its place there arose the greatest of all medieval African empires, that of Mali. Ghana lingered on under Berber – and Muslim – rule until 1240, when the king of Mali, Sundiata Keita, finally conquered it. Sundiata was a Mandingo, one of a group of Negro peoples who still live in present-day Mali.

The rulers of Mali were Muslims, and Timbuktu, already a notable trading centre, became a centre of Muslim culture and learning as well. After a period during which the Mossi kingdom of the upper Volta region overran part of Mali and sacked Timbuktu, Mali regained its power under Sulaiman, king from about 1341 to 1360.

The Mali empire finally succumbed to combined onslaughts from the Tuareg tribes in the north and the Mossi from the south during the 1400s.

1296 Edward I of England deposes John Balliol from Scottish throne.
Interregnum in Scotland (until 1306).
Conflict between Philip IV of France and Pope Boniface VIII over papal powers in France (ends 1303).
1297 Battle of Cambuskenneth: Scottish patriot William Wallace defeats English army.
1298 Edward I defeats Wallace at battle of Falkirk and reconquers Scotland
Albert I, Holy Roman Emperor (to 1308) following defeat and death of Adolf at battle of Göllheim.
1300 Wenceslas II, King of Poland.
1301 Edward I of England invests his baby son Edward as Prince of Wales.
Osman, founder of the Ottoman Turks, defeats the Byzantines.
1302 Battle of Courtrai: burghers of Flanders defeat the flower of French chivalry and save their country from French occupation.
Papal Bull *Unam Sanctam* declares papal authority to be supreme.
1303 Guillaume de Nogaret, emissary of Philip IV of France, captures Pope Boniface VIII at Anagni, Italy, and ill-treats him; the Pope is rescued by the citizens of Anagni, but dies soon after in Rome.
Benedict XI, Pope (to 1304).
1304 Petrarch, Italian poet, born (dies 1374).
1305 Clement V, Pope (Bertrand de Got, Archbishop of Bordeaux) (to 1314).
The 'Babylonian Captivity': the papal see removed from Rome to Avignon, France (until 1377).
The English capture and execute William Wallace.
1306 Philip IV expels the Jews from France.
New Scottish rebellion against English rule led by Robert Bruce.
Robert I, the Bruce crowned King of Scotland (to 1329) at Scone.
1307 Edward I dies on march north to crush Robert Bruce.
Edward II, King of England (to 1327).
1308 Henry VII, Holy Roman Emperor (to 1313).
1310 English barons appoint 21 peers – the Lords Ordainers – to manage Edward II's household.
1312 Order of Knights Templars abolished for malpractices.
1314 Battle of Bannockburn: Robert Bruce defeats Edward II and makes Scotland independent.
Louis X, the Quarrelsome, King of France (to 1316).
Louis IV, Holy Roman Emperor (to 1347); civil war with his rival, Frederick of Austria.

The Hundred Years' War

The long struggle between England and France known as the Hundred Years' War lasted from 1337 to 1453, and was actually a series of wars. The main cause was a claim by English kings to the throne of France. There were four periods in the war:

1337–1360: Edward III of England claimed the French throne through his mother, Isabella of France. After the naval victory of Sluys and the land victories of Crécy and Poitiers, Edward secured a large part of France under the Treaty of Brétigny.

1360–1396: The French gradually recaptured most of France, as England lost its best generals, Edward III and his son Edward the Black Prince. A truce made in 1389 was extended in 1396 for 28 years.

1415–1422: Henry V revived the English claim to the French throne, and in a swift campaign compelled the partly insane French King Charles VI to make him his heir. Henry married Charles's daughter Catherine, but died in 1422 leaving a baby as his heir.

1422–1453: War flared up again. The English scored initial victories, but the peasant girl Jeanne d'Arc put new faith into the French armies, and by 1453 Calais was the only English possession left in France.

Between the mid-12th and early 14th centuries many magnificent cathedrals were built in France. Among them were Laon, Notre Dame in Paris, Bourges, Rheims, Amiens, Le Mans and, perhaps most famous of all, Chartres (left). They are built in the style known as Gothic, with tall pointed arches, and many contain beautiful stained glass. Money for cathedral building came from rich and poor and the people of Chartres are said to have harnessed themselves to the carts which carried the great limestone blocks to the cathedral from the quarry.

1315 Swiss defeat Leopold of Austria at battle of Morgarten.
1316 John XXII, Pope (to 1334).
The papacy sends eight Dominican friars to Ethiopia in search of Prester John, a legendary Christian emperor.
Philip V, the Tall, King of France (to 1322).
1317 France adopts the Salic Law, excluding women from succession to the throne.
1318 Swiss make peace with the Habsburgs.
1320 Tughluk Dynasty in Delhi (until 1413), founded by the Turk Ghidyas-ud-din Tughluk.
1322 Charles IV, the Fair, King of France (to 1328).
1325 Traditional foundation date of Tenochtitlán (now Mexico City) by the Aztecs.
1326 First Polish War: the Teutonic Knights defeat the Poles in 1333.
Queen Isabella and Roger Mortimer sail from France with an army to rebel against Edward II of England.
1327 Parliament declares Edward II deposed, and his son accedes to the throne as Edward III. Edward II is murdered nine months later.
Holy Roman Emperor Louis IV invades Italy and declares Pope John XXII deposed.
1328 Philip VI, King of France (to 1350); first king of the House of Valois.
1329 David II, King of Scotland (to 1371), succeeding his father, Robert Bruce.
1332 Edward Balliol, son of John Balliol, attempts to seize the throne of Scotland, with the help of the English; he is driven back over the border.
1333 Edward III invades Scotland on Balliol's behalf and defeats the Scots at battle of Halidon Hill.
Emperor Daigo II of Japan overthrows the Hojo family of shoguns and sets up period of personal rule (to 1336).
1334 Benedict XII, Pope (to 1342).
1335 Pope Benedict XII issues reforms of the monastic orders.
1336 Revolution in Japan: Daigo II is exiled.
Ashikaga family rule Japan as shoguns (until 1568); period begins with civil war lasting until 1392.
1337 Edward III of England, provoked by French attacks on his territories in France, declares himself king of France. Beginning of 'The Hundred Years' War' between England and France (ends 1453).
1338 Declaration of Rense: Electors of the Holy Roman Empire declare the empire to be independent from the papacy.
Treaty of Coblenz: alliance between England and the Holy Roman Empire.

Right: The battle of Crécy, the first major engagement of the Hundred Years' War. English soldiers under Edward III defeated a much larger number of French under Philip VI near Abbeville, in northern France, in 1346. The supremacy of the English longbow won the day.

Flagellants in procession being whipped and blessed, a custom that grew up in the late 1200s and the 1300s, particularly at the time of the Black Death. Flagellation, or whipping, was a form of penance for sins, designed to reduce the punishment one would otherwise receive in the next world.

The Black Death

The Black Death was a fearful epidemic of bubonic plague which caused havoc throughout Europe. The outbreak started in China and spread along the trade routes to the west, carried by the fleas on rats. In 1347 it appeared in Cyprus, and by the following year had spread to France, Italy, Germany, and England. In 1349 it was in Poland, Scandinavia, and Scotland, and in 1351 it ravaged Russia.

Altogether about 25,000,000 Europeans died – about a quarter of the continent's population. The Black Death caused a great shortage of labour, and wages rose enormously: in England men received an average of 50 per cent more, and women 100 per cent more. The result was to strengthen the position of the humbler workers, and to hasten the end of the feudal system on which medieval society was based.

The Hanseatic League

Traders in the Middle Ages formed associations for mutual protection, often of merchants from the same town. In Germany, a guild of this kind was known as a *Hanse*, and German traders in the 1100s established hanses in most of the important ports of the Baltic and North Seas.

Gradually the hanses of several towns began to link up for trading purposes, and under the leadership of two cities, Lübeck and Cologne, they formed the powerful Hanseatic League, an alliance of nearly 100 towns. In its heyday the League dominated the foreign trade of Denmark, Norway, and Sweden, and almost dominated that of London: any town which refused to give trading concessions to the League had its own trade boycotted wherever the League had influence.

The Hanseatic League began to lose power in the late 1400s, in the face of strong competition from other countries, and by 1600 it had little strength left.

The seal of Danzig, a leading Hanseatic town on the Baltic Sea.

1340	Naval victory at Sluys gives England the command of the English Channel.
	English Parliament passes four statutes providing that taxation shall be imposed only by Parliament.
1341	Sulaiman, King of Mali (to 1360).
	Italian poet Petrarch (Francesco Petrarca) is crowned Poet Laureate at the Capitol in Rome.
1342	Clement VI, Pope (to 1352).
1343	Peace of Kalisch gives the Teutonic Knights land cutting off Poland from access to the Baltic Sea.
1344	First known use of the term Hanseatic League.
1346	Edward III of England invades France with a large army and defeats an even bigger army under Philip VI at the battle of Crécy.
	Stephen Dushan, King of the Serbs, is crowned 'Emperor of the Serbs and Greeks'.
	Battle of Neville's Cross: David II of Scotland defeated and captured by the English.
1347	The English capture Calais.
	The Black Death (bubonic plague) reaches Cyprus from eastern Asia.
	Charles IV, Holy Roman Emperor (to 1378).
	Italian patriot Cola da Rienzi assumes power in Rome, taking the title of 'tribune'; but is soon driven from office.
1348	Edward III establishes the Order of the Garter.
	The Black Death ravages Europe.
	Black Death reaches England.
1349	Persecution of the Jews in Germany.
1350	John II, King of France (to 1364).
	Pedro the Cruel, King of Castile (to 1369).
1351	The Black Death sweeps Russia.
	The English remove the Pope's power to give English benefices to foreigners.
1353	Statute of Praemunire: English Parliament forbids appeals to the Pope.
1354	Rienzi returns to power in Rome and is killed by his opponents.
1356	The Golden Bull: new constitution for the Holy Roman Empire, providing for seven electors.
	Edward the Black Prince, son of Edward III, defeats the French at the battle of Poitiers, capturing King John II.
1357	The French Estates-General, led by the merchant Etienne Marcel, attempts a series of reforms.
	The Scots ransom David II from the English.
1358	The *Jacquerie*, revolt by French peasants: it is suppressed by the Regent Charles, son of John II.
1360	Treaty of Brétigny ends the first stage of the Hundred Years' War: Edward III gives up claim to French throne.

John of Gaunt

John of Gaunt was an English prince who had a quiet but dominating effect on English politics during the second half of the 14th century. The third surviving son of Edward III, he was born at Ghent, in Flanders: *Gaunt* is a corruption of this name.

John was created earl of Richmond, and married Blanche, daughter of the duke of Lancaster. On Lancaster's death John inherited his estates, and was given the title too. Blanche died in 1369, and two years later John married Constance, daughter of Pedro I of Castile and Léon. At this time John virtually ruled England, because Edward III was growing senile and his heir, Edward the Black Prince, was also ill. By 1377 both Edwards were dead, leaving the Black Prince's 10-year-old son Richard II as king, with John of Gaunt as regent.

From 1386 to 1388 John led an expedition to Castile to try to overthrow its ruler, Juan I, whose father had murdered Pedro and usurped the throne. It failed, and John returned to England, where his loyalty to his nephew played a large part in keeping the ineffective Richard on his throne.

Constance lived until 1394, but in the 1370s John had several children by Katherine Swynford, believed to be a sister-in-law of the poet and diplomat Geoffrey Chaucer. After Constance died John married Katherine, and their illegitimate children, the Beauforts, were declared legitimate. It was through the Beauforts that Henry VII derived his shadowy claim to the throne.

After John of Gaunt died in 1399, his son Henry by his first marriage overthrew his cousin Richard II and made himself king as Henry IV.

The Ming Dynasty

The Yuan Dynasty which swept into power in China under the warrior-kings Genghis Khan and Kublai Khan ended in weakness and dissipation. The last Mongol emperor, Sun Ti, was superstitious and immoral; bad administration coupled with years of famine led to a general uprising, headed by Chu Yuan-chang, a peasant's son who had become a monk. After 13 years of campaigning he captured the capital and proclaimed a new dynasty, Ming, meaning 'brightness', in 1368. His 30-year reign as Emperor T'ai Tsu brought order back to the country. The third Ming emperor, Ch'eng Tsu, rebuilt the Great Wall and erected many of the great palaces of Peking. The closing years of the dynasty were marked by bad government; in 1644 the Manchus from Manchuria swept over the Great Wall, and the Ming Dynasty came to an end.

The Great Schism

When Pope Urban V decided the papacy should return to Rome from its long exile in Avignon, he found Rome poor and so went back to Avignon. His successor, Gregory XI, also visited Rome, where he died in 1378, but he too favoured Avignon. Under mob pressure the cardinals elected an Italian pope, Urban VI, who then proved cruel and autocratic.

A few months later 13 cardinals quietly left Rome, met at Fondi between Rome and Naples, and elected a rival pope, Clement VII. This divided the Church in what is known as the Great Schism. Clement and his successor Benedict XIII, elected in 1394, were based at Avignon, and are generally described as *anti-popes* – that is, popes not correctly elected. France, Scotland, and parts of Germany and Italy under French influence recognized the Avignon popes, others acknowledged the Roman popes.

In 1409 the College of Cardinals called the Council of Pisa, consisting of 500 delegates from all over Europe. The council formally deposed both popes and elected another, Alexander V. But the other popes refused to resign, and the schism was a triple one.

Alexander V died in 1410, and his successor, John XXIII, proved to be another unscrupulous man. Finally, the Council of Constance in 1417 deposed him, persuaded the Roman pope Gregory XII to resign, and won over the supporters of Benedict XIII of Avignon. A new pope, Martin V, was chosen, and the Great Schism was over.

Tamerlane (Timur the Lame), the Tatar ruler descended from Genghis Khan. From Samarkand he ruled over a kingdom in central Asia and conquered India, Baghdad, and Egypt before his death in 1405.

1363 Philip the Bold, son of John II, becomes Duke of Burgundy.
Mongol leader Tamerlane (Timur the Lame) begins the conquest of Asia.
1364 Charles V, the Wise, becomes King of France (to 1380), on the death in London of his father, John II, in captivity.
1367 Confederation of Cologne: 77 Hanse towns prepare for struggle with Denmark.
1368 Rebellion led by Chu Yüan-chang overthrows the Yüan (Mongol) Dynasty in China.
Ming Dynasty in China (to 1644).
1369 Tamerlane (Timur the Lame) becomes king of Samarkand.
Second stage of war between England and France begins.
1370 Peace of Stralsund establishes the power of the Hanse towns, with the right to veto Danish kings.
Edward the Black Prince sacks Limoges.
Gregory XI, Pope (to 1378).
1371 Robert II, King of Scotland (to 1390): the first Stuart monarch.
1372 French troops recapture Poitou and Brittany.
Naval battle of La Rochelle: French regain control of the English Channel.
1373 John of Gaunt, Duke of Lancaster, son of Edward III, leads new English invasion of France.
1374 John of Gaunt returns to England and takes charge of the government: Edward III in his dotage, the Black Prince ill.
1375 Truce of Bruges ends hostilities between England and France.
1376 The Good Parliament in England, called by Edward the Black Prince, introduces many reforms of government.
Death of Edward the Black Prince, aged 45.
The *Civil Dominion* of John Wyclif, an Oxford don, calling for Church reforms.
1377 Richard II, son of the Black Prince, King of England (to 1399).
Pope Gregory XI returns to Rome, ending the Babylonian Captivity' in Avignon.
1378 The Great Schism (ends 1417): rival popes elected.
Urban VI, Pope at Rome (to 1389).
Clement VII, antipope at Avignon (to 1394).
Wenceslas IV, Holy Roman Emperor (to 1400).
1380 Charles VI, King of France (to 1422).
1381 Peasants' Revolt in England.
1382 John Wyclif is expelled from Oxford because of his opposition to Church doctrines.
John I, King of Portugal (to 1433), founder of the Avis Dynasty.
The Scots, with a French army, attack England.

Henry the Navigator

Prince Henry the Navigator (1394–1460), the third son of King John of Portugal, took part in 1415 in the campaign in which Spain captured the North African port of Ceuta from the Moors. This expedition aroused Henry's interest in Africa and exploration.

From 1419 onwards Henry despatched a series of expeditions down the western coast of Africa. He went on one or two voyages himself, but spent most of his time organizing and financing the exploration fleets. About 1439 he retired to Sagre, in southern Portugal, where he erected an observatory, and founded a college of navigation. He assembled a team of geographers and navigators, and developed ships suitable for voyages of exploration.

Before Henry began his campaign, the farthest Portugese navigators had gone was Cape Bojador, opposite the Canary Islands. By the time he died, one of his captains, Pedro de Sintra, had reached as far south as the coast of present-day Sierra Leone.

In those days many people believed that farther south the sea grew boiling hot, or that ships could fall off the edge of the Earth; one of Henry's main achievements was overcoming such fears among his men.

Opposite: Princess Isabella of France goes to meet her husband, King Richard II of England. The tyrannical and wildly extravagant Richard was forced to abdicate in favour of his cousin Henry of Bolingbroke, who had the support of Parliament and people.

1386 Battle of Sempach: Swiss defeat and kill Leopold III of Austria.
John of Gaunt leads an expedition to Castile, which he claims in his wife's name; fails 1388.
1387 Poet Geoffrey Chaucer begins work on *The Canterbury Tales.*
1389 Truce halts fighting between England, and the French and Scots.
Richard II, aged 22, assumes power.
Boniface IX, Pope at Rome (to 1404).
1390 Robert III, King of Scotland (to 1406).
Turks complete conquest of Asia Minor.
1392 The I Dynasty in Korea (to 1910).
Charles VI of France becomes insane.
1394 Benedict XIII antipope at Avignon (to 1423).
Prince Henry the Navigator, son of John I of Portugal, pioneer of exploration, born; founds naval institute at Sagres, 1439; dies 1460.
Richard II leads expedition to subdue Ireland; returns to England 1395.
1396 Richard II marries the seven-year-old Princess Isabella of France.
Ottoman Turks conquer Bulgaria.
1397 Union of Kalmar unites Norway, Denmark, and Sweden under one king, Eric of Pomerania
1398 Tamerlane ravages kingdom of Delhi, 100,000 prisoners massacred; returns home 1399.
Absolute rule of Richard II.
1399 Death of John of Gaunt.
Gaunt's eldest son, Henry of Bolingbroke, lands in Yorkshire with 40 followers, and soon has 60,000 supporters: Richard II is deposed. Bolingbroke becomes Henry IV, King of England (to 1413).
1400 Richard II murdered at Pontefract Castle.
Owen Glendower proclaims himself Prince of Wales and begins rebellion.
Holy Roman Emperor Wenceslas IV is deposed for drunkenness.
1401 Tamerlane conquers Damascus and Baghdad.
1402 Henry IV enters Wales in pursuit of Glendower.
Tamerlane overruns most of Ottoman Empire.
1403 Battle of Shrewsbury: rebellion by the Percy family: Henry IV defeats and kills Harry 'Hotspur' Percy.
1404 Innocent VII, Pope at Rome (to 1406).
1405 French soldiers land in Wales to support Glendower: initial successes.
Death of Tamerlane.
1406 Gregory XII, Pope at Rome (to 1415).
James I, King of Scotland (to 1437); captive in England from 1406 to 1423.
Henry, Prince of Wales, defeats Welsh.
1409 Council of Pisa, called to resolve the Great Schism, declares the rival popes deposed and elects a third.

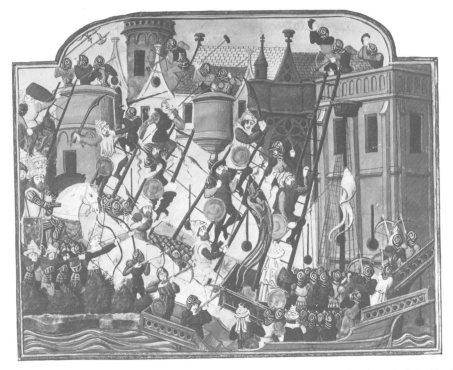

Turkish forces storming the walls during the siege of Constantinople in 1453. The city was battered by cannon fire for six weeks before being attacked on three sides from land and sea, and overrun. Its capture marked the end of the Byzantine Empire. Under Turkish rule its lands became the most backward in Europe.

Left: Jeanne d'Arc (Joan of Arc) the young peasant girl who put new heart into France during the Hundred Years' War, at the siege of Paris in 1430. Jeanne believed she heard voices and saw visions, guiding her to go to the uncrowned king of France and demand to lead his soldiers. Clad in armour, she led a small army to drive English occupation forces from Orléans and Rheims, and persuaded the king to be crowned. In 1430 she was captured by the Burgundians who handed her over to the English; the next year she was burned as a witch.

The End of Byzantium

About 1300 a Turkish leader named Osman founded a principality on the Black Sea coast of Asia Minor. His followers and successors, known as Ottomans, gradually extended their conquests over Asia Minor, and crossed into Europe in 1345, to help the Byzantine Emperor John Cantacuzene in a civil war.

Once in Europe, the Ottoman Turks quickly increased their holdings. By 1400, after a series of campaigns, they had conquered Macedonia, Serbia, and Bulgaria, and had reduced the Byzantine Empire to a small region around Byzantium (Constantinople), about the same size as present-day Turkey-in-Europe.

Byzantium was saved for a while by the Mongol conqueror Tamerlane, 'Timur the Lame', a descendant of Genghis Khan. He overran most of the Ottoman Empire in 1402, and even after he died civil war ravaged the Ottoman Empire. But in 1451 a grim and relentless Sultan, Mohammed II, the Conqueror, ascended the Ottoman throne. In 1453 he besieged Constantinople with 150,000 men.

The city was bombarded by a great force of artillery for six weeks, and attacked on three sides by Turkish forces on land and in warships. The last of the Byzantine emperors, Constantine XI, had only 8000 men. Even so, the tremendous fortifications enabled the defenders to hold out for 54 days before the Turks burst in, and Constantine was killed. After three days of massacre and looting the Turks began converting the city into a capital for their empire, and renamed it Istanbul.

The fall of Constantinople is generally reckoned as marking the end of the Middle Ages. Many of Constantinople's scholars fled to the West, encouraging the revival of learning and classical knowledge which is known as the Renaissance.

1409 Alexander V, antipope at Pisa (to 1410).
1410 Sigismund, Holy Roman Emperor (to 1437).
 Battle of Tannenberg: Ladislaus II of Poland defeats the Teutonic Knights.
 John XXIII (Baldassare Cossa), antipope at Pisa (to 1415).
1412 Jeanne d'Arc (Joan of Arc) born; dies 1431.
1413 Henry V, King of England (to 1422).
1414 Council of Constance (until 1417) called by John XXIII, deposes John, persuades Gregory XII to resign, and isolates Benedict XIII.
1415 Henry V invades France, and defeats the French at Agincourt.
1416 Death of Owen Glendower.
1417 Martin V, Pope (to 1431): end of the Great Schism.
1420 Treaty of Troyes: Henry V, acknowledged as heir to the French throne, marries Charles VI's daughter Catherine.
1422 Deaths of Henry V of England and Charles VI of France.
 Henry VI, King of England (to 1461).
 Charles VII, King of France (to 1461); known as Dauphin until 1429.
1424 John, Duke of Bedford, regent for Henry VI of England, defeats the French at Cravant.
1428 English begin siege of Orléans.
1429 Jeanne d'Arc, appointed military commander raises siege of Orléans: Charles VII crowned king of France at Rheims.
1430 Burgundians capture Jeanne d'Arc and hand her over to the English.
1431 Khmer city of Angkor abandoned.
 Jeanne d'Arc burned as a witch at Rouen.
 Eugene IV, Pope (to 1447).
 Henry VI of England crowned king of France in Paris.
1434 Cosimo de Medici becomes ruler of Florence.
1437 James I of Scotland murdered at Perth.
 James II, King of Scotland (to 1460).
1438 Albert II, Holy Roman Emperor (to 1439).
 Inca Empire established in Peru.
1439 Council of Basle deposes Pope Eugene IV.
 Felix V, antipope (to 1449).
1440 Frederick III, Holy Roman Emperor (to 1493).
 Johannes Gutenberg invents printing from movable type.
1447 Nicholas V, Pope (to 1455).
1451 Mohammed II, Sultan of Turkey (to 1481).
 Christopher Columbus born; dies 1506.
1453 Hundred Years' War ends: England's only French possession is Calais.
 Henry VI becomes insane.
 Ottoman Turks capture Constantinople: end of the Byzantine Empire and of the Middle Ages.

The Renaissance

THE RENAISSANCE MARKS the beginning of what historians think of as the modern period of history. *Renaissance* is a French word meaning 'rebirth', and at one time historians thought there was a rebirth of learning following the darkness of the medieval period. It would probably be fairer to say there was a great increase in learning and in the practice of the arts, but scholarship had persisted since Classical times, particularly in the Church and among Arabs who carried on Greek traditions.

As with all changes and movements, the exact beginning of the Renaissance is hard to establish. A convenient date is 1453, when the fall of Constantinople to the Ottoman Turks sent the remaining scholars of the Byzantine Empire fleeing westwards for safety.

Their learning, which with the development of printing spread rapidly, boosted the questioning of established ideas in religion, art, and science. Scholarship began to develop independently of the Church, and the human rather than divine in life and art was underlined; the well-rounded individual became an ideal. The challenge of fresh ideas also gave impetus to explorers, who began to open up new lands and trade routes, and to the religious leaders who set in motion the Reformation.

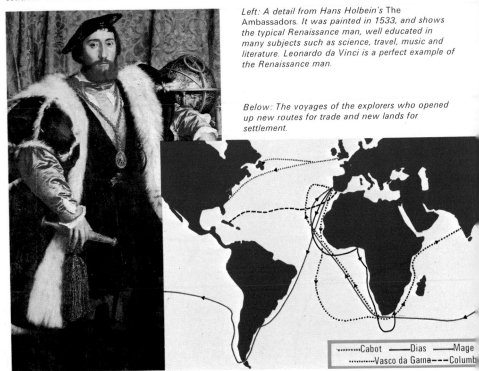

Left: A detail from Hans Holbein's The Ambassadors. *It was painted in 1533, and shows the typical Renaissance man, well educated in many subjects such as science, travel, music and literature. Leonardo da Vinci is a perfect example of the Renaissance man.*

Below: The voyages of the explorers who opened up new routes for trade and new lands for settlement.

·······Cabot ———Dias ———Mage
··········Vasco da Gama———Columb

EUROPE		ASIA	
1454	Printing by movable type perfected		
1455	Wars of the Roses in England (to 1485)		
1459	Ottoman Turks conquer Serbia	1467	Start of civil wars in Japan
1467	Charles the Bold, Duke of Burgundy	1472	Venetians destroy Smyrna
			Battle of Otluk-beli
1492	Spain conquers Granada	1475	Turks conquer Crimea
1494	Statute of Drogheda		
1497	Jews expelled from Portugal	1498	Vasco da Gama reaches India
1499	Treaty of Basle		
1501	France and Spain occupy Naples	1509	Battle of Diu
		1513	Portuguese reach Canton
1519	Charles V, Holy Roman Emperor (to 1556)	1514	War between Turkey and Persia
1520	Field of Cloth of Gold	1516	War between Ottoman Empire and Egypt
1521	Diet of Worms		(until 1517)
1523	Gustavus I, King of Sweden, elected		
1527	Sack of Rome by Spaniards and Germans	1526	Mughal Empire founded
1531	Schmalkaldic League formed		
1532	Religious Peace of Nuremberg		
1533	Ivan IV rules Russia (to 1584)		
1534	Act of Supremacy	1534	Turks capture Baghdad and Mesopotamia
1545	Pope Paul III opens Council of Trent	1549	St Francis Xavier introduces Christianity
			to Japan
		1556	Akbar the Great defeats Hindus at battle
1561	Mary Queen of Scots returns to Scotland		of Panipat
1562	Religious wars in France (to 1598)	1557	Portuguese settle at Macao
1564	Reign of terror begins in Russia		
1568	Netherlands begins revolt against Spain		
1572	Massacre of St Bartholomew's Day	1571	Battle of Lepanto
		1573	Venice abandons Cyprus
1581	Union of Utrecht	1577	Akbar the Great unifies northern India
1582	Introduction of Gregorian Calendar		
1588	Defeat of Spanish Armada		
1589	Henri IV, King of France (to 1610)	1590	Peace between Turkey and Persia
			Hideyoshi unifies Japan
		1592	Hideyoshi invades Korea
1598	Edict of Nantes		Akbar the Great conquers Sind
		1600	Tokugawa period in Japan
		1603	Persia conquers Tabriz, Erivan, Shirvan,
			and Kars
			Tokugawa Ieyasu shogun of Japan
		1604	French East India Company founded
1605	Gunpowder Plot discovered		Russians begin to settle Siberia

The Renaissance

The defeat of the 'Invincible Armada' which Philip II of Spain sent to invade England in 1588. The heavily armed Spanish fleet of about 130 warships was out-manoeuvred and out-gunned by the faster English ships. At night the English caused panic among the anchored Spanish ships by sending fireships floating into them. The Spanish fled northwards, rounding Britain to head to Spain, as they lacked access to a deep-water port in the Channel. Fewer than 60 vessels of the Armada returned home. The English lost not one ship.

Right: England's King Henry VIII arriving at the Field of Cloth of Gold, near Calais, in June 1520, to meet the French King François I. Despite the splendid pageantry, no political alliance resulted from the meeting.

AFRICA

1455	Cadamosto explores West Africa (to 1457)
1468	Sonni Ali captures Timbuktu; Songhai Empire founded in West Africa
1471	Portuguese take Tangier from Muslims
1472	Portuguese discover Fernando Pó
1482	Portuguese settle Gold Coast
1488	Bartholomew Diaz rounds Cape of Good Hope
1505	Portuguese colonize Mozambique
1517	Ottoman Turks capture Cairo; end of Mameluke Empire
1520	Portuguese mission to Ethiopia (to 1526)
1534	Turks capture Tunis
1535	Charles V conquers Tunis
1554	Turks conquer coast of North Africa; completed in 1556
1571	Bornu Empire in Sudan reaches greatest height (until 1603)
1574	Turkey regains Tunis from Spain
1578	Battle of Al Kasr Al-kabil
1591	Songhai Empire destroyed by Spanish and Portuguese mercenaries
1595	First Dutch settlements on Guinea Coast

AMERICAS AND ELSEWHERE

1492	Christopher Columbus crosses Atlantic and discovers West Indies
1493	Newly discovered lands divided between Spain and Portugal
1494	Treaty of Tordesillas
1497	John Cabot discovers Newfoundland
1498	Columbus discovers Trinidad and South America
1500	Pedro Cabral claims Brazil for Portugal
1501	Amerigo Vespucci explores coast of Brazil (to 1502)
1502	Columbus discovers Nicaragua
1513	Vasco Nuñez de Balboa discovers Pacific Ocean
1521	Hernán Cortés conquers Tenochtitlán
1522	First circumnavigation of the world by Magellan's expedition
1533	Francisco Pizarro conquers Peru
1535	Jacques Cartier navigates St Lawrence River (to 1536) Spaniards explore Chile (to 1537)
1541	Hernando de Soto discovers Mississippi River
1567	Portuguese settle at Rio de Janeiro
1577	Francis Drake sails round world (to 1580)
1586	Francis Drake sails to West Indies
1603	Samuel de Champlain explores St Lawrence River
1606	William Jansz sights Australia
1607	English found colony of Virginia Henry Hudson explores in Canada
1608	Champlain founds settlement of Quebec

Printing

Few inventions have had a greater impact on the world than printing. The first printing, using wood-blocks carved by hand, was done by the Chinese in the AD 700s, and a Chinese printer named Pi Sheng made movable type from pottery 300 years later.

Printing as we know it, from movable metal type, was the invention of a goldsmith of Mainz in Germany, Johannes Gutenberg. Several people were experimenting in the 1440s, but it was Gutenberg who brought his process to perfection by about 1454. His invention consisted of a typemould for casting the individual letters, a press adapted from the wine-press of the day, and a suitably sticky ink. The press could print about 300 sheets a day.

Printing enabled books to be produced more quickly, cheaply, and accurately than by hand-copying, so boosting the spread of knowledge.

Above: Federico da Montefeltro, Duke of Urbino, painted by the Renaissance artist Piero della Francesca. Opposite: Ivan III, known as 'the Great', laid the foundations of the Russian empire.

Left: Johannes Gutenberg, inventor of printing from movable metal type, checking a printed sheet. This relief from the Gutenberg monument in Mainz, Germany, shows a printing shop with a press of the kind Gutenberg designed (which stayed virtually unchanged until the 1800s), ink daubers, and sheets hanging up to dry.

Wars of the Roses

The struggle for the throne between rival families of Edward III's descendants owes its name to the badges of the warring factions, a white rose for the house of York, and red for the house of Lancaster.

The war began in 1455 when Richard, Duke of York, challenged the right to the throne of the Lancastrian Henry VI, a pious but weak man, subject to bouts of insanity. Richard's son Edward became king in 1461; Henry regained the throne briefly in 1470. On Edward IV's death in 1483, his son Edward V and his supporters were displaced by the young king's uncle Richard, Duke of Gloucester. Edward was sent to the tower and his uncle became King Richard III.

The struggle ended with the battle of Bosworth Field in 1485 when Richard III was killed and the throne was seized by the Lancastrian Henry VII, the first of the Tudors. In the first few years of his reign he eliminated all his rivals, and married Edward IV's daughter Elizabeth to strengthen his claim.

1454 Richard, Duke of York, is regent of England while Henry VI is insane.
Printing with movable type is perfected in Germany by Johannes Gutenberg.

1455 Henry VI recovers. Richard of York is replaced by Somerset and excluded from the Royal Council.
Wars of the Roses – civil wars in England between royal houses of York and Lancaster (until 1485).
Battle of St Albans. Somerset defeated and killed.
Calixtus III, Pope (to 1458).
Cadamosto, Venetian sailor, explores the Senegal and Gambia rivers, and discovers Cape Verde Islands (1456).

1456 Turks capture Athens.

1458 Pius II, Pope (to 1464).
Matthias Corvinus, King of Hungary (to 1490).
George Podiebrad, King of Bohemia (to 1471).

1459 Ottoman Turks conquer Serbia.

1460 Battle of Westfield. Richard of York is defeated and killed.
Earl of Warwick (the Kingmaker) captures London for the Yorkists.
Battle of Roxburgh: James II of Scotland is killed
James III, King of Scotland (to 1488).
Battle of Northampton: Henry VI is captured by Yorkists.
Turks conquer Morea.

1461 Battles of Mortimer's Cross and Towton: Richard's son, Edward of York, defeats Lancastrians and becomes king.
Edward IV, King of England (to 1483).
Louis XI, King of France (to 1483).
Turks conquer Trebizond, last surviving Greek state.

1462 Ivan III (the Great), Duke of Moscow (to 1505).
Castile captures Gibraltar from Arabs.

1463 Ottoman Turks and Venetians at war (until 1479).

1464 Paul II, Pope (to 1471).
Edward IV marries Elizabeth Woodville.

1465 Henry VI imprisoned by Edward IV.
League of the Public Weal. Dukes of Alençon, Berri, Burgundy, Bourbon, and Lorraine conspire against Louis XI.

1466 Peace of Thorn. Poland gains much of Prussia from the Teutonic Knights.
Warwick's quarrels with Edward IV begin.
Warwick forms alliance with Louis XI.

1467 Charles the Bold becomes Duke of Burgundy, chief rival to Louis XI.
Period of civil war begins in Japan and lasts for more than 100 years.

Charles the Bold

Burgundy in the 1400s was the most important of the semi-independent provinces which made up the kingdom of France. It lay in the eastern part of the country, and part of it was outside the French frontiers, being known as Franche-Comté, or 'free county'. The duchy also included Artois, Flanders, and Brabant, in modern Belgium.

Charles the Bold, who succeeded to the dukedom in 1467 at the age of 34, was one of the most ambitious Burgundian rulers. He wanted to gain the lands which lay between the two halves of his duchy, and make himself a king. He extended his possessions, engaged in almost continual conflict with Louis XI of France – nominally his overlord – and formed an alliance with Edward IV of England. But his ambitions brought him into conflict with the Swiss.

In 1476 Charles occupied Grandson, on Lake Neuchâtel, and hanged the Swiss garrison. Bern and its allies routed Charles's army there, and later at Morat. At Nancy, in Lorraine, in January 1477 Charles was defeated and killed.

Lorenzo the Magnificent

Of all Italy's great families the Medici was probably the most powerful. From the early 1200s they were leading political figures in Florence, and in the 14th century amassed an enormous fortune by banking and moneylending. The three golden balls which pawnbrokers use as a sign are from the Medici coat of arms.

The most famous of all was Lorenzo, who became joint ruler of Florence with his brother Giuliano when their father died in 1469. On Giuliano's death in 1478 Lorenzo became sole ruler, but would take only the usual title Florence gave its overlords, *magnifico signore*; from this comes the name by which he is best known, Lorenzo the Magnificent.

A clever statesman, Lorenzo lived up to his title by the style in which he lived. He was the patron of writers, artists, and scientists, and under his rule Florence became one of the most beautiful and prosperous cities of Italy.

Ferdinand and Isabella

A royal marriage brought about the union of Spain. In 1469 Ferdinand, son of John II of Aragon, married Isabella, half-sister of Henry IV of Castile. These were the two biggest kingdoms in Spain, Castile covering almost three-quarters of the modern country. In 1474 Henry died, and Isabella and Ferdinand succeeded as joint rulers of Castile; five years later Ferdinand inherited Aragon, and made Isabella joint ruler of that also. The two controlled all Spain except for the kingdom of Navarre in the north and the Moorish emirate of Granada.

Ferdinand and Isabella were bigoted Roman Catholics: under their rule the Inquisition was established in Spain, directed mainly against the Jews. In 1492 they expelled 200,000 Jews from the country, and captured Granada. In the same year Isabella sponsored Christopher Columbus's voyage to the West.

Of their five children Juana, heiress to Castile, was mad but her son Charles succeeded to the throne; Catherine of Aragon married Henry VIII of England.

Opposite above: Charles the Bold of Burgundy.
Below: The unification of Spain after 1469.

Map key:
- Spanish kingdoms
- Territory acquired by kings of Aragon

Map labels: NAVARRE, Toulouse, ARAGON, Barcelona, Madrid, PORTUGAL, Lisbon, CASTILE, Baleares, GRANADA

1468	Margaret of York marries Charles the Bold. Sonni Ali captures Timbuktu and founds the Songhai Empire in West Africa.
1469	Marriage of Ferdinand of Aragon and Isabella of Castile, uniting Spain.
1470	Warwick turns Lancastrian: he defeats Edward IV and restores Henry VI. Turks seize Negroponte from the Venetians.
1471	Battle of Barnet. Edward IV defeats and kills Warwick. Henry VI dies, probably murdered, in the Tower of London. Sixtus IV, Pope (to 1484). The Portuguese, under Alfonso V, take Tangier from the Muslims. Vladislav of Poland elected King of Bohemia after the death of Podiebrad.
1472	Venetians destroy Smyrna. Battle of Otluk-beli. Turks, under Mohammed II, defeat the Persian ruler, Uzan Hasan, chief ally of Venice. Fernando Po discovered by the Portuguese.
1473	Sistine Chapel built by Giovanni de Dolci.
1474	Louis XI goes to war against Charles the Bold. Alliance between Charles the Bold and Edward IV of England. Triple alliance of Florence, Venice, Milan. War between Charles the Bold and the Swiss Confederation (ends 1477). Isabella succeeds to throne of Castile. A nautical almanack for 1474–1506 by the German astronomer Regiomontanus describes the method of finding longitude by using lunar distances.
1475	Edward IV invades France. Peace of Piéquigny between England and France. Birth of Leonardo da Vinci. Turks conquer the Crimea.
1476	William Caxton sets up printing press at Westminster.
1477	Maximilian, son of Frederick III, marries Mary, daughter of Charles the Bold. Battle of Nancy. Charles the Bold is defeated and killed by the Swiss.
1478	Spanish Inquisition established by Ferdinand and Isabella with the consent of Sixtus IV: its main aim is to punish so-called 'converted' Jews who still practise their old faith in secret. Lorenzo de Medici, ruler of Florence (to 1492). Pazzi Conspiracy against the Medicis. Giuliano de Medici assassinated. Ivan III conquers Novgorod and incorporates it into duchy of Moscow. Hungary gains Moravia and Silesia. Turks conquer Albania.

Age of Exploration

Exploration has always been partly spurred on by curiosity, the desire to know what lies in the unknown. But in the 1400s the great impetus to exploration was trade. At that time great quantities of spices were used to preserve and flavour meat in winter, and Europe relied heavily on spices imported from the Spice Islands in the east, now called the Moluccas. But the spices had to travel overland through the Near East, and could be bought only at great expense.

From the time of Prince Henry the Navigator, Portuguese seamen were exploring the west coast of Africa, seeking a sea route to India. In 1487–1488 Bartolomeu Dias became the first European to sail round the Cape of Good Hope, and he helped to plan Vasco da Gama's expedition 10 years later. Da Gama rounded the Cape and sailed across the Indian Ocean to Calicut, on the west coast of India. His route-proving expedition was followed by a trading voyage commanded by Pedro Alvares Cabral, who returned with a valuable cargo of pepper.

Before da Gama's successful voyage a Genoese navigator, Christopher Columbus, had persuaded Queen Isabella of Spain to finance an expedition to find a westward route to the Indies. Columbus was using ancient, inaccurate maps and thought the world much smaller than it is. In 1492 he sailed across the Atlantic Ocean and discovered a group of islands which he called the Indies (now the West Indies), believing them to be his goal.

Columbus never did realize he had found a whole new continent, even though a later explorer, Amerigo Vespucci, reported that this must be so in 1502, four years before Columbus died. Vespucci's opinion prompted Martin Waldseemüller, a German map-maker, to say in 1507 that the 'new world' should be named America 'because Amerigo discovered it'.

Above: Little ships like these took the explorers of the 1400s and 1500s on their epic voyages to the Indies and the Americas. This is a Portuguese caravel, no more than 70 feet (21 m) long; on the right is the Santa Maria, Christopher Columbus's flagship, which was about 117 feet (36 m) long.

The first round-the-world voyage was the inspiration of a Portuguese navigator, Ferdinand Magellan (1480–1521). Out of favour with his own country, Magellan offered his services to Spain whose ruler, Emperor Charles V, provided a fleet for the voyage.

Magellan set sail in 1519 with five ships, aiming for the south of South America, where he was sure there was a route to the western ocean. Despite tremendous storms Magellan found his route – the strait that now bears his name – and sailed into a calm sea which he named Pacific; he had lost one ship, and one had turned for home. Magellan sailed across the Pacific to the Philippines, where he was killed in a skirmish with the natives. The epic voyage was completed by Captain Sebastian del Cano with one ship and 17 men.

1479 Ferdinand succeeds to the throne of Aragon. Spain united by the formal union of Aragon and Castile.
Ferdinand V of Castile, King of Aragon (to 1516); known as the Catholic king.
Treaty of Constantinople: Venice agrees to pay tribute to the Ottoman Empire for trading rights in the Black Sea.

1480 Ivan III, known as 'the Great', ends allegiance to the Tatars.
Turks besiege Rhodes, held by the Knights of St John.

1481 Death of Mohammed II, founder of the Ottoman Empire.

1482 Portuguese navigator Diego Cao explores the Congo River (until 1484).
Portuguese establish settlements on the Gold Coast (Ghana).

1483 Death of Edward IV.
Edward V, King of England; he is deposed by his uncle, Richard, Duke of Gloucester.
Richard III, King of England (to 1485).
Edward V and his brother are murdered in the Tower of London.
Charles VIII, King of France (to 1498).

1484 Caxton prints *Morte D'Arthur*, the poetic collection of legends about King Arthur compiled by Sir Thomas Malory.
Innocent VIII, Pope (to 1492).

1485 Battle of Bosworth Field: Henry Tudor, Earl of Richmond, defeats and kills Richard III. He becomes Henry VII, King of England (to 1509), and first of the Tudor monarchs.
Hungary captures Vienna and acquires lower Austria: Hungary becomes the most powerful state in central Europe.

1486 Maximilian of Habsburg King of Germans.
Henry VII of England marries Elizabeth of York; unites the houses of York and Lancaster.

1488 Diaz rounds the Cape of Good Hope.
James IV, King of Scotland (to 1513).

1492 Ferdinand V of Castile conquers Granada and ends Muslim influence in Spain.
Alexander VI (Roderigo Borgia), Pope (to 1503).
Christopher Columbus crosses the Atlantic and discovers the West Indies.

1493 The Songhai Empire reaches its greatest heights under Askia Mohammed who takes over much of the Mandingo Empire.
Pope Alexander VI divides newly discovered lands between Spain and Portugal.
Maximilian I, Holy Roman Emperor (to 1519).

1494 Charles VIII invades Italy.
Treaty of Tordesillas: Spain and Portugal move pope's line of demarcation farther west.

This drawing by the artist Holbein shows the first two Tudor kings of England, Henry VII (right) and his son Henry VIII. When Henry VII seized the English throne in 1485, he took over a kingdom drained of resources by thirty years of civil war. He was a clever ruler and left the country rich and stable. Under Henry VIII England became a major European power. When the Pope refused to annul his first marriage (to his brother's widow) Henry broke with the Roman Church and made himself head of the Church of England.

Above: Hernán Cortés, the greatest of the Spanish conquistadores (conquerors), entering the Aztec capital of Tenochtitlan (now Mexico City) in 1521.

The American Civilizations

Three important civilizations were flourishing among the American Indians before Europeans arrived in the late 1400s.

The Aztecs of Mexico founded their capital, Tenochtitlán, in 1325 where Mexico City now stands. They had a religion which required many sacrifices, and fought wars to obtain prisoners for those sacrifices. They were fine architects, and had evolved a system of picture writing.

The Maya of Central America had a much older civilization; it developed from around 500 BC to a peak in the AD 700s. The Maya reached a high standard of architecture, mathematics, and astronomy, but were weak politically and were in decline by the 1400s.

The Inca of Peru ruled an empire in the Andes of perhaps as many as seven million people. They were fine architects, potters, and metal-workers, with well-organized government and superb roads. The Spanish *conquistadors* took more than 30 years to subdue them.

1495 Charles VIII enters Naples. The Holy League – Milan, Venice, Maximilian, Pope Alexander VI, and Ferdinand V – forces him to withdraw.
1496 Henry VII of England joins the Holy League. Commercial treaty between England and Netherlands.
1497 John Cabot discovers Newfoundland.
1498 Louis XII, King of France (to 1515).
Vasco da Gama of Portugal reaches India.
Columbus discovers Trinidad and South America.
Savonarola burned at the stake.
1499 Louis XII of France, invades Italy.
1500 Louis XII conquers Milan. Treaty of Granada: Louis and Ferdinand V agree to divide Naples.
Pedro Cabral claims Brazil for Portugal.
1501 France and Spain occupy Naples.
Amerigo Vespucci explores the coast of Brazil (until 1502).
Russia and Poland at war. Russia gains Lithuania and border territories (1503).
1502 Margaret, daughter of Henry VII, marries James IV of Scotland.
War breaks out between France and Spain.
Columbus discovers Nicaragua.
Shah Ismail (dies 1524) founds the Safavid dynasty in Persia.
1503 Battles of Cerignola and Garigliano. France defeated.
Julius II, Pope (until 1513).
1505 Treaty of Blois. France keeps Milan but cedes Naples to Spain; Spain now has control of southern Italy.
Portuguese trading posts established on the Malabar coast.
The Portuguese found Mozambique.
Basil III, ruler of Moscow (to 1533).
1506 Christopher Columbus dies in poverty.
1507 Martin Waldseemüller produces a world map: for the first time it shows South America as separate from Asia and uses the name *America* after Amerigo Vespucci.
1508 The League of Cambrai. Emperor Maximilian, Louis XII, and Ferdinand V ally against Venice.
1509 Henry VIII, King of England (to 1547).
Battle of Diu establishes Portuguese control of Indian seas.
1510 Pope Julius II and Venice form Holy League to drive Louis XII out of Italy.
1511 Ferdinand V and Henry VIII join Holy League.
1512 Swiss join the League and drive French out of Milan.
Selim I, Sultan of Turkey (to 1520).
Russia and Poland at war (until 1522).
1513 Battle of Novara: French driven out of Italy.
Leo X (Giovanni de Medici), Pope (to 1521).

The Reformation

The revival of learning known as the Renaissance played a large part in the religious movement which we know as the Reformation. Men who had studied philosophy began to question the Church's teachings, while the leadership and administration of the Church were already being strongly criticized. The supreme power of the Church in religion was being challenged by many heretical sects, which called for greater reliance on Bible teachings and simplicity of worship.

The Reformation really began in Germany in 1517, when an Augustinian monk, Martin Luther, nailed a protest against the sale of indulgences (pardons for sin) on the door of a church in Wittenberg. Luther quickly found support, and although Pope Leo X and the Holy Roman Emperor Charles V tried to suppress the new movement, it rapidly gathered ground.

Switzerland, Scandinavia, Scotland, and some of the many small German states soon adopted the new religion, called Protestantism because its followers were protesting against abuses in the Roman Church. In England the break with Rome came when Pope Clement VII refused to allow King Henry VIII to divorce his wife, Catherine of Aragon, so that he could remarry and have a son. Cranmer, Archbishop of Canterbury, pronounced the divorce which was eventually confirmed by Parliament; in 1534, the Act of Supremacy made the King head of the Church in England. He did not adopt Protestant beliefs, but his people, freed from papal interference, did so. Henry took over the wealth of the monasteries, which were dissolved, thus destroying the power of the Church.

The Roman Catholic Church replied to the Reformation with its own Counter-Reformation, which began in 1560 and introduced much-needed reforms.

Opposite top: A Peruvian sacrificial knife, made of gold inlaid with turquoises.

Opposite bottom: An Aztec turquoise mask. The civilizations of Central and South America were plundered ruthlessly by the early explorers and Spanish conquistadors soon ruled over them.

Left: Martin Luther (1483–1546), an Augustinian monk, began the Reformation in 1517 with his 95 Theses challenging the sale of indulgences.

Right: John Calvin (1509–1564), a French theologian originally named Jean Chauvin, introduced the Reformation to Switzerland. His teachings spread across western Europe.

Left: Ignatius Loyola (1491–1556) was a Spanish soldier who in 1534 founded a new religious order, the Society of Jesus (the Jesuits), principally to spread a Catholic or Counter-Reformation.

1513 The Portuguese reach Canton, China.
Vasco Nunez de Balboa discovers the Pacific.
Battle of Flodden Field. James IV of Scotland killed.
James V, King of Scotland (to 1542).
1514 Mary, sister of Henry VIII, marries Louis XII.
War breaks out between Turkey and Persia.
Battle of Chaldiran: Persians defeated:
1515 Thomas Wolsey, Archbishop of York, is made Lord Chancellor of England and Cardinal.
Francois I, King of France (to 1547).
Battle of Marignano: the French defeat the Swiss and regain Milan.
1516 Treaty of Noyon between France and Spain: French relinquish claims to Naples.
War between Ottoman Empire and Egypt (until 1517).
Battle of Marjdabik: Selim defeats Egyptians.
Charles I, King of Spain (to 1556).
1517 The Reformation begins: Martin Luther nails his 95 Theses, protesting against the sale of indulgences, on the church door at Wittenberg.
Ottoman Turks capture Cairo: end of Mameluke Empire; Syria and Egypt are added to the Ottoman Empire.
1519 Reformation begins in Switzerland, led by Ulrich Zwingli.
Charles V (Charles I of Spain), Holy Roman Emperor (to 1556), on the death of Maximilian I.
1520 Field of Cloth of Gold: Francois I of France meets Henry VIII of England but fails to gain his support against Holy Roman Emperor Charles V.
Secret treaty between Henry VIII and Charles V.
Suleiman I, sultan of Turkey (to 1566). Turkish power at its height.
1521 Diet of Worms: Martin Luther is condemned as a heretic and is excommunicated.
Henry VIII receives the title 'Defender of the Faith' from Pope Leo X for his opposition to Luther.
France and Spain at war over rival claims to Italy (until 1529).
Belgrade is captured by the Turks.
Ferdinand Magellan dies in the Philippines.
Hernan Cortés conquers the Aztec capital, Tenochtitlán (Mexico City).
1522 Battle of Biocca: Charles V defeats the French, driving them out of Milan.
One ship from Magellan's expedition completes the first circumnavigation of the world.
1523 Clement VII, Pope (to 1534).
Gustavus Vasa of Sweden leads revolt against Danish rulers and is elected Gustavus I, King of Sweden.
1524 France invades Italy and recaptures Milan.

The Mughal Empire

Although the great days of the Mongol Empire came to an end in the 1300s after the death of Kublai Khan, it had a brief revival in the west under Tamerlane, who died in 1405. Even then the Mongol strength was not altogether exhausted, and it had a final revival with a descendant of Tamerlane, Babar, king of Kabul in Afghanistan.

In the 1520s Babar invaded India, and at the battle of Panipat made himself master of the Punjab. He had soon established a new Mongol empire in India, which goes under the name of the Mughal Empire – from a Persian version of the word 'Mongol' – to distinguish it from the earlier Mongol conquests. Babar died in 1530, only four years after Panipat, but his empire lasted until the mid-1700s, when the British took over as supreme power. At its height the Mughal Empire covered almost all of modern India, Pakistan, and Bangladesh.

Left: Babar, the first Mughal emperor of India. Part Turkish and part Mongol by birth, a descendant of Timur the Lame, he conquered Delhi at the battle of Panipat in 1526. He thus established the foundations of the Mughal empire in India.

The Conquest of Peru

The mighty Inca empire of Peru, although well-organized and well-governed, was conquered by fewer than 200 Spanish adventurers led by Francisco Pizarro, his three brothers and a fellow soldier, Diego de Almagro.

The Spaniards sailed to Peru in 1531. Although the Inca had a large army, the Spaniards had guns, and Pizarro was helped by the fact that a civil war was raging when he arrived. By treachery he seized the Inca emperor, Atahualpa, held him to ransom, and when the ransom was paid had Atahualpa strangled. Within three years the Spaniards were masters of Peru, though it was to be 30 years before the last vestiges of Inca rebellion were stamped out.

Opposite: The title page of Martin Luther's German translation of the Bible. Luther thought that everyone should have the chance to read and understand the Bible for himself. Luther gained much support from people who were starting to question the teachings and practices of the Catholic Church, and this movement became known as the Reformation, with the followers of the ideas of Luther being called Protestants.

The Schmalkaldic League

In 1530 a group of Protestant German rulers, headed by Philip of Hesse and the Elector of Saxony, met at Schmalkalden in Thuringia to consider a defensive alliance against their Roman Catholic overlord, the Emperor Charles V, and his allies. The result was the Schmalkaldic League, founded early in 1531. Fifteen years later Charles declared war on the league, which he defeated in 1547.

The league broke up, but in 1552 Duke Maurice of Saxony compelled Charles to accord temporary freedom of worship pending a full-scale conference. The conference, held in 1555, resulted in a permanent settlement, the Peace of Augsburg. This allowed states and cities freedom to introduce the Reformation, while giving them equal rights with Catholic states.

1525 Battle of Pavia: Francois I is captured.

1526 Treaty of Madrid: François I is to give up claims to Milan, Genoa, and Naples but fails to keep the Treaty.
League of Cognac: alliance between François I, Pope Clement VII, Francesco Sforza of Milan, Venice, and Florence against Charles V.
Battle of Mohacs: Turks defeat and kill Louis II of Bohemia and Hungary.
Ferdinand of Austria, brother of Charles V, succeeds to the Bohemian throne.
Dispute over Hungarian succession between Ottoman Empire and Ferdinand (until 1528).
Battle of Panipat: Babar defeats last Delhi sultan and founds the Mughal (Mongol) Empire.

1527 Sack of Rome by Spanish and German troops: Pope Clement VII is captured.

1528 Ferdinand of Austria succeeds to the Hungarian throne.

1529 Henry VIII dismisses Lord Chancellor Thomas Wolsey for failing to obtain the Pope's consent to his divorce from Catherine of Aragon.
Sir Thomas More appointed Lord Chancellor.
Henry VIII summons the 'Reformation Parliament' and begins to cut the ties with the Church of Rome.
Peace of Cambrai between France and Spain: France renounces claims to Italy.
Treaty of Barcelona between Pope Clement VII and Charles V.
The Turks unsuccessfully besiege Vienna.

1530 Knights of St John established at Malta by Charles V.
Thomas Wolsey dies.
Charles V crowned emperor by Pope Clement VII, the last Imperial coronation by a pope.
Civil war in Switzerland between Catholic and Protestant cantons: Protestants are defeated.

1532 Sir Thomas More resigns over the question of Henry VIII's divorce.
Religious Peace of Nuremberg: Protestants allowed to practise their religion freely.
Calvin starts Protestant movement in France.
Turks invade Hungary but are defeated.

1533 Henry VIII marries Anne Boleyn and is excommunicated by Pope Clement VII.
Thomas Cranmer, Archbishop of Canterbury.
Peace between Suleiman I and Ferdinand of Austria.
Francisco Pizarro captures the Inca capital, Cuzco, and conquers Peru.
Ivan IV, the Terrible, ruler of Russia, succeeds at the age of three (to 1584).

1534 Act of Supremacy: Henry VIII declared supreme head of the Church in England.

The Renaissance

The development of Renaissance art took many
different forms and directions. *Left:* The Nativity *by
the pioneer Giotto. Below: Michelangelo's* Pietà
is a triumph of the High Renaissance.
*Bottom right: The dome of Florence Cathedral by
Brunelleschi. Bottom left: A detail from the* Virgin
and Child *by Durer, painted at a time when
Renaissance ideas had reached as far as northern
Europe.*

The Renaissance

During the Middle Ages, the Christian Church was the main source of scholarship and the main sponsor of the arts. For this reason, all learning had a strong religious bias. But in the 1200s the foundation of the universities of Bologna, Paris, and Oxford brought study to a much wider group of people. The breadth of their knowledge was increased by a revival of interest in the writings of ancient Greece and Rome, a revival which led historians of the 1800s to describe the movement as the *Renaissance,* the rebirth of learning.

A key date in the Renaissance was 1397, when Manuel Chrysoloras of Constantinople became the first professor of Greek at Florence University. Italian scholars quickly seized on the works of the ancient philosophers, which dealt with questions not answered by the Christian Church. From this came *humanism,* the belief that man, and not God, controlled his own fate.

The example of Greek and Roman sculptors, with their realistic portrayal of the human form, led to major changes in art. The Florentine painter Giotto (1266–1337) pioneered the change from a stiff, formal style of medieval art to showing men and women on canvas as they really are. In the *Quattrocento* – the 1400s – Italian art produced great masters like the painter Massacio, the sculptor Donatello – who made the first bronze statue since Roman times – and the architect Brunelleschi.

The period of the 1500s is known as the High Renaissance, during which Italian artists produced their finest work. The period is dominated by three men: Michelangelo, Leonardo da Vinci, and Raphael. All three were skilled in many arts, the Renaissance ideal being a 'universal man', but the greatest all-rounder was Leonardo, who was a superb painter, sculptor, architect, engineer, musician, and inventor.

1534 Ignatius Loyola founds the Society of Jesus (Jesuits).
Paul III, Pope (to 1549).
The Turks capture Tunis, Baghdad, and Mesopotamia.

1535 Sir Thomas More is executed for failing to take the Oath of Supremacy.
Death of Francesco Sforza: Milan comes under direct Spanish control.
War between France and Spain (until 1538).
Jacques Cartier navigates the St Lawrence River (and in 1536).
The Spaniards explore Chile (to 1537).

1536 Anne Boleyn is executed: Henry VIII marries Jane Seymour.
Suppression of monasteries in England under the direction of Thomas Cromwell, completed 1539. Pilgrimage of Grace – Catholic uprising in the north of England – suppressed.
Calvin leads Protestants in Geneva.
France invades Savoy and Piedmont.
France forms alliance with Turkey.

1537 Jane Seymour dies after the birth of a son, the future Edward VI.

1538 Truce of Nice between France and Spain.

1539 Truce of Frankfurt between Charles V and Protestant princes.

1540 Henry VIII marries Anne of Cleves following negotiations by Thomas Cromwell.
Henry VIII divorces Anne of Cleves and marries Catherine Howard.
Thomas Cromwell executed on charge of treason.
Philip, son of Charles V, made duke of Milan.
Pope Paul III officially recognizes Society of Jesus.

1541 John Knox brings the Reformation to Scotland.
Hernando de Soto discovers the Mississippi.
Turks conquer Hungary.

1542 Catherine Howard is executed.
Battle of Solway Moss: James V, King of Scotland, is killed.
Mary Stuart, Queen of Scotland (to 1567).

1543 Henry VIII marries Catherine Parr.
Alliance between Henry VIII and Charles V against Scotland and France.

1544 Henry VIII and Charles V invade France.
Treaty of Crépy between Spain and France.

1545 Pope Paul III opens the Council of Trent which, under Jesuit guidance, is to reform the Roman Catholic Church.

1547 Edward VI, King of England (until 1553): Duke of Somerset acts as Protector.
Henri II, King of France (until 1559).
Battle of Mühlberg: Charles V defeats Schmalkaldic League.

The Magnificent Lawgiver

The greatest ruler of the Ottoman Empire was Suleiman I, who came to the throne in 1520 and reigned for 46 years. To the Turks he became known as *Kanuni*, the Lawgiver, because of his reforms of justice and administration; to the western countries he was 'the Magnificent' because of the splendour of his court and his many military victories in Europe.

In a series of brilliant campaigns Suleiman captured Belgrade and the island of Rhodes, and overran Hungary. He waged three great campaigns against Persia, gaining control of Iraq, but the eastern frontier remained a problem. Under him Ottoman naval strength grew formidable. He died in 1566, while he was besieging a Hungarian fortress.

Left: The forces of Suleiman the Magnificent besieging the Hungarian fortress of Szigetvár in 1566. Suleiman himself died during the siege.

Ivan the Terrible

Ivan IV, Grand Duke of Muscovy from the age of three, became the first ruler to take the title of *Tsar* (caesar, or emperor) of all Russia. Ivan extended his rule eastward to absorb Siberia, and established trade relations with the western nations.

But his capacity for good rule was marred by his excessive cruelty. His secret police, the Oprichniks, tortured and murdered all who were suspected of treason. The people of Novgorod, accused of rebellion, were put to the sword. Ivan had seven wives, one of whom died under suspicious circumstances. In a fit of rage Ivan killed his eldest son, who was just as cruel, and spent his remaining years in remorse, interspersed with cruelty and violence. He died insane in 1584.

Emperor Charles V

Charles V (1500–1558) was the most powerful member of the Habsburg family, which controlled the Holy Roman Empire for more than 600 years. From his father, Philip of Burgundy, Charles inherited Burgundy and most of present-day Belgium and the Netherlands. In 1516 he inherited the thrones of Aragon and Castile through his mother, Juana of Castile, who was insane. He ruled Spain as Charles I.

In 1519 Charles's paternal grandfather, the Emperor Maximilian I, died; Charles inherited the vast Austrian lands, and in 1520 was crowned Holy Roman Emperor. He also ruled Sardinia, Sicily, and Naples. In 1556 Charles abdicated, leaving Spain to his son, Philip II, and the Empire to his brother, Ferdinand I.

1547 Ivan IV crowned *Tsar* (emperor) of Russia.
1548 Holy Roman Emperor Charles V annexes the Netherlands.
1549 Introduction of uniform Protestant service in England with Edward VI's *Book of Common Prayer*.
St Francis Xavier in Japan (until 1551), introduces Christianity.
1550 Julius III, Pope (until 1555).
Fall of Duke of Somerset: Duke of Northumberland succeeds as Protector.
1551 Turkey and Hungary at war (until 1562).
Archbishop Cranmer publishes Forty-two Articles of religion.
Treaty of Friedewalde between Saxony and France.
1552 War between Charles V and Henri II of France (until 1556).
France seizes Toul, Metz and Verdun.
Peace of Passau between Saxony and Holy Roman Empire.
1553 On death of Edward VI Lady Jane Grey proclaimed queen of England by Duke of Northumberland: reign lasts nine days.
Mary I, daughter of Henry VIII and Catherine of Aragon, Queen of England (to 1558).
Restoration of Roman Catholic bishops in England.
1554 Execution of Lady Jane Grey
Mary I marries Philip, heir to throne of Spain.
Turks conquer coast of North Africa (completed 1556).
1555 England returns to Roman Catholicism: Protestants are persecuted and about 300, including Cranmer, are burned at the stake.
Paul IV, Pope (to 1559).
Religious Peace of Augsburg: Protestant princes are granted freedom of worship and the right to introduce the Reformation into their territories.
1556 Abdication of Charles V (dies 1558): Spain and its colonies, the Netherlands, Naples, Milan, and Franche-Comté to go to his son Philip; the office of Emperor and the Habsburg lands to go to his brother, Ferdinand.
Philip II, King of Spain (to 1598).
Alliance between Pope Paul IV and Henri II.
Battle of Panipat: Akbar the Great defeats Hindus.
1557 Battle of St Quentin: France is defeated by Spain and England.
Portuguese settle at Macao, China.
Livonian War (until 1582) involves Poland, Russia, Sweden, and Denmark in a dispute over the succession to the Balkan territories.
Russia invades Poland.

Above: Mary I of England. A devout Catholic, she restored Catholicism in England and her persecution of Protestants gave her the nickname 'Bloody Mary'. Below: Charles V of Spain.

115

Above: The battle of Lepanto in 1571 was the last great naval engagement in which galleys – oared warships – played a major part. It ended Turkish predominance in the Mediterranean Sea.

The Great Siege

In 1530 the Knights of St John, ousted from Rhodes by the Turks, were given Malta as their home. They remained at war with the Turks, whom they regarded as infidels and so sworn enemies. In 1565 the Ottoman sultan Suleiman the Magnificent ordered an attack on Malta in an attempt to exterminate the order.

A large Turkish fleet, with four times the number of men the defenders had, besieged the island in May. The fighting raged until September, when in the face of reinforcements from Sicily the Turks withdrew, badly mauled. The hero of the siege was the Grand Master of the Order, Jean Parisot de la Vallette, who founded a new, heavily fortified city, named Valletta after him and now the island's capital.

1558 England loses Calais, last English possession in France.
Death of Mary I; Elizabeth I, daughter of Henry VIII and Anne Boleyn, Queen of England (to 1603).
Repeal of Catholic legislation in England.
Mary Queen of Scots marries Francois, Dauphin of France.
Ferdinand I, Holy Roman Emperor (to 1564).
1559 Francois II, King of France (to 1560).
Pius IV, Pope (to 1565).
Treaty of Cateau-Cambrésis between Spain and France ends the Habsburg-Valois wars: France gives up all conquests except Toul, Metz, and Verdun; Spain now controls virtually all Italy.
1560 Treaty of Berwick between Elizabeth I and Scottish reformers.
Charles IX, King of France (to 1574).
Treaty of Edinburgh among England, France, and Scotland.
1561 Mary Queen of Scots, widowed, returns to Scotland.
1562 Religious wars in France between the Huguenots (French Protestants) and Roman Catholics (until 1598).
Truce between Ferdinand I and Turkey.
1563 The Thirty-nine Articles, which complete establishment of the Anglican Church.
Ivan the Terrible conquers part of Livonia.
1564 Peace of Troyes between England and France.
Maximilian II, Holy Roman Emperor (to 1576).
William Shakespeare and Galileo Galilei born.
Reign of terror begins in Russia.
1565 Turks besiege Malta without success.
Portuguese attack French colony and found Rio de Janeiro (1567).
1566 Pope Pius V (later Saint), Pope (to 1572).
Selim II, Sultan of Turkey (to 1574).
1567 Murder of Lord Darnley, husband of Mary Queen of Scots, probably by Earl of Bothwell.
Mary Queen of Scots marries Bothwell, is imprisoned, and forced to abdicate.
James VI, King of Scotland (to 1625).
1568 Netherlands revolt against Spain (independence gained 1648).
Mary Queen of Scots escapes to England and is imprisoned by Elizabeth I.
1569 Union of Lublin merges Poland and Lithuania.
1570 Peace of St Germain: Huguenots given conditional freedom of worship.
Turks attack Cyprus.
Ivan IV ravages Novgorod.
1571 Battle of Lepanto: Combined papal and Venetian fleet under Don John of Austria defeats the Turks under Ali Pasha.

The Battle of Lepanto

In 1570 the Ottoman Turks invaded the island of Cyprus, then owned by Venice. The Venetians, weakened by years of fighting the Turks, appealed for help. Possession of Cyprus would allow the Turks to dominate the Mediterranean. So Pope Pius V assembled a fleet of 208 galleys and six galleasses (huge oar-driven ships with 44 guns), from the navies of Venice, Spain, and the Papal States, under the command of Don John of Austria. This fleet met 230 Turkish galleys off Lepanto, Greece, on October 7, 1571.

The fight lasted three hours. All but 40 of the Turkish galleys were destroyed or captured; the Christians lost only 12 ships. Lepanto was the end of the Turkish threat to Europe from the sea.

The Great Armada

The execution of the Catholic Mary Queen of Scots in 1587 led Philip II of Spain, long an enemy of Protestant England, to plan to invade the island and restore the English to the faith of Rome. He assembled a huge fleet, which the proud Spaniards called the *Invincible Armada.*

Sir Francis Drake destroyed part of this Armada in Cadiz Harbour, but Philip rebuilt his fleet and despatched it in July 1588. The Spanish, commanded by the inexperienced and seasick Duke of Medina Sidonia, sailed first to pick up an army from the Spanish territory of the Netherlands.

A scratch English fleet under Lord Howard of Effingham and including Drake, Sir John Hawkins, and Sir Martin Frobisher was waiting for the Armada and harried it up the English Channel. After a hard-fought battle off the French port of Gravelines, the English drove the Armada into the North Sea. Sidonia sailed round Britain back to Spain; more than half his ships were lost, many wrecked by storms.

Day of Terror

The ambition of one woman, Catherine de Médicis, led to one of the worst massacres in France's history. Catherine, widow of Henri II, exercised complete control over her son, Charles IX, who was only 10 when he became king. But in 1572 it seemed that Charles, then 22, was coming under the influence of the Huguenot leader, Admiral Gaspard de Coligny. Huguenot was the name given to Protestants in France.

An attempt to have Coligny assassinated having failed, Catherine planned a mass killing of leading Huguenots, who were in Paris for the marriage of Henri of Navarre to Catherine's daughter Marguerite. The massacre began at dawn on St Bartholomew's Day, August 24, 1572, two days after the attempt on Coligny's life. This time Coligny did not escape, though the Queen spared the lives of Henri of Navarre and the Prince de Condé. The massacre was repeated throughout France and the number of Huguenots killed may have been as high as 20,000 in two days.

Opposite: The medal to commemorate the defeat of the Spanish Armada in 1588.

Left: A scene in Paris during the Massacre of St Bartholomew's Day, August 24, 1572. About 20,000 French Protestants were murdered.

Mary, Queen of Scots

Mary became queen at the age of one week when her father, James V of Scotland, died; she was brought up in France – her mother was a Guise – and at the age of 16 she married the Dauphin, soon to be Francois II. He died two years later.

In 1561 Mary returned to Protestant Scotland where she married her cousin Lord Darnley, like her a Roman Catholic. Tiring of Darnley, Mary made a friend of her private secretary, the Italian musician David Rizzio. In 1566 Rizzio was assassinated, partly at Darnley's instigation.

Soon after, Mary became friendly with James Hepburn, Earl of Bothwell. In 1567 Darnley died when his house was blown up, and Bothwell was held to be responsible. Mary's prompt marriage to Bothwell was the signal for a rebellion, and Mary was forced to abdicate in favour of her baby son by Darnley, James VI. She fled for safety to Elizabeth I of England, whose heir she was.

The English held Mary in custody, fearing a Roman Catholic conspiracy to make her queen and depose Elizabeth. Finally in 1587 Mary was implicated in just such a plot, and was executed for treason.

1571 Bornu Empire in the Sudan (until 1603) reaches its greatest height under Idris III.
1572 Gregory XIII, Pope (to 1585).
Massacre of St Bartholomew: mass murder of Protestants (Huguenots) in France on St Bartholomew's Day.
1573 Venice abandons Cyprus and makes peace with Turkey.
Don John recaptures Tunis.
1574 Henri III, King of France (to 1589).
Turkey regains Tunis from Spain.
1576 Rudolf II, Holy Roman Emperor (to 1612).
Pacification of Ghent: Netherlands provinces unite to drive out the Spaniards.
Protestantism forbidden in France.
1577 Alliance between England and Netherlands.
Akbar the Great completes the unification and annexation of northern India.
Francis Drake sails around world (to 1580).
1578 Duke of Parma subdues the southern provinces of the Netherlands.
Battle of Al Kasr Al-kabil: Portuguese defeated by the Muslims.
1579 Northern provinces of the Netherlands form Union of Utrecht.
1580 Spanish conquer Portugal.
1581 Union of Utrecht declares itself the Dutch Republic, independent of Spain, and elects William of Orange as its ruler.
Poland invades Russia.
1582 Gregorian calendar introduced into Roman Catholic countries.
Peace between Russia, and Poland and Sweden.
1584 William of Orange is murdered.
England sends aid to the Netherlands.
Alliance of Bern, Geneva, and Zurich against Roman Catholic cantons.
Fedor I, Tsar of Russia (to 1598).
1585 England sends troops to the Dutch Republic.
Sixtus V, Pope (to 1590).
'War of the Three Henrys' – Henri III of France, Henri of Navarre and Henri of Guise.
1586 Expedition of Sir Francis Drake to the West Indies.
Conspiracy against Elizabeth I involves Mary Queen of Scots.
1587 Execution of Mary Queen of Scots.
England at war with Spain.
Sir Francis Drake destroys Spanish fleet at Cadiz.
Savoy and the Catholic cantons form an alliance with Spain.
1588 The Spanish Armada is defeated by the English fleet under Lord Howard of Effingham, Sir Francis Drake, and Sir John Hawkins:

Renaissance astronomers overturned Man's idea of his place in the Universe. Using the accurate observations of Tycho Brahe (left), who lived from 1546 to 1601, Johannes Kepler (top left) began in 1609 to publish his laws of motion, which explained the apparently irregular movements of the planets. At the same time, Galileo Galilei (top right) was observing the heavens with a telescope for the first time. He discovered four of the thirteen moons of Jupiter with its aid. His studies convinced him of the truth of the idea that the Earth moves round the Sun; but the Church imprisoned him for asserting this 'heresy'.

Calendar Change

The calendar we use today was worked out by astronomers in the service of Pope Gregory XIII in the 1580s. Up to that time the calendar in use, introduced by Julius Caesar in 46 BC, had provided for a year that was 11 minutes and 14 seconds longer than the actual year, the time the Earth takes to orbit the Sun. So after more than 1600 years the calendar was 10 days ahead of the seasons.

On Pope Gregory's orders October 5, 1582 was made October 15, which corrected the error. To prevent it recurring, the Pope decreed that century years which could not be divided by 400 would not be leap years (i.e. not have an extra day as expected). Roman Catholic countries adopted the new calendar at once but many Protestant countries did not change until 1700. Britain did so in 1752, and Russia only in 1918.

'The War of the Three Henrys'

'The War of the Three Henrys' which raged from 1585 to 1589 was the eighth of a series of religious wars which ravaged France in the 1500s. The Roman Catholic King Henri III, his heir the Protestant Henri of Navarre, and the leader of the Holy Catholic League, Henri Duke of Guise, each headed a powerful army.

The war began because Henri III, under the influence of Guise, banned the Protestant religion. Navarre won several battles, and when Guise seized Paris, intending to depose the King, Henri III found himself powerless and had to flee to Blois for safety. In desperation, he invited Guise to a conference, and there had him murdered. At once the forces of the League attacked Henri, bent on revenge, and he had to make peace with Navarre and the Protestants.

Henri III and his heir, Navarre, were advancing to retake Paris, when a fanatical monk, Jacques Clément, assassinated the King. Henri of Navarre became king as Henri IV, but had to fight several more battles and adopt the Roman Catholic faith before he could confirm his claim to the throne. The wars of religion were eventually ended by the Edict of Nantes in 1598.

Opposite: Akbar the Great (in red and blue) awaits the Persian ambassador in 1562. Akbar, Babar's grandson and the greatest of the Mughal emperors of India, ruled from 1556 to 1605, almost exactly contemporary with Elizabeth I of England (reigned 1558–1603). He enlarged the empire to include all northern India.

1588 war between Spain and England continues until 1603.
Henri of Guise is murdered.
1589 Henri III of France is murdered and the Protestant leader Henri of Navarre succeeds to the throne as Henri IV (to 1610).
Antonio of Crato, with British support, lands in Portugal and marches on Lisbon to reconquer the throne: he is defeated by the Spaniards.
1590 Peace between Turkey and Persia.
Battle of Ivry. Henri IV victorious against the Roman Catholic party.
1591 Songhai Empire is destroyed by Spanish and Portuguese mercenaries in the service of Morocco.
1592 Clement VIII, Pope (to 1605).
Hideyoshi invades Korea with plans to conquer China, but is forced to withdraw (1593).
Akbar the Great conquers Sind.
1593 Diet of Uppsala in Sweden upholds Martin Luther's doctrines.
War between Austria and Turkey (until 1606).
1595 Treaty of Teusina between Sweden and Russia: Sweden gains Estonia.
1596 Battle of Keresztes: Turkish victory in Hungary.
1597 Irish rebellion under Hugh O'Neill, Earl of Tyrone (put down 1601).
1598 Edict of Nantes ends civil wars in France by giving Protestant Huguenots equal political rights with Roman Catholics.
Philip III, King of Spain (to 1621).
Treaty of Vervins between France and Spain: all conquests restored to France.
Boris Godunov, Tsar of Russia (to 1605).
1599 Confederation of Vilna: alliance formed between Orthodox and Dissidents in Poland.
Irish rebels defeat the Earl of Essex; he returns to England and disgrace.
1600 Elizabeth I grants charter to English East India Company.
Battle of Sekigahara: Tokugawa Ieyasu defeats rivals to become ruler of Japan; he establishes a military and administrative headquarters at Edo (Tokyo).
1601 Elizabethan Poor Law charges the parishes with providing for the needy.
Essex attempts rebellion, and is executed.
1602 Savoy attacks Geneva: Protestant cantons ally with France.
Dutch East India Company formed.
Holy War between Persia, under Shah Abbas I and Turkey (until 1618).
1603 Ieyasu appointed shogun of Japan.
James VI, King of Scotland becomes James I of England (to 1625).

Don Quixote, the romantic knight created by Spain's greatest novelist, Miguel de Cervantes Saavedra, tilts at a windmill 'giant'. Cervantes (1547–1616) had to flee to Italy after killing a man in self defence. He became a soldier, and took part in the battle of Lepanto. He was a slave of the Turks for five years. Book I of Don Quixote *was published in 1605, Book II in 1615. An amusing and shrewd commentary on people and experience,* Don Quixote *is one of the world's most translated books.*

A New Continent

Little more than a hundred years after the discovery of the New World, another unknown continent was found – and once again the discoverer did not realize what he had come across.

The Dutch navigator Willem Jansz had set out from the Netherlands in 1606 aboard the *Duifken* ('Little Dove') to sail to the island of New Guinea, rumoured to be rich in gold. Jansz reached the southern coast of the island, and then turned south, touching land again on Cape York Peninsula in northern Australia. He sent a party ashore and they found 'wild, cruel black savages'. Jansz thought he was still off New Guinea, but he had stumbled across the *Terra Australis Incognita* – 'Unknown Southern Land' – which geographers for centuries had insisted must exist.

Dutch Independence

The city-states known usually as the Low Countries because they were so close to sea-level – now the Netherlands and Belgium – came into the possession of the dukes of Burgundy during the 1500s. The dukes were Habsburgs, and through inheritance the lands went to the Habsburg Philip II of Spain.

Philip, an ardent Roman Catholic, tried to put down the Protestant religion in his Dutch possessions, and as a result the Dutch revolted. The Spaniards soon brought most of the area that is now Belgium – whose people were mostly Roman Catholics – under control, but the northern provinces, under their leader William the Silent, Prince of Orange, declared themselves the Republic of the United Netherlands. The English came to the aid of the Dutch in 1585, but without lasting success. Dutch independence was finally won in 1648.

Japan in Isolation

The year 1600 saw a power struggle in Japan end with the victory of the Tokugawa family, whose head, Tokugawa Ieyasu, was appointed shogun – military dictator – in 1603. Ieyasu established his military headquarters at Edo – renamed Tokyo in 1868 – which effectively became the capital of Japan. The emperors maintained their court at the nominal capital, Kyoto.

The Tokugawa family remained in power as shoguns until 1868. At the start, the family feared the presence of Christian missionaries who had been welcomed into Japan, and persecution of Christians began in 1612. Gradually the Tokugawa shoguns drove out the missionaries, and the European traders who were established there.

By 1641 only the Dutch, isolated on an island in Nagasaki Harbour, retained a trading post in Japan. Japan was virtually cut off from the world, and remained so until the United States forced a trade treaty at gunpoint in 1854.

1603 Samuel de Champlain explores the St Lawrence river.
1604 Time of Troubles in Russia (to 1613).
French East India Company founded.
Hampton Court Conference: no relaxation by the Church towards Puritans; James bans Jesuits.
England and Spain make peace.
Russians begin settlement of Siberia and found Tomsk.
1605 Paul V, Pope (to 1621).
Gunpowder Plot to blow up English Parliament is discovered; Guy Fawkes and other conspirators arrested and tried.
Fedor II, Tsar of Russia, deposed and murdered.
1606 Laws passed in England against Roman Catholics.
Basil Shuisky, Tsar of Russia (to 1610).
Several attempts by pretenders to gain the Russian throne; Cossack and peasant uprisings (until 1608).
Treaty of Zsitva-Torok between Turks and Austrians: Austria abandons Transylvania but ceases to pay tribute to Turkey.
Willem Jansz sights Australia.
1607 English Parliament rejects proposals for union between England and Scotland.
English colony of Virginia is founded at Jamestown by John Smith.
Henry Hudson begins voyage of discovery to eastern Greenland and Hudson River.
1608 Protestant Union formed in Germany and led by Frederick IV.
French explorer Samuel de Champlain founds settlement of Quebec.
1609 Twelve Years Truce ends fighting between Spain and the United Provinces; it ensures the virtual independence of the Netherlands.
The Catholic League led by Maximilian of Bavaria is formed in opposition to the Protestant Union.
Poland intervenes in Russia during the Time of Troubles (until 1618).
Johannes Keppler publishes his first two laws of planetary motion.
1610 The Great Contract: James I to receive an annual income of £200,000.
Galileo Galilei reveals stellar observations, made for the first time with a telescope.
Henri IV assassinated; Louis XIII, King of France (to 1643).
Henry Hudson discovers Hudson Bay.
Tea introduced to Europe.
Basil Shruisky is deposed and the Russian throne offered to Wladyslaw, son of Sigismund, King of Poland.

United Provinces (Netherlands Republic)
Spanish Netherlands (the future Belgium)
Neighbouring countries
FRIESLAND
Haarlem OVERYSSEL
The Hague GELDERLAND Duisberg
Rotterdam
BRABANT
Bruges Ghent
Brussels
FLANDERS Liège
HAINAULT
Arras
LUXEMBURG
Luxemburg
DUTCH INDEPENDENCE

The Age of Kings

THE PERIOD from the assassination of Henri IV of France to the eve of the American War of Independence has been called 'the Age of Kings' because the march of events was dominated by a number of outstanding rulers, many of whom possessed dictatorial powers which they believed were theirs by right. The idea of the 'Divine Right of Kings' was clearly stated by James I of England; but it was in England that the very concept of kingship was most strongly challenged. James's son Charles I was beheaded for 'treason against the State', and all future British monarchs had greatly restricted powers.

In France, the picture was very different. Three kings named Louis – XIII, XIV, XV – whose reigns between them spanned 164 years, exercised absolute power directly or through their ministers. The history of Russia in this period is dominated by Peter the Great, that of Sweden by his enemy Charles XII. The rivalries of Frederick the Great of Prussia and the Empress Maria Theresa led to Europe being ravaged by war. But the power of all these sovereigns was too great for their countries' good, and was to lead to the decline of monarchy. A growing emphasis on the supremacy of reason over religion in human affairs, a legacy of the Renaissance, assisted this decline and aided the spread of scientific knowledge.

The battle of Blenheim, 1704. Far left: English troops attacking the village of Blindheim, Bavaria from which the battle is named. Centre: French troops are surrounded and cut to pieces. Right: Austrian troops attack.

EUROPE

1611	Authorized Version of Bible completed
	Plantation of Ulster
1614	Estates-general summoned in France
1618	Thirty Years' War (to 1648)
1624	Richelieu chief minister in France
1640	Portuguese revolt against Spain
1641	Irish Catholic revolt
1642	Civil War in England (to 1646)
1648	Treaty of Westphalia
	Revolt of Fronde in Paris (to 1649)
1649	Charles I of England executed
	Commonwealth in England (to 1660)
	Serfdom established in Russia
1651	Battle of Worcester
1652	Anglo-Dutch war (to 1654)
1660	Charles II regains English throne
1661	Louis XIV absolute monarch in France
1665	Great Plague in London
	Second Anglo-Dutch war (to 1667)
1666	Great Fire of London
1672	William III rules Netherlands
1683	Siege of Vienna by Turkish forces
1686	League of Augsburg formed
1688	England's 'Glorious Revolution'
1689	Peter I, Tsar of Russia (to 1725)
1690	Battle of the Boyne in Ireland
1700	Great Northern War (to 1721)
1701	Act of Settlement in Britain
	War of Spanish Succession (to 1713)
1704	Battle of Blenheim
1707	Act of Union
1715	First Jacobite uprising
1733	War of Polish Succession (to 1735)
1739	John Wesley founds Methodists
1740	War of Austrian Succession (to 1748)
1745	Jacobite rebellion
1755	Lisbon earthquake kills 30,000
1756	Seven Years' War (to 1763)
1762	Catherine II, Tsarina of Russia (to 1796)
1772	First partition of Poland
1773	Pope Clement XIV suppresses Jesuits
	Peasant uprising in Russia (to 1775)

ASIA

1615	Tribes in Northern China form military organizations (to 1620)
1621	Nurhachi expels Ming
1623	Dutch massacre English at Amboina
1630	Turks take Hamadan, in Persia
1637	Russian explorers cross Siberia and reach Pacific Ocean
1638	Turks conquer Baghdad
1644	Manchu dynasty in China (to 1912)
1645	Turkey and Venice at war over Crete
1656	Venetians rout Turks off Dardanelles
1661	English acquire Bombay
	Koxinga takes Formosa
1669	Venice surrenders Crete to Turkey
	Hindu religion prohibited by Aurangzeb, Emperor of India
1676	Treaty of Zuravno; Turkey gains Polish Ukraine
	Sikh uprising in India (to 1678)
1683	Cheng Chin surrenders Formosa
1689	Treaty of Nerchinsk between Russia and China
1707	Death of Aurangzeb leads to disintegration of Mughal Empire
1724	State of Hyderabad achieves independence from Mughals
1730	Maratha government in India (to 1735)
1736	Russia, Austria fight Turkey (to 1739)
	Chi'en Lung Emperor of China (to 1795)
1737	Nadir Shah takes Afghanistan
1739	Nadir Shah sacks Delhi
1747	Nadir Shah assassinated
1751	Robert Clive takes Arcot in India
	Chinese conquer Tibet
1756	'Black Hole of Calcutta'
1757	British rule established in India
1761	Afghans defeat Marathas at Panipat

Above: A Danish guardsman from the Thirty Years War, carrying a matchlock musket.

Below: Japanese torturing Christian missionaries as part of a campaign against Christianity carried on by shogun Iemitsu to consolidate Tokugawa rule.

AFRICA

1618 French explorer Paul Imbert reaches Timbuktu

1626 First French settlements on Madagascar

1645 Capuchin monks ascend Congo River

1652 Capetown founded by the Dutch

1660 Rise of Bambara Kingdoms on upper Niger
1662 Portuguese cede Tangier to England

1686 Louis XIV of France announces annexation of Madagascar
1705 Turkish authority overthrown in Tunis

1713 Asiento Treaty starts most active period of British slave trade
1715 French take Mauritius

AMERICAS

1619	First American parliament meets at Jamestown, Virginia
	First Negro slaves arrive in Virginia
1620	Pilgrim Fathers reach Cape Cod and found New Plymouth
1626	Dutch found New Amsterdam
1630	Period of English settlement in Massachusetts (to 1642)
1633	Colony of Connecticut founded
1642	Montreal founded by the French
1654	Portuguese take Brazil from Dutch
1655	England seizes Jamaica from Spain
1664	England seizes New Amsterdam from Dutch, changing name to New York
1675	King Philip's War in New England (to 1676)
1681	Sieur de La Salle explores Mississippi River (to 1682)
1686	Dominion of New England formed
1692	Salem witchcraft trials in New England
739	Britain captures Porto Bello
744	King George's War (to 1748)
745	British capture Louisburg in Canada
755	French and Indian War (to 1763)
759	Britain captures Quebec
763	Chief Pontiac leads Indian uprising
1765	Stamp Act in American colonies
1767	Townshend Acts impose tax on imports
	Mason-Dixon line established
1770	Boston Massacre
1773	Boston Tea Party

ELSEWHERE

1616	Dutch navigator Willem Schouten rounds Cape Horn
1642	Abel Tasman discovers Van Diemen's Land (now Tasmania)
1699	William Dampier sails along north-west coast of Australia
1722	Dutch navigator Jacob Roggeveen discovers Samoa and Easter Island
1728	Danish navigator Vitus Bering explores Bering Strait
1768	English navigator James Cook discovers and explores east coast of Australia; lands in New Zealand (1769)
1770	James Cook discovers Botany Bay
1772	James Cook on second voyage (to 1775); crosses Antarctic Circle and circumnavigates Antarctica

Above: Gustavus Adolphus, the 'Lion of the North', king of Sweden from 1611 to 1632.
Left: Velazquez's portrait of Philip IV of Spain (1621–1665).
Opposite: A compound microscope, used by the 17th-century English scientist Robert Hooke. The first such microscope was invented about 1590 by a Dutch spectacle-maker.

Progress of Science

The 'Age of Kings' was also the age of considerable scientific thought and development. In particular, thinking men challenged literal interpretation of Scripture and began to trust to the results of their own observation and experiment.

Galileo Galilei (1564–1642), the Italian scientist, caused a furore when he asserted the truth of the theory put forward a hundred years earlier by the Polish astronomer Nicolaus Copernicus: that the Earth is not the centre of the universe, but revolves about the Sun. The Inquisition forced Galileo to recant such 'heresies'.

The Frenchman René Descartes (1596–1650) reached equally powerful conclusions in philosophy, emphasizing reason rather than traditional Church argument. At first he doubted all knowledge, even of self, but concluded because he could think, he must exist – '*Cogito, ergo sum*'. Descartes was also one of the founders of 'mechanistic philosophy', which explains the universe in terms of purely mechanical laws.

On the more practical side, many basic discoveries and inventions were made at this time. They included the discovery of logarithms by the Scottish mathematician John Napier in 1614; that of the circulation of the blood by the English physician Sir William Harvey in 1616; and the invention of the barometer by the Italian Evangelista Torricelli in 1643.

The Pilgrim Fathers

In 1620 the little ship *Mayflower* sailed from Plymouth in England with 102 passengers – men, women, and children bound for the New World and religious freedom. Most of them were Puritans who had fallen foul of the religious laws of England; some had been in exile in the Netherlands.

The expedition reached Cape Cod Bay in Massachusetts after a 65-day voyage, and finally landed on part of the rocky shore which had been given the name Plymouth a few years earlier. By the time the party reached its proposed settlement numbers were reduced to 99 – five people had died and two babies had been born.

These early settlers, forerunners of the colonists who were to form the independent United States 150 years later, are generally known as the Pilgrim Fathers, a term first used in 1799. They settled the first permanent colony of Europeans in New England, and the *Mayflower Compact* by which they governed themselves was to become famous.

1611 James I's authorized version of the Bible is completed.
Plantation of Ulster: English and Scottish Protestant colonists settle in Ulster.

1612 Matthias, Holy Roman Emperor (to 1619).

1613 Michael Romanov, Tsar of Russia (to 1645) founder of the Romanov dynasty.

1614 James I dissolves the 'Addled Parliament' which has failed to pass any legislation.
Estates-general summoned in France to curb the nobility – last such meeting until 1789.

1615 Tribes in northern China begin to form military organizations; later called *Manchus*.

1616 Willem Schouten, Dutch navigator, rounds Cape Horn.

1617 Treaty of Stolbovo between Russia and Sweden.

1618 'Defenestration of Prague' (incident when Bohemians claiming independence threw two Catholic governors from a window) sparks off Thirty Years' War; general conflict in Europe lasts until 1648.
Paul Imbert, French explorer, reaches Timbuktu.

1619 Ferdinand II, Holy Roman Emperor (to 1637).
Bohemians depose Ferdinand II and elect Frederick V ('the Winter King') as ruler.
First American parliament meets at Jamestown, Virginia.
First Negro slaves arrive in Virginia.

1620 Battle of the White Mountain: Frederick V is defeated by Maximilian of Bavaria.
Pilgrim Fathers reach Cape Cod, Massachusetts, in the *Mayflower* and found New Plymouth.

1621 Philip IV, King of Spain (to 1665).
Dutch West Indies Company is founded.
Nurhachi expels the Ming and sets up Manchu capital at Liaoyang.

1622 James I dissolves Parliament for asserting its right to debate foreign affairs.
Spain occupies Valtelline Pass; war with France follows.
Battles of Wimpfen and Rochst: Protestant forces defeated by Count Tilly.
Execution of Christian missionaries in Japan reaches its height (to 1624).

1623 Duke of Buckingham and Charles, Prince of Wales, visit Spain on unsuccessful attempt to negotiate a marriage treaty.
Urban VIII, Pope (to 1644).
Massacre of English by the Dutch at Amboina in the Moluccas Islands.

1624 Alliance between James I and France: Parliament votes supplies for war against Spain.
Cardinal Richelieu becomes Chief Minister in France (to 1642).

The Thirty Years' War

The Thirty Years' War lasted from 1618 to 1648, and was really a series of wars. It began with a quarrel between the Protestant and Roman Catholic princes of Germany over who should become the next Holy Roman Emperor. The Roman Catholic Ferdinand, King of Bohemia, was elected in 1617, but was deposed as king by supporters of the Protestant Frederick, Elector Palatine, two years later.

Ferdinand soon crushed Frederick, but Christian IV, the Protestant King of Denmark, intervened in 1625. By 1629 he too was defeated and withdrew from the war. Gustavus Adolphus of Sweden, with financial backing from the Roman Catholic leader of France, Cardinal Richelieu, intervened in 1630, but was killed two years later after winning several victories.

The Swedes carried on the fight with military aid from Richelieu, who feared the growing power of Ferdinand more than he supported his religion. The political scene grew ever more confused, with Denmark and Sweden, both Protestant, locked in combat, and France fighting on the same side as the Protestant Netherlands.

War in Germany was ended by the Peace of Westphalia, which gave France part of Alsace, and Lorraine. Germany was devastated, with cities ruined and millions dead.

The Lion of the North

One of the greatest champions of the Protestant cause was Gustavus Adolphus, King of Sweden, nicknamed the 'Lion of the North' because of his prowess in war. From the moment he became king in 1611 at the

Gustavus Adolphus inspects his armoury during an attack. The light guns which he introduced could be moved quickly around the battlefield, and revolutionized artillery warfare.

age of 16, he was involved in war – at first with Poland, Denmark, and Russia. He soon settled the quarrel with Denmark and Russia, but the war with Poland dragged on until 1629, when he gained victory. By then Gustavus was acknowledged one of the great warriors of the age.

In 1630 he decided to intervene in the Thirty Years' War, in which the Protestants were having a bad time. Some of his opponents sneered at the leather-jerkined King, calling him the 'Snow King' and saying he would melt as he came to the warmer south. But the 'Snow King' overwhelmed and killed one of the most successful generals on the Roman Catholic side, the Count of Tilly. In 1632, at the battle of Lützen, Gustavus met the even more redoubtable Albrecht von Wallenstein whom he defeated; but Gustavus died leading a cavalry charge.

Below: Cardinal Richelieu, chief minister to Louis XIII of France from 1624 to 1642. Born Armand Jean du Plessis, he was consecrated bishop of Lucon in 1607 at the age of only 22. As Louis' minister, he raised France and its King to great power.

1624	Virginia becomes a crown colony.
1625	Charles I, King of England (to 1649).
	Charles I marries Henrietta Maria, sister of Louis XIII of France; dissolves Parliament which fails to vote him money.
	Christian IV, Protestant King of Denmark, enters the war against Ferdinand II.
1626	Battle of Dessau: Catholic forces under von Wallenstein defeat Protestants.
	Battle of Lutter: Christian IV defeated.
	Dutch found New Amsterdam (New York).
1627	Siege of La Rochelle: Huguenots at La Rochelle besieged by Richelieu.
	Charles I raises forced loan to aid Huguenots.
	A new constitution in Bohemia confirms hereditary rule of the Habsburgs.
	Imperial forces under Counts Tilly and Wallenstein subdue most of Protestant Germany.
1628	Petition of Right: Charles I forced to accept Parliament's statement of civil rights in return for finances.
	Duke of Buckingham assassinated.
	Huguenots surrender to Richelieu, losing all political power.
	William Harvey demonstrates circulation of the blood.
1629	Charles I dissolves Parliament and rules personally until 1640.
	Treaty of Lübeck between Ferdinand II and Christian IV.
	Edict of Restitution issued by Ferdinand II entitles Catholics to reclaim Protestant lands.
1630	England makes peace with France and Spain.
	Gustavus Adolphus II, King of Sweden, enters war against Ferdinand II.
	About 16,000 colonists from England begin to settle in Massachusetts, in a migration lasting till 1642.
	Turks, under Murad IV, take Hamadan.
1631	City of Magdeburg sacked by Catholic forces under Tilly.
	Battle of Leipzig (Brietenfeld): Swedish and Saxon forces defeat Tilly.
1632	Battle of Lützen: Swedish victory, but Gustavus Adolphus II is killed.
1634	Wallenstein dismissed; later murdered.
	Battle of Nördlingen: Swedes defeated by imperial forces.
	Treaty of Polianov between Russia and Poland.
1635	Treaty of Prague: Ferdinand II revokes Edict of Restitution and makes peace with Saxony. Treaty is accepted by most Protestant princes.
	France declares war on Spain.
1637	Ferdinand III, Holy Roman Emperor (to 1657).
	Russian explorers reach the Pacific Ocean, having crossed Siberia.

The Arts

The first half of the 17th century saw the rise of what is called the Baroque period in the arts. Painters, sculptors, and architects aimed at spectacular, grand effects, and also at realism rather than formality in creating pictures. Outstanding portrait painters of the period included two Dutchmen, Sir Anthony Van Dyk (1599–1641) and Sir Peter Paul Rubens (1577–1660)–both Flemish painters who found wealth and honours in England– and the Spaniard Diego Velazquez (1599–1660).

In architecture, the outstanding names are those of two Italians, Giovanni Lorenzo Bernini (1598–1680), who designed the elaborate canopy over the main altar at St Peter's, Rome; and Francesco Borromini (1599–1667), designer of many churches. In England, Inigo Jones (1573–1652) went against the prevailing trend by producing simple but elegantly proportioned buildings.

In music, the period is important for the development of opera and oratorio. The first opera was *Dafne*, by the Italian composer Jacopo Peri (1561–1633), produced in 1594 and now lost. The Venetian Claudio Monteverdi (1567–1643) and his pupil Francesco Cavalli (1602–1667) were the principle developers of this new art form. Oratorio, a form of opera with sacred themes and no acting or scenery, developed simultaneously for performance on holy days.

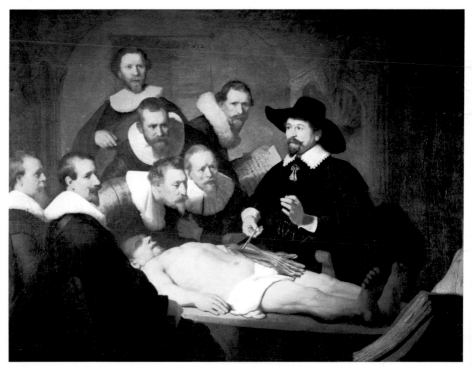

Above: The Taj Mahal at Agra, in India, was built to the order of the Mughal Emperor Shah Jahan from 1632 to 1653 as a tomb for his beautiful wife.

Opposite: The Anatomy Lesson of Professor Nicolaes Tulp *by Rembrandt van Rijn (1606–1669).*

English Civil War

The English Civil War which raged from 1642 to 1646 arose from disputes between King Charles I and Parliament, between high Churchmen and Puritans, over several issues. Charles's idea that the 'Divine Right of Kings' put him above the law annoyed a defiant Parliament which he dissolved three times. He favoured bishops while others, especially Scots, wanted a more Puritan worship. And in desperate need of money for armies, he imposed taxes which provoked stern resistance. Parliament raised an army and civil war broke out.

Charles scored many victories at first, but in 1644 the Parliamentarians – called *Roundheads* from their close-cropped hair – gained the upper hand over the Royalists, known as *Cavaliers* from their superiority in cavalry. Two final defeats in 1645 led Charles to surrender to the Scots, who handed him over to his enemies. In 1649 he was tried for treason, condemned and beheaded. From then on the army rather than Parliament assumed control, under a leading general, Oliver Cromwell.

1638 Scottish Presbyterians sign the Solemn League and Covenant.
Turks conquer Baghdad.
Shimbara uprising and slaughter of Japanese Christians virtually stamps out Christianity in Japan.

1639 First Bishops' War between Charles I and the Scottish Church; ends with Pacification of Dunse.

1640 Charles I summons the 'Short' Parliament; dissolved for refusal to grant money.
Second Bishops' War; ends with Treaty of Ripon.
The Long Parliament of Charles I (until 1660).
Revolt in Catalonia against Spain (until 1659).
Revolt of the Portuguese against Spain, led by João Ribeiro with French support.

1641 Triennial Act requires Parliament to be summoned every three years.
Star Chamber and High Commission abolished by Parliament.
Catholics in Ireland revolt; some 30,000 Protestants massacred.
Grand Remonstrance of Parliament to Charles I.

1642 Charles I attempts to arrest five members of Parliament but fails; he rejects Parliament's Nineteen Propositions.
Civil War in England between Cavaliers (Royalists) and Roundheads (Parliamentarians) (until 1646); opens with battle of Edgehill.
Second battle of Leipzig: Swedish victory.
Montreal founded by the French.
Abel Tasman sights Van Diemen's Land (Tasmania) and New Zealand.

1643 Solemn League and Covenant is signed by English Parliament.
Louis XIV, King of France at age of 5; Cardinal Mazarin chief minister. Louis reigns until 1715.
Battle of Rocroi: France defeats Spain.
Denmark and Sweden at war for Baltic supremacy (until 1645).

1644 Battle of Marston Moor: Oliver Cromwell defeats Prince Rupert.
Manchu (Ta Ch'ing) dynasty begins; lasts until 1912.

1645 Formation of Cromwell's New Model Army.
Battle of Naseby: Charles I defeated by Parliamentary forces.
Turkey and Venice at war (until 1664) over Turkish designs on Candia (Crete).

1646 Charles I surrenders to the Scots.

1647 Scots surrender Charles I to the English Parliament; he is captured in turn by the army but escapes to the Isle of Wight; makes secret treaty with Scots.

Aurangzeb

The reign of the Mughal Emperor Aurangzeb, which lasted from 1658 to 1705, provides an example of how the force which builds up an empire can also bring about its eventual destruction.

Aurangzeb was clever, efficient, ruthless, and a bigoted Muslim. He began his reign by imprisoning his ailing father, Shah Jahan, and killing his brothers who were his rivals for the throne. A series of conquests enabled him to extend the Mughal Empire to cover nearly all of present-day India and Pakistan, and even part of Afghanistan. But he never fully subdued the Mahrattas of the Deccan, the peninsular part of India, and by the time he died his authority was challenged almost everywhere in the empire.

Aurangzeb's religious fanaticism led him to persecute the Hindu population, instead of conciliating it as his grandfather Akbar had done. This more than any other action hastened the break-up of the Empire which followed his death at the age of 88.

East India Companies

In the 1600s and 1700s trade with the East Indies – a term then used to include India and the islands of south-eastern Asia – offered splendid opportunities for profit, and following it up was left to private enterprise rather than to governments. In eight countries trading firms known as East India Companies were formed, of which three – English, French, and Dutch – were important. The English company was granted its charter by Elizabeth I in 1600; the Dutch company was founded in 1602 with a capital of more than half a million pounds.

The Dutch company gained control of most of the islands later known as the Dutch East Indies, and now forming Indonesia. The English and French companies were rivals for power in mainland India, and eventually the French tried to drive out the English. This move failed, and the English company ended up ruling most of India. In the 1800s this company's affairs were taken over by the British government.

Below: The trial of Charles I of England, from a book of 1684 titled A true Copy of the Journal of the High Court of Justice for the Tryall of King Charles I. *Although the monarchy was restored in 1660, royal power in England was diminished for ever.*

Opposite: The Mughal Emperor of India, Aurangzeb, receiving the head of one of his brothers, whom he had killed as rivals for the throne. Aurangzeb's bigoted, ruthless rule contributed to the break-up of the Mughal Empire.

1648 Scots invade England; defeated by Cromwell at battle of Preston; Pride's Purge: Presbyterians expelled from Parliament which is now known as the 'Rump'.

Treaty of Westphalia ends Thirty Years' War; Dutch and Swiss republics recognized as independent.

Revolt of the Fronde or *parlement* faction in Paris against Louis XIV (suppressed 1649).

1649 Charles I is tried and executed.

The Commonwealth (until 1660) — England governed as a republic.

Cromwell harshly suppresses Catholic rebellions in Ireland.

Serfdom completely established in Russia.

1650 Second revolt of Fronde is suppressed.

Charles II lands in Scotland; proclaimed king.

1651 Charles II invades England; defeated in battle of Worcester and escapes to France.

First Navigation Act: England gains virtual monopoly of foreign trade.

1652 Anglo-Dutch war (until 1654).

Spain intervenes in Fronde revolt against Louis XIV (to 1653).

Barcelona surrenders to Philip IV; end of Catalan revolt.

Capetown founded by the Dutch.

1653 Cromwell dissolves the 'Rump' and becomes Lord Protector of England.

1654 Treaty of Westminster between England and Dutch Republic.

Portuguese take Brazil from the Dutch.

1655 England divided into 12 military districts by Cromwell.

England seizes Jamaica from Spain.

Sweden declares war on Poland.

1656 First Villmergen War in Switzerland between Protestant and Catholic cantons.

England and Spain at war (until 1659).

Battle of Warsaw: Swedish victory; Russia, Denmark, and Holy Roman Empire declare war on Sweden.

Turks routed by Venetians off Dardanelles.

1657 Dutch Republic and Portugal at war (to 1661).

1658 Oliver Cromwell dies; succeeded as Lord Protector by son Richard.

Battle of the Dunes: England and France defeat Spain; England gains Dunkirk.

Leopold I, Holy Roman Emperor (to 1705).

1659 Richard Cromwell forced to resign by the army; 'Rump' Parliament restored.

Treaty of the Pyrenees between France and Spain: settles borders and confirms supremacy of France over Spain.

1660 Convention Parliament restores Charles II to the English throne.

The Absolute Monarch

Louis XIV of France ruled for longer than any other European monarch – 72 years – and wielded more power than any of his contemporaries. He became king at the age of five in 1643, and began to rule in his own right when he was 24.

Louis typified the concept of absolutism – rule with no restraints imposed by the constitution, or by a legislature. He once summed up his position in the words 'L'état, c'est moi' – I am the state. He had a small council of ministers, but they did as the King willed.

The magnificence in which the King lived in his new palace at Versailles earned him the nickname of *Le Grand Monarque*. But another of his titles, the 'Sun King' – from a rôle he once danced in a court ballet – was more appropriate because of his position as the centre of the political universe in France.

Louis's rule was not always wise; he fought four wars, which gained him little for their cost in money and lives. He persecuted the Huguenots until 400,000 of them, many of France's best craftsmen, fled the country. When he died in 1715, having outlived both his eldest son and his grandson, he left a troubled, impoverished country.

Above: Louis XIV of France, by the court portrait painter Hyacinthe Rigaud (1659–1743). Rigaud brings out clearly the pomp and wealth of Le Grand Monarque, *as Louis was often called.*

Plague and Fire

Two disasters struck London during the 1660s. The first was an outbreak of bubonic plague, the last and worst of a series which had started in the 1300s. The Great Plague, as it was called, began late in 1664, and raged for over a year; more than 75,000 people died and many fled to the country.

Hardly had the disease died down than a fire broke out in a bakery near London Bridge. Many of London's houses were built of wood, and the fire rapidly gained a hold. It burned from September 2 to 9 1666, destroying most of the city, including 13,000 houses, St Paul's Cathedral and 84 churches, the Guildhall, markets, wharves, and even shipping on the river Thames. It was stopped by blowing up buildings to make gaps the fire could not cross.

Opposite: The charred and smoking ruins of London after the Great Fire of 1666. This picture gives some idea of the extent of the devastation, in which about 14,000 buildings were destroyed. The halting of the fire was helped by the King, Charles II, and his brother the Duke of York, later James II. Sir Christopher Wren was one of the men chosen to supervise the rebuilding. His greatest achievement was his design for the new St Paul's Cathedral, the old Cathedral having been destroyed in the fire.

1660 Charles II, King of England and Scotland (to 1685).
Treaty of Oliva: Poland cedes Livonia to Sweden.
Treaty of Copenhagen: Denmark surrenders territory to Sweden.

1661 Treaty of Kardis: Russia and Sweden restore all conquests to each other.
Clarendon Code: 'Cavalier' Parliament of Charles II (to 1665) passes a series of repressive laws against Nonconformists.
Death of Cardinal Mazarin; Louis XIV of France becomes absolute monarch.
English acquire Bombay.
Chinese general Koxinga takes Formosa.
Turkey and Empire at war (until 1664).

1662 Act of Uniformity passed in England.

1664 England seizes New Amsterdam from the Dutch; its name changed to New York.
Battle of St Gotthard: Austrians under Count Raimund Montecuccoli defeat Turks.
Treaty of Vasvar between Holy Roman Empire and Turkey.

1665 Great Plague in London.
Second Anglo-Dutch war (until 1667); English fleet defeats the Dutch off Lowestoft.
Newton discovers laws of gravitation.

1666 Great Fire of London.

1667 Dutch fleet defeats the English in the Medway river.
Treaties of Breda among Netherlands, England, France, and Denmark.
War of Devolution: France invades Spanish Netherlands.
Treaty of Andrussovo: Russia gains Smolensk and eastern Ukraine from Poland.

1668 Triple Alliance of England, Netherlands, and Sweden against France.
Treaty of Lisbon: Spain recognizes Portugal's independence.
Treaty of Aix-la-Chapelle ends War of Devolution; France keeps most conquests in Flanders.

1669 Venice surrenders Candia (Crete) to Turkey.
Hindu religion prohibited and Hindus persecuted by Aurangzeb, Emperor of India.
Death of Rembrandt.

1670 Secret Treaty of Dover between Charles II of England and Louis XIV of France to restore Roman Catholicism to England.
Hudson's Bay Company founded.
Uprisings by peasants and Cossacks in Russia (to 1671).

1672 Third Anglo-Dutch war (until 1674).
France at war with Netherlands (until 1678): French troops invade southern Netherlands.

Sir Isaac Newton

Isaac Newton, a professor at Cambridge University, did more than any other man to advance scientific knowledge in the 17th century. The principles he stated were to be the basis of physics for centuries.

In a burst of brilliant inspiration in 1665–1667 – before he was 26 – Newton made three momentous discoveries. The first was the theory of gravitation – that all bodies exert a pull on one another proportional to their size. Arising out of this were his three laws of motion (governing bodies moving or at rest, the effect of acceleration, and the equality of action and reaction). These principles are the basis of classical dynamic theory. Newton's second discovery was that white light is made up of rays of coloured light. The third was a new branch of mathematics, the calculus.

Newton did not publish his discoveries for many years, until the astronomer Edmund Halley persuaded him to do so in 1687. Newton became Master of the Mint in 1699 and was knighted by Queen Anne in 1705.

Peter the Great

Peter I (1672–1725), known as *the Great*, was made joint tsar of Russia with his feeble-minded half-brother, Ivan V, in 1682. Ivan's sister Sophia ruled as regent, and Peter lived away from court. In 1689 Peter seized power, and banished Sophia to a convent; he allowed Ivan to live quietly until he died in 1696.

A military enthusiast, Peter fought several successful wars. He captured the Black Sea port of Azov from the Turks in 1696. In the Great Northern War (1700–1721) he captured territory which gave Russia access to the Baltic Sea.

Peter's greatest achievement was the modernization of Russia. He toured western Europe in 1696–1697 to study how other peoples lived, and returned home to begin many reforms. His court followed western ways, and the Russians were ordered to wear a more western style of dress. Peter reorganized the army, founded a navy, developed trade, industry, and the civil service, and built canals and roads.

Top left: Sir Isaac Newton, whose Law of Universal Gravitation was the climax of the scientific era. It also sparked off new philosophical ideas in men like John Locke, who set out to prove that mankind, too, was governed by a universal law of equality and independence. Newton's discoveries influenced many areas other than simply science.

Opposite: Peter the Great of Russia. Only one year of Peter's 43-year reign passed without war. Nobles and peasants alike could be drafted into the army for life. Even the church bells of Moscow were melted down to make cannon for his army. His ambition was to forge a great military power from the backward country which he had inherited. He succeeded in this aim, and his internal reforms changed the country from within as well so that under his rule Russia rose in many ways to be a power in western Europe. Peter had achieved his ambition.

The Obstinate Governor

Peter Stuyvesant, the last Dutch governor of the North American city of New Amsterdam, was an obstinate and dictatorial man. Employed by the Dutch West India Company, which administered Dutch colonies in America, he incorporated New Amsterdam as a city, but let no one else share power.

During the Dutch wars with England in the 1660's, Stuyvesant ordered his citizens to resist an English attack but nobody would obey him; in September 1664, he capitulated without a shot being fired. The English renamed the city New York after James, Duke of York.

1672 William III (of Orange) becomes hereditary *stadholder* (ruler) of Netherlands (until 1702).
Treaty of Stockholm between France and Sweden.
Poland and Turkey at war for control of the Ukraine (until 1676).

1673 Test Act aims to deprive English Roman Catholics and Nonconformists of public office.

1674 Holy Roman Empire declares war on France in defence of the Dutch.
Treaty of Westminster between England and the Netherlands.

1675 Battle of Fehrbellin: Swedish forces defeated by Frederick William (the Great Elector)' of Brandenburg.
King Philip's War (to 1676): American Indians attack settlers in New England.

1676 Sikh uprisings in India (until 1678).
Treaty of Zuravno between Poland and Turkey; Turkey gains Polish Ukraine.
Fedor III, Tsar of Russia (to 1682).

1677 William III of the Netherlands marries Mary, daughter of James, Duke of York, heir to the English throne.
Russia and Turkey at war (until 1681).

1678 'Popish Plot' in England: Titus Oates falsely alleges a Catholic plot to murder Charles II.
Treaty of Nimwegen ends Franco-Dutch war.

1679 Act of Habeas Corpus passed in England, forbidding imprisonment without trial.
Parliament's Bill of Exclusion against the Roman Catholic Duke of York blocked by Charles II; Parliament dismissed.
Charles II rejects petitions (to 1680) calling for a new Parliament; petitioners become known as *Whigs*; their opponents (royalists) known as *Tories*.

1680 Chambers of Reunion established by Louis XIV of France to annex territory; France occupies Strasbourg, Luxemburg, Lorraine (1683).

1681 Whigs reintroduce Exclusion Bill; Charles II dissolves Parliament.
Treaty of Radzin: Russia gains most of Turkish Ukraine.

1682 Turkey and Austria at war (until 1699).
Ivan V, Tsar of Russia (to 1689).

1683 Siege of Vienna by Turkish forces; city is relieved by German and Polish troops.
Koxinga's grandson, Cheng Chin, surrenders Formosa to the Manchus.

1684 Holy League formed by Pope Innocent XI: Venice, Austria, and Poland united against Turkey.
France occupies Trier in the Rhineland.

1685 Louis XIV revokes Edict of Nantes: all religions except Roman Catholicism forbidden.

Above: Louis XIV built the palace of Versailles as a home for his huge court. It was a palace of such splendour that it cost more than £150 million and took 47 years to complete. The facade measures 1361 ft (3158 m) long, and the entire palace is surrounded by vast formal gardens. A huge retinue of over 5000 courtiers, mostly nobles, lived at the palace, with another 5000 servants living close by. Versailles was a fit setting for a monarch commonly known as the 'Sun King'.

The League of Augsburg

The League of Augsburg was a coalition of European princes against Louis XIV of France, who was claiming part of the Palatinate, one of the German states. The chief members of the League were the Holy Roman Emperor Leopold I, the kings of Sweden and Spain, and the electors of Bavaria, the, Palatinate, and Saxony. Pope Innocent XI secretly promised support. The Netherlands supported the League, and when William of Orange became king of England in 1689 England joined as well.

The War of the League of Augsburg lasted from 1689 to 1697. The Treaty of Ryswick restored the conquered territory except for parts of Alsace and Strasbourg, which remained French.

The Salem Witches

Superstition and credulity led to North America's last trials for witchcraft in 1692, in the little village of Salem, Massachusetts. The witchcraft scare began when a Negro slave girl named Tituba told some stories of voodoo (the traditional West African spirit religion) to some friends who had nightmares as a result. A doctor who was called in to examine the girls said they must be bewitched.

Trials of Tituba and others were held before Judge Samuel Sewall. Cotton Mather, a colonial preacher who was convinced that witchcraft existed, led the prosecution. The witchcraft scare lasted about a year, during which time 19 people, mostly women, were found guilty and executed – one man by the barbarous medieval custom of being pressed to death by heavy weights. About 150 other people were jailed. Judge Sewall later confessed that he thought his judgments had been wrong.

Below: Map of the League of Augsburg.

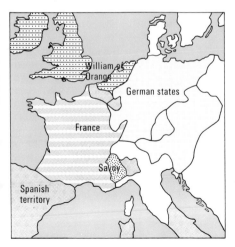

1685	more than 50,000 Protestant (Huguenot) families leave France.
	James II, King of England and VII of Scotland (to 1688).
	Rebellion by Charles II's illegitimate son, Duke of Monmouth, against James II put down.
1686	James II disregards Test Act: Roman Catholics appointed to public office.
	League of Augsburg formed between Holy Roman Empire, Spain, Sweden, Saxony, Bavaria, and the Palatinate against France.
	Austrians advance on Budapest.
	Venetians take Morea.
1687	James II of England issues Declaration of Liberty of Conscience: extends toleration to all religions.
	Battle of Mohács: Turks defeated; Habsburg succession to Hungarian throne confirmed.
1688	England's 'Glorious Revolution': William III of Orange is invited to save England from Roman Catholicism; he lands in England; James II flees to France.
	Austrians capture Belgrade.
1689	War of the League of Augsburg (until 1697); France invades the Palatinate.
	Convention Parliament issues the Bill of Rights; establishes a constitutional monarchy in Britain; bars Roman Catholics from the throne.
	William III and Mary II, joint monarchs of England and Scotland (to 1694).
	Toleration Act grants freedom of worship to dissenters in England.
	Grand Alliance of the League of Augsburg, England, and the Netherlands.
	Peter I (the Great), Tsar of Russia (to 1725).
1690	Battle of the Boyne: William III of Great Britain defeats exiled James II in Ireland.
	Battle of Beachy Head: France defeats Anglo-Dutch fleet.
	Turks retake Belgrade from Austrians.
1691	Pope Innocent XII, Pope (to 1700).
1692	Massacre of Glencoe: Campbells slaughter MacDonalds in Scotland on pretext of disloyalty to William III.
	Battle of La Hogue: France defeated by Anglo-Dutch fleet.
	Salem witchcraft trials in New England.
1694	Death of Mary II; William III, sole ruler of England and Scotland (to 1702).
1696	Peter the Great of Russia makes incognito visits to Western Europe (until 1697).
1697	Treaty of Ryswick among France, England, Spain, and the Netherlands.
	Battle of Zenta: Eugène of Savoy defeats Turks.

The Spanish Succession

It had long been realized that the sickly, insane Charles II of Spain, product of centuries of intermarriage, would never have a son. His death in 1700 provoked a crisis as the rulers of Europe rallied behind three claimants in a struggle for power. Each was related to Charles through the female line.

Charles himself had favoured Philip of Anjou, grandson of Louis XIV of France; but the rulers of Austria, the Netherlands, and England favoured the Archduke Charles of Austria, son of the Holy Roman Emperor Leopold I. A third candidate was Leopold's grandson, the Prince Elector Joseph Ferdinand of Bavaria. The main concern of Austria and its allies was to prevent France gaining too much power in Europe.

Fighting began in 1702, with the Austrian faction, known as the Grand Alliance, on one side, and France, Bavaria, Cologne, Mantua, and Savoy together on the other. The campaigns which followed were distinguished by the brilliant tactics of the English general John Churchill, Duke of

The battle of Blenheim, in south Germany, at which the Duke of Marlborough and Prince Eugène of Savoy led the English and Austrian forces to defeat the French. The battle was a terrible blow to French pride; it saved Vienna and ended Louis XIV's hopes of defeating Austria.

Marlborough, and his colleague Prince Eugène of Savoy, commanding the Austrian armies. The main fighting took place in Bavaria, Italy, and on the borders of France and Flanders. The Alliance won the victories of Blenheim, Ramillies, Turin, Oudenarde, and Malplaquet. Fighting also spread to North America, where it is known as Queen Anne's War, while the British seized the Spanish possessions of Gibraltar (in 1704) and Minorca (in 1709).

The Treaty of Utrecht ended the war in 1713. Philip was acknowledged as king of Spain, provided France and Spain were never united; England gained Nova Scotia and Newfoundland from France, and Gibraltar and Minorca from Spain. The Treaty of Rastatt and Baden in 1714 gave the Spanish Netherlands (modern Belgium) to Austria, after establishing the Dutch border.

The Austrian commander, Prince Eugène of Savoy.

The Act of Union

When James VI of Scotland became king of England as James I in 1603 he united the two kingdoms under one monarch – but they remained independent in government. In 1701 the English Parliament passed an Act of Settlement to ensure that future sovereigns would be Protestants. Because William and Mary, and Mary's sister Anne, were childless, the succession devolved on Sophia, Princess of Hanover, and granddaughter of James I.

But the Act did not mention Scotland – and so in 1707 an Act of Union was passed by the parliaments of both countries, formally uniting England and Scotland under the name of Great Britain, with one Parliament, but separate legal systems and Churches. Sophia and her descendants were to rule the new united kingdom.

Sophia of Hanover died a few months before Anne, and her son George became king as George I. The Roman Catholic Stuart descendants of the exiled James II were specifically excluded. James II's son James 'the Old Pretender' landed in Scotland, in 1708 and 1715, in vain attempts to regain the throne for the Stuarts.

1698 Charles II of Spain names Prince Elector of Bavaria as his heir.
1699 Treaty of Karlowitz: Austria receives Hungary from Turkey; Venice gains Morea and much of Dalmatia; Poland receives Podolia and Turkish Ukraine.
Death of Prince Elector of Bavaria.
1700 Charles II of Spain names Philip of Anjou, grandson of Louis XIV of France, as heir; he succeeds as Philip V (to 1746).
Great Northern War caused by rivalry between Russia and Sweden for supremacy in the Baltic (until 1721).
Battle of Narva: Russians defeated by Charles XII, King of Sweden.
Clement XI, Pope (to 1721).
1701 Act of Settlement establishes Protestant Hanoverian succession in Britain.
Death of exiled James II.
Grand Alliance formed among England, the Netherlands, Holy Roman Emperor Leopold I, and the German states against France.
War of the Spanish Succession (until 1713).
Frederick III, Elector of Brandenburg, is crowned Frederick I, King of Prussia.
Charles XII of Sweden invades Poland.
1702 Anne, Queen of England and Scotland (to 1714).
1703 Methuen Agreement: trade treaty between England and Portugal.
Hungarian revolt begins against Austria; led by Francis II Rákóczi (until 1711).
1704 British fleet captures Gibraltar from Spain.
Battle of Blenheim: allies under Duke of Marlborough and Prince Eugène defeat French.
Isaac Newton, English physicist, publishes *Optics*.
1705 Joseph I, Holy Roman Emperor (to 1711).
1706 Battle of Ramillies: French forces defeated by Duke of Marlborough.
Battle of Turin: Prince Eugène defeats French in Italy.
Treaty of Altranstädt between Augustus II, King of Poland, and Charles XII of Sweden.
1707 Act of Union unites England and Scotland under the name of Great Britain.
Battle of Almanza: Allied forces defeated by Spain.
Death of Aurangzeb leads to disintegration of Mughal Empire.
1708 Battle of Oudenarde: French defeated by allied forces under Duke of Marlborough and Prince Eugène.
Charles XII of Sweden invades Russia.
1709 Battle of Malplaquet: French defeated but more than 20,000 Allied troops killed.

Johann Sebastian Bach

The Bachs were a German family which, over a period of 200 years, contained more than 40 musicians. The greatest of them was the composer Johann Sebastian Bach (1685–1750), who was in turn court organist at Weimar, *Kapellmeister* (musical director) at Köthen, and from 1723 until his death cantor (choirmaster) of St Thomas's Church, Leipzig.

Bach was known throughout Germany as the greatest organist and improviser of his day. Yet contemporaries regarded his second son, Carl Philipp Emanuel, as a finer composer.

The Swedish Meteor

At the end of the 17th century Sweden held control of the Baltic Sea, and three of its rivals – Denmark, Poland, and Russia – formed an alliance to break its power. In 1700 they launched a three-pronged attack on Swedish possessions. But the 18-year-old Swedish King, Charles XII, surprised them, hitting back with a speed and generalship which earned him the nickname of 'the Swedish Meteor'.

Above: Johann Sebastian Bach.
Below: King Charles XII, 'the Swedish Meteor'.

Within months he forced the Danes to make peace and inflicted a crushing defeat on Russia. A six-year campaign forced the Polish king to abdicate in favour of an ally of Charles's, Stanislaus Leszczynski. Charles then made the mistake of invading Russia. Like Napoleon and Hitler in later centuries, he was defeated by Russia's sheer size and its bitter winters.

A military defeat at Poltava in the Ukraine at the hands of Peter the Great ended the campaign. After five years' exile Charles returned to Sweden to carry on the war, and died in battle in 1718. The Peace of Nystadt (1721) restored some possessions to Sweden which it had lost during the war, and established Russia as a leading European power.

Above: The Empress Maria Theresa of Austria.
Below: Louis XV of France, great-grandson of Louis XIV, succeeded to the throne at the age of 5. During his reign France was involved in several costly and unsuccessful wars, its administration and finances became steadily worse, and the ordinary people became increasingly discontented.

1709 Battle of Poltava: Peter I of Russia defeats Charles XII of Sweden.
1711 Duke of Marlborough dismissed as Allied commander.
Charles VI, Holy Roman Emperor (to 1740).
Peace of Szatmar between Austria and Hungary.
1713 Pragmatic Sanction issued by Emperor Charles VI to guarantee the succession of his daughter, Maria Theresa.
Treaty of Utrecht ends War of Spanish Succession; France recognizes Protestant succession in Britain; cedes Newfoundland, Nova Scotia, and Hudson Bay territory; Spanish Netherlands ceded temporarily to the Netherlands; Britain gains the *asiento*, contract to supply slaves to Spanish America, and gains Gibraltar and Minorca.
Papal Bull *Unigenitus*, condemns Jansenists.
Frederick William I, King of Prussia (to 1740) establishes a standing army of more than 80,000 men.
1714 George I, King of Great Britain and Ireland, first Hanoverian monarch (to 1727).
Treaty of Rastatt and Baden between Austria and France cedes Spanish Netherlands to Austria.
1715 Louis XV, King of France (to 1774); Duke of Orléans regent until 1723.
First Jacobite uprising in Scotland (until 1716) in support of James Edward (the Old Pretender).
1717 Spain seizes Sardinia from Austria.
1718 Spain seizes Sicily from Savoy.
Quadruple Alliance (until 1719) of Austria, Britain, France, and Netherlands against Spain.
Treaty of Passarowitz ends war between Turkey and Austria.
1720 Collapse of John Law's Mississippi Company in France.
'South Sea Bubble': South Sea Company fails in England, causing financial panic.
Treaty of the Hague between Quadruple Alliance and Spain.
Treaties of Stockholm among Sweden, Prussia, Hanover, Denmark, Savoy, Poland (and 1721).
1721 Administration of Sir Robert Walpole, Britain's first prime minister (to 1742).
Treaty of Nystadt between Russia and Sweden confirms Russia as a great power.
1724 State of Hyderabad, India, achieves independence from Mughals.
1725 Treaty of Vienna between Spain and Austria.
Treaty of Hanover: alliance between Britain, France, Prussia, Sweden, Denmark, and the Netherlands.

The Austrian Succession

The War of the Austrian Succession (1740–1748) was caused by the death of the last male descendant of the Habsburg family, the Holy Roman Emperor Charles VI, in 1740. He left his vast Austrian lands to his daughter, Maria Theresa, whose succession the leading rulers of Europe had agreed to support. But three other rulers at once claimed his lands: Charles Albert, Elector of Bavaria; Philip V, King of Spain; and August III, King of Poland and Elector of Saxony. War broke out when the Prussian King Frederick II, the Great, occupied Silesia, the richest Austrian province. He was soon supported by Bavaria, France, Poland, Sardinia, Saxony, and Spain – Maria Theresa by Hungary, Britain, and the Netherlands.

In 1742 Charles Albert of Bavaria was elected emperor as Charles VII. Soon after, Maria Theresa yielded most of Silesia to Prussia, which withdrew from the war. The following year a British and Hanoverian army defeated the French at Dettingen.

Charles VII died in 1745, and Maria Theresa's husband, Francis Stephen of Lorraine, was elected emperor as Francis I. This act secured Maria Theresa's position in Europe, but the war dragged on until 1748 when the Treaty of Aix-la-Chapelle restored all conquered lands with the exception of Silesia, which remained in Prussian hands consolidating their power.

Jean-Jacques Rousseau

Jean-Jacques Rousseau (1712–1778) was one of the most versatile and influential Frenchmen of the mid-18th century. Born in Geneva, Switzerland, of Huguenot (Protestant) parents, he worked in turn as a lawyer's clerk, an engraver, a servant, and a music teacher. At several stages in his life he made his living as a music-copyist, and wrote operas and articles on music.

It was through his political thinking that Rousseau had his greatest influence. In *The Social Contract* (1762) and several novels he called for reforms in education and politics. His works inspired many of the leaders of the French Revolution.

Rousseau was also a pioneer of the *Romantic* movement, in which writers, artists, and musicians emphasised emotion rather than reason. His views influenced writers like William Wordsworth, William Blake, and Johann von Goethe. His autobiography, *Confessions*, was published after his death.

The Polish Succession

The death in 1733 of Augustus II, Elector of Saxony and King of Poland, plunged Europe into war over his successor. The Poles chose Stanislaus Leszczynski, who had been king from 1704 to 1709 with the backing of Charles XII of Sweden. Russia and Austria forced the Poles to accept Augustus's son, Augustus III.

But the French King, Louis XV, had married Stanislaus's daughter and so supported his father-in-law. For a year France, supported by Spain and Sardinia, fought Austria and Russia who prevailed, so that Augustus III became king.

The 'Forty-Five'

The exiled Stuarts continued to claim the British throne even after their abortive rebellion of 1715. Their supporters, mostly Roman Catholics, became known as *Jacobites*, from the Latin name for James, Jacobus. The exiled James II died in 1701, leaving his claim to his son James, known as the 'Old Pretender', but he failed to secure the support of the French.

In 1745 James's son, Charles Edward, the 'Young Pretender', landed in Scotland with a handful of followers. He quickly raised an army among the Highland clans and entered Edinburgh with 2000 men. Defeating a British army at Prestonpans, Charles marched into England, but the support on which he counted was not forthcoming. In Scotland the Stuart forces were crushed in April 1746 at Culloden by an army led by the Duke of Cumberland.

Charles fled to France and frittered away the rest of his life until his death in 1788.

The French philosopher, author, and musician Jean-Jacques Rousseau sitting in his garden.

1725 Catherine I, widow of Peter the Great, succeeds to throne of Russia.
1726 Administration of Cardinal Fleury, chief minister in France (to 1743).
1727 George II, King of Great Britain (to 1760).
Spain at war with Britain and France (until 1729).
1730 Maratha government becomes pre-eminent in India (to 1735).
1733 First family pact between Bourbons of France and of Spain.
War of Polish Succession between France and Spain, and Austria and Russia (until 1735).
1734 France invades Lorraine.
1735 Preliminary Treaty of Vienna ends War of Polish Succession.
1736 Russia and Austria at war with Turkey (to 1739).
Nadir Shah, ruler of Persia (to 1747); conquers Afghanistan and invades northern India (1738).
Chi'en Lung, Emperor of China (to 1799).
1738 Treaty of Vienna formally resolves War of Polish Succession; Lorraine to be ceded to France on death of Stanislaus I, defeated claimant to Polish throne.
1739 War of Jenkins' Ear between Britain and Spain (until 1741).
British Admiral Edward Vernon captures Porto Bello in the West Indies from Spain.
Treaty of Belgrade ends Austro-Russian war against Turkey.
Nadir Shah sacks Delhi.
John Wesley founds Methodist movement.
1740 Frederick II, the Great, King of Prussia (to 1786).
Death of Charles VI ends male line of Habsburgs; Maria Theresa succeeds to thrones of Austria, Bohemia, and Hungary.
Frederick the Great of Prussia seizes Silesia.
War of Austrian Succession (until 1748): caused by rival claims of Bavaria, Spain, and Saxony to the Austrian throne.
1741 Alliance of Nymphenburg among France, Bavaria, Spain, Saxony, and Prussia.
Sweden and Russia at war (until 1743).
1742 Charles VII, Holy Roman Emperor (to 1745).
Treaty of Berlin between Prussia and Austria.
1743 Battle of Dettingen: French defeated by army under George II of England.
Treaty of Abö between Sweden and Russia.
1744 Frederick the Great invades Bohemia; driven out by Austrian and Saxon forces.
King George's War between Britain and France in North America (until 1748).
1745 'The Forty-Five': Jacobite rebellion in England and Scotland led by Charles Edward Stuart ('the Young Pretender').

Above: The city of Quebec, seen from a ferry house across the St Lawrence river, painted in 1754. At this time the city belonged to the French. Five years later, during the Seven Years' War, it was captured by a British force under General Wolfe. He scaled the cliff to the Plains of Abraham (on the left) and surprised the French. Both Wolfe and the French commander Montcalm died.

The Seven Years' War

The Seven Years' War from 1756 to 1763 was a power struggle between two European blocs: Austria, France, Russia, and Sweden on one side; Britain, Hanover, and Prussia on the other. Britain and France also fought for territory in India and North America.

The war began when Frederick the Great of Prussia attacked Saxony and Bohemia, and was himself attacked by Austria and its allies. At one stage Frederick seemed about to be overpowered, but brilliant victories at Rossbach and Leuthen in 1757 saved him from destruction, and Britain and Hanover came to his aid. In 1762 Peter III became ruler of Russia and was happy to make peace; Austria followed suit in 1763.

In North America, the British won control of Canada by the battle of Quebec in 1759. In India, the soldiers of the British East India Company, commanded by one of its clerks, Robert Clive, won a series of victories ensuring British supremacy.

The Peace of Paris, signed in 1763 by Britain, France, and France's ally Spain, gave Britain Canada, French territory east of the Mississippi River, and Florida; Spain received Louisiana, the French territories west of the Mississippi, and Minorca, in the Mediterranean Sea. In India, France gave up most of its territory to Britain. The Treaty of Hubertsburg, signed between Prussia and Austria the same year, confirmed Prussian possession of Silesia.

Below: Benjamin Franklin flew a kite in a thunderstorm to show that lightning is a form of electricity. Current ran down the wet string, sparking from a key attached to its end.

1745 Alliance among Austria, Saxony, Britain, and the Netherlands against Prussia.
Bavaria, defeated, withdraws claims to Austrian throne.
Battle of Fontenoy: French defeat British forces in War of Austrian Succession.
Battles of Hohenfriedberg and Soor; Austrians defeated.
Francis I, Holy Roman Emperor (to 1765).
Treaty of Dresden between Prussia and Austria.
British capture Louisburg, French fortress in Canada.

1746 Battle of Culloden: Jacobites defeated.

1747 Nadir Shah assassinated; his general, Ahmad Shah, becomes ruler of Afghanistan.

1748 Treaty of Aix-la-Chapelle ends War of Austrian Succession: Prussia keeps Silesia.

1751 English soldier Robert Clive seizes Arcot; ends French plans for supremacy in southern India.

1752 Chinese invade and conquer Tibet.
Benjamin Franklin invents lightning conductor.

1755 Earthquake in Lisbon kills some 30,000 people.
The French and Indian War between Britain and France in North America (until 1763).

1756 Treaty of Westminster: alliance between Britain and Prussia.
Treaty of Versailles: alliance between France and Austria.
Start of Seven Years' War: caused by colonial rivalry between Britain and France, and by rivalry between Austria and Prussia.
'Black Hole of Calcutta': Siraj-ud-Daulah, Nawab of Bengal, captures Calcutta and imprisons 146 British in small room; most die.

1757 Russia joins alliance with France and Austria.
Battles of Rossbach and Leuthen: Prussia defeats French and Austrian armies.
Robert Clive captures Calcutta.
Battle of Plassey: Clive defeats Nawab of Bengal; establishes British rule in India.

1758 Battle of Zorndorf: Russians defeated by Prussians.

1759 Britain captures Quebec; French general Marquis de Montcalm and British general James Wolfe killed.
Battle of Quiberon Bay: French defeated. .
Battle of Kunersdorf: Austrian victory.

1760 George III, grandson of George II, King of Great Britain and Ireland (to 1820).

1761 Battle of Panipat: Afghan forces defeat Marathas.

1762 Britain declares war on Spain.
Treaty of St Petersburg between Russia and Prussia.

The Unknown Southern Land

Although Willem Jansz in 1606 and Abel Tasman in 1642 had made some discoveries in Australia, explorers still sought a *Terra Australis Incognita* (unknown southern land) as large as the continents of the northern hemisphere. The brilliant navigation of the British sailor Captain James Cook disproved the existence of Terra Australis, while his voyages resulted in the correct charting of much of the Pacific and its previously unmapped islands.

Cook was sent out to the southern seas in 1768 to observe the transit of Venus from Tahiti. He then sailed eastwards to New Zealand and charted its coasts correctly for the first time. Before he returned home, he decided to have a look at the east coast of New Holland, as Australia was known. He found the coast in April 1770, and landed in a bay where he found so many plants that he named it Botany Bay. He also saw a strange animal 'which went only upon two legs, making vast bounds'. No European had seen a kangaroo before.

Cook was to make two more voyages exploring and charting – in 1772–1775, and 1776–1779 – before being killed in Hawaii.

Below: A painting reconstructs the death of Captain James Cook in a scuffle with Hawaiian islanders in 1779. Cook had successfully mapped much of the South Seas, confirming that Australia was a continent, before his untimely death. Right: A beautifully carved Maori house-pole from New Zealand, whose coastline Cook charted.

Right: The French philosopher Voltaire (François Marie Arouet, 1694–1778), as an old man. He was one of France's greatest satirical writers.

Voltaire

Voltaire was the pen-name of the French writer, philosopher, and historian François Marie Arouet (1694–1778), whose opinions and writings played a large part in events leading to the French Revolution.

Jailed twice for writing satires on members of the French royal court, Voltaire took refuge for a time in England. He was impressed by the country's freedom of thought, and wrote a book on his return advising the French to copy the English way of life. The storm this aroused forced Voltaire to leave Paris and live in Lorraine. He finally settled in Switzerland, where he continued to campaign for religious tolerance and respect for the rights of man, particularly in France.

Voltaire returned to Paris in 1778 after an absence of 28 years and was given a hero's welcome. He died shortly after.

1762 French philosopher Jean-Jacques Rousseau publishes *The Social Contract*.
Catherine II (the Great), Tsarina of Russia (to 1796).

1763 Peace of Paris among Britain, France and Spain ends Seven Years' War; Britain gains Canada and virtually all lands east of the Mississippi River.
Peace of Hubertsburg among Prussia, Saxony, and Austria.
North American Indian uprising against the British led by Ottawa chief, Pontiac.

1764 Spinning jenny invented by Englishman, James Hargreaves.

1765 Stamp Act passed by English Parliament imposes a tax in the American colonies on publications and legal documents.
Joseph II, Holy Roman Emperor (to 1790), co-regent until 1780 with his mother, Maria Theresa.

1766 English Parliament repeals Stamp Act.

1767 Townshend Acts: tax imposed on various imports into North America.
Mason-Dixon line established between Maryland and Pennsylvania; separates free states from slave states.
Confederation of Bar: anti-Russian association is formed in Poland.
Russia and Turkey at war (until 1774).
James Cook, English navigator on first voyage (to 1771), discovers and explores east coast of Australia, calling it New South Wales.

1770 Boston Massacre: British troops fire on mob in Boston; five citizens killed.
Townshend Acts repealed; tax on tea imported into North America is kept.

1771 Russia conquers the Crimea.
Carl Scheele discovers oxygen.

1772 First Partition of Poland among Russia, Prussia, and Austria.

1773 Boston Tea Party: citizens, disguised as North American Indians, dump tea into Boston Harbour.
Pope Clement XIV suppresses Society of Jesus (Jesuits).
Peasant uprising in Russia led by Cossack Pugachev (suppressed 1775).

1774 Louis XVI, King of France (to 1792).
Treaty of Kuchuk Kainarji between Russia and Turkey; Russia gains Black Sea ports and the right to represent Greek Orthodox Church in Turkey.
'Intolerable Acts': British Parliament passes series of repressive acts against North American colonies. First Continental Congress meets at Philadelphia to protest.

The Age of Revolution

REVOLUTIONS OF TWO KINDS – peaceful and bloody – dominated the period from 1775 to 1848. The peaceful changes were the moves from doing work by hand to doing it with machines and mechanical sources of power, which brought about the Industrial Revolution. This began in Britain around the middle of the 1700s, and has continued and accelerated since throughout the world.

The other revolutions were against bad or tyrannical government. The first was the American War of Independence, in which 13 of Britain's North American colonies broke away from rule by the mother-country. The second, encouraged by the American example, was the French Revolution, which overturned the dictatorship of the French kings and put forward the ideals of 'Liberty, Equality, and Fraternity' – though the revolutionaries did not keep to them. But the ideals remained influential throughout the next century.

The movement of ideas and belief which had been dominant until this time, the Enlightment, with its emphasis on reason and natural law, gave place in the social ferment to the Romantic movement in the arts which favoured emotions before reason, and free and individual expression. Romanticism popularized the ideals of the French Revolution.

The storming of the Bastille, a fortress-prison in Paris, on July 14, 1789, marked the start of the French Revolution.

EUROPE

1778	France joins war against Britain
	War of Bavarian Succession (to 1779)
1780	Gordon riots in London
	Armed Neutrality of the North
1783	First successful hot-air balloon
1787	Assembly of Notables dismissed
1789	French Revolution begins
1791	New Constitution in France
1792	Austria and Prussia fight France
	National Convention in France
	France declared a republic
1793	Reign of Terror in France (to 1794)
1795	Directory rules France (to 1799)
	Third partition of Poland
1797	Treaty of Campo Formio
1798	Rebellion at Vinegar Hill, Ireland
1799	Five nations unite against France
	Consulate rules France (to 1804)
1800	Volta invents electric battery
1801	Act of Union creates United Kingdom
1802	Bonaparte created First Consul
1804	Bonaparte crowns himself Emperor
1805	Third coalition against France
	Battles of Trafalgar and Austerlitz
1806	Napoleon dissolves Holy Roman Empire
1808	Peninsular War (to 1814)
1809	Battle of Corunna
1811	Luddite riots in England (to 1812)
1812	Napoleon's Russian campaign
1813	Battle of Leipzig
1814	Napoleon exiled to Elba
1815	Hundred Days: Battle of Waterloo
1819	*Zolverein* begins in Germany
1820	Neapolitan revolution
1821	Greek War of Independence (to 1829)
1823	Spanish revolution crushed
1825	Egyptian forces invade Greece
1830	July Revolution in Paris
1831	Leopold I becomes King of Belgians
1834	'Tolpuddle Martyrs' in England
	Carlist Wars in Spain (to 1839)
1846	Irish potato famine at its worst
1848	Year of revolutions in Europe

ASIA

1774	Warren Hastings appointed first Governor-General of India
1775	War between British and Marathas in India (to 1782)
1777	Christianity introduced in Korea
1782	Treaty of Salbai
1783	India Act gives Britain control in India
1787	Rice riots in Edo, Japan
1792	China invades Nepal
1793	Indian judicial system reorganized
1794	Qajar Dynasty in Persia (to 1925)
1796	British conquer Ceylon from Dutch
1799	Bonaparte invades Syria
	Tippoo Sahib killed; British control most of southern India
1800	Russia annexes Georgia
1804	Serbian nationalists revolt in Turkey (to 1815)
1805	Christian literature forbidden in China
1809	Afghanistan's first agreement with Britain
1811	Stamford Raffles administers Batavia and Java (to 1816)
1814	Kurozumi sect founded in Japan (first modern Shinto sect)
	India and Nepal fight over borders (to 1816)
1823	Treaty of Erzerum
1824	First Anglo-Burmese War (to 1826)
1826	Russia and Persia at war (to 1828)
1833	Mohammed Ali gains Syria
1839	British occupy Aden
	Opium War between Britain and China
1842	Hong Kong ceded to Britain
1845	Anglo-Sikh Wars in India (to 1848)

*Below: The Prussian General von Blucher,
Wellington's ally at Waterloo.
Bottom: The battle of Bunker Hill, in June 1775,
was the first battle of the War of Independence.*

AFRICA

1787	British acquire Sierra Leone
1792	Denmark the first country to prohibit slave trade
1795	British take Cape of Good Hope from Dutch
	Mungo Park explores Gambia River and reaches Niger River (1796)
1798	Bonaparte leads French army into Egypt (until 1799)
	Battle of the Pyramids
	Battle of the Nile
1801	Islamic kingdom of Sokoto founded in West Africa
1802	Portuguese explorers cross Africa from West to East (1811)
1805	Mohammed Ali appointed *pasha* of Egypt
	Mungo Park explores Niger River
1811	Mamelukes massacred in Cairo
1815	France prohibits slave trade
1818	Zulu empire founded in South Africa
1822	Egypt completes conquest of Sudan
	Liberia founded
1824	War in Gold Coast (to 1827)
1832	War between Egypt and Turkey (to 1833)
1835	The Great Trek (to 1837)
1838	Boers defeat Zulus in Natal
1843	Natal becomes British colony
1842	British defeat Boers
1846	Zulu reserves set up in Natal

AMERICAS

1774	'Intolerable Acts'
	First Continental Congress meets
1775	American War of Independence (to 1783)
	Battles of Lexington and Concord
	Battle of Bunker Hill
1776	Declaration of Independence
1780	Peruvian Indians revolt against Spain
1781	Cornwallis surrenders at Yorktown
1783	Treaty of Paris
1787	United States Constitution signed
1789	George Washington, first President of United States (to 1797)
1791	American Bill of Rights
	Canada Act divides Canada into French- and English-speaking territories
	Toussaint l'Ouverture leads revolt in Haiti
1794	Jay's Treaty
1803	'Louisiana Purchase'
	Ohio becomes 17th North American State
1804	Meriwether Lewis and William Clark explore north-western United States,
1810	Argentina independent
1811	Paraguay and Venezuela independent
1812	Britain and United States at war over shipping and territory (to 1814)
1819	Spain cedes Florida to United States
	Simón Bolivar secures independence of Great Colombia
1820	Missouri Compromise
1821	Mexico and Peru independent
1822	Brazil independent
1825	Bolivia independent
1836	Texas independent of Mexico
1839	Rebellions in Upper and Lower Canada
1840	Upper and Lower Canada united
1842	Webster-Ashburton Treaty
1846	Oregon Boundary Treaty
	United States-Mexico war (to 1848)
1848	Californian gold rush begins

ELSEWHERE

1788	First convicts transported from Britain to Australia
1790	Mutiny on the *Bounty* first British settlers colonize Pitcairn Island
1793	First free settlers arrive in Australia
1802	Matthew Flinders circumnavigates Australia (to 1803)
1803	Settlers begin to arrive in Tasmania
1807	Slave trade abolished in British Empire
1820	American missionaries reach Hawaii
1833	Slavery abolished in British colonies
1834	South Australia and Victoria settled (to 1837)
1840	Treaty of Waitangi in New Zealand
1843	First Maori War (to 1848)

Above: The clash at Lexington, Massachusetts, on April 19, 1775.

American Independence

The American War of Independence lasted from 1775 to 1783. At the end of it 13 ex-British colonies formed the United States of America; they were Connecticut, Delaware, Georgia, Massachusetts, Maryland, North Carolina, New Hampshire, New Jersey, New York, Pennsylvania, Rhode Island, South Carolina, and Virginia.

The colonies already made their own local laws, but the British Parliament kept control of financial matters, and particularly trade. The colonies had to use their own or British ships and to trade mainly with Britain or British colonies.

After the Seven Years' War which brought Britain the French possessions in North America, Britain felt it necessary to keep a standing army there and taxed the colonies to pay for it. The colonists objected to taxation without representation in Parliament. The British tried imposing

taxes on newspapers, tea, paper, lead, and paint, but had to repeal all bar the tea tax when the colonists refused to buy British goods as a protest.

On December 16, 1773 a band of colonists disguised as Indians boarded British ships in Boston harbour and threw cargoes of tea overboard. To this 'Boston tea party', the British Parliament retorted with the so-called 'Intolerable Acts', which included closing the port of Boston.

The First Continental Congress at Philadelphia in September 1774 protested at the Acts, and the colonies decided not to buy British goods. British troops were sent from Boston to destroy an arms cache held by the colonists at nearby Concord. Just after dawn on April 19, 1775, at Lexington on the road to Concord, the troops were confronted by armed colonists. The opening 'shot heard round the world' was fired and war began. The British retreated from Concord to

Johann Wolfgang von Goethe (1749–1832), a major figure in the Romantic movement.

Boston, and in June won the battle of Bunker Hill, near Boston, despite heavy losses. The Second Continental Congress assembled in May 1775, and on July 4, 1776 issued the Declaration of Independence, largely drafted by Thomas Jefferson, claiming complete freedom from British rule.

In 1777 the British gained an important victory at Brandywine Creek, in Pennsylvania, but a few weeks later another British army, under General John Burgoyne, was forced to surrender at Saratoga, New York. France entered the war on the American side, followed later by Spain.

The end came when the British under Cornwallis surrendered to the American commander-in-chief, George Washington, at Yorktown, Virginia, on October 19, 1781. The Treaty of Paris (September 3, 1783) formally recognized the independence of the United States; Washington was elected first president in 1789.

1774 Warren Hastings, Governor of Bengal, is appointed first Governor-General of India.
1775 War of American Independence (until 1783); George Washington leads American troops. Battles of Lexington and Concord: British troops retreat to Boston; battle of Bunker Hill: British victory.
Catherine the Great reorganizes local government in Russia.
War between British and Marathas in India (until 1782).
British engineers James Watt and Matthew Boulton form partnership to produce first commercial steam engines.
1776 British troops evacuate Boston.
Declaration of Independence drawn up by American colonies in Philadelphia adopted by Continental Congress.
Viceroyalty of Rio de la Plata formed by Argentina, Bolivia, Paraguay, Uruguay.
Wealth of Nations published by Scottish economist Adam Smith.
1777 Battle of Saratoga: British army under General John Burgoyne surrenders to American General Horatio Gates.
1778 France enters American War of Independence in support of the colonists.
War of Bavarian Succession (until 1779): bloodless war between Prussia and Austria.
Death of French philosopher Voltaire.
1779 Spain joins Americans against Britain.
France and Spain besiege Gibraltar without success (until 1783).
1780 Riots against Roman Catholics in London; led by Protestant Lord George Gordon.
British capture Charleston, S. Carolina.
Armed Neutrality of the North formed by Russia, Denmark, Sweden, Netherlands, to protect neutral shipping from British interference.
Peruvian Indians, led by Inca Tupac Amarú, revolt against Spain; put down by 1783.
1781 British troops under General Charles Cornwallis besieged by French and American forces at Yorktown, Virginia; British surrender.
Joseph II introduces religious toleration in Austria and abolishes serfdom.
Austro-Russian alliance against Turkey.
1782 Treaty of Salbai ends war between British and Marathas.
1783 Treaty of Paris ends American War of Independence; Britain recognizes independence of American colonies.
Russia annexes Crimea.
French brothers Joseph and Jacques Montgolfier build first successful hot-air balloon.

The Age of Revolution

The head of King Louis XVI is displayed to the cheering crowds. Louis had tried to escape with his family in 1791, but was recaptured and was eventually guillotined in 1793.

The French Revolution

The French Revolution which broke out in 1789 not only transformed the government of France but also shook the Establishment throughout Europe, and led to many changes in ideas of government.

Causes: By 1789 France was deeply in debt because of expensive wars, and badly governed by an élite of the nobility, who lived in luxury while many poor people starved. Faced with national bankruptcy, the King, Louis XVI, decided to summon the Estates General, a national parliament which had not met since 1614. It consisted of three 'Estates' – 300 noblemen, 300 clergy, and 600 commoners. Each Estate had one vote, which meant that the nobility and the clergy could outvote the commoners. So the commoners formed a national Constituent Assembly, pledged to make a new constitution for France.

Mob Violence: Louis planned to dismiss the Assembly. This aroused the fury of the Paris mob, which stormed the fortress-prison of the Bastille on July 14, 1789. Louis had to give way, and the Assembly proceeded to bring in many reforms.

The Republic: Louis conspired with his allies in Austria and Prussia, and in June 1791 tried to flee the country. He was captured and taken back to Paris. War with Austria and Prussia followed in April·1792. In August the Paris mob attacked the King in the Palace of the Tuileries, butchering his guards and imprisoning him. French victory against the Prussians in the battle of Valmy encouraged the revolutionaries. A new assembly, the National Convention, declared the monarchy abolished and set up a republic on September 21.

Death and Terror: Power in the Convention passed to a political group called the

Girondins, who had Louis tried for treason and executed. But during 1793 a more extremist group, the Jacobins, gained power. The Girondins were executed, and a Committee of Public Safety ruled the country, headed by Maximilien Robespierre. Under his influence anyone suspected of opposing the new regime was executed, in a bloodbath known as the 'Reign of Terror'. In July 1794 Robespierre himself was accused and guillotined, and the Terror gradually died away. In 1795 a new two-chamber assembly was elected, and order returned gradually to France.

Left: The French revolutionary leader Georges Danton.

Right: Maximilien Robespierre, one of the leaders of the Reign of Terror in 1793–1794, and (below) the guillotine on which he and so many others perished.

1784 India Act: British Prime Minister William Pitt (the Younger) establishes government control of political affairs in India.

1785 League of German Princes formed by Frederick the Great against Joseph II of Austria.

1787 Assembly of Notables in France dismissed after refusing to introduce financial reforms.
Russia and Turkey at war (until 1792).
New Constitution of the United States drawn up and signed at Philadelphia.
Famine causes rice riots in Edo, Japan.

1788 First convicts transported from Britain to New South Wales, Australia.
Gustavus III of Sweden at war with Russia (until 1790) to consolidate his rule.

1789 Estates-General meets at Versailles, France.
French Revolution begins.
Third Estate (representatives of the middle class) forms National Assembly; as Constituent Assembly it governs France until 1791.
Storming of the Bastille in Paris.
George Washington, first President of the United States (to 1797).

1790 Treaty of Wereloe ends Russo-Swedish war.
Leopold II, Holy Roman Emperor (to 1792).

1791 Flight and capture of Louis XVI of France and family; Louis accepts new Constitution; Constituent Assembly replaced by Legislative Assembly.
Treaty of Sistova between Austria and Turkey.
Canada Act divides Canada into French- and English-speaking territories.
Bill of Rights: first 10 amendments to US Constitution.
Negro slave revolt against French in Haiti led by Toussaint l'Ouverture.

1792 Coalition of Austria and Prussia against France.
Francis II, Holy Roman Emperor (to 1806).
France declares war on Austria and Prussia; battle of Valmy: French defeat Prussians.
National Convention governs France (until 1795); France is declared a republic.
Treaty of Jassy between Russia and Turkey.
China invades Nepal after Gurkhas menace Tibetan borders.

1793 Louis XVI is executed; his wife, Marie Antoinette subsequently beheaded.
Revolutionary France declares war on Britain, the Netherlands, and Spain.
Royalist uprising in La Vendée, France.
Reign of Terror (to 1794); France ruled largely by Maximilien Robespierre and the Committee of Public Safety.
Conscription in France for revolutionary army.
Second partition of Poland between Russia and Prussia.

Members of the Jacobin clubs terrorized France during the French Revolution.

Above: The first vaccination against the widespread scourge of smallpox was performed by the English physician Edward Jenner on May 14, 1796. He inoculated a healthy eight-year-old boy with a mild form of the disease called cowpox. Seven weeks later Jenner inoculated the boy with fluid from a smallpox sore, but he remained healthy. Immune substances developed by his body cells to fight the cowpox prevented his catching smallpox.

The Rights of Man

The writings of the Englishman Thomas Paine were a major influence on the French and American revolutions. Born in Norfolk in 1737, the son of an English Quaker, Paine met the American statesman Benjamin Franklin in London, and on his advice emigrated to the American colonies. There he began writing pamphlets and articles supporting colonial independence, and served in the colonial army during the American War of Independence.

In 1787 Paine returned to Britain, where in 1791 and 1792 he published *Rights of Man*, supporting republicanism and the ideals of the growing revolution in France. Accused of treason, Paine escaped to France; he was welcomed as a hero and elected to the National Convention. But he criticized the bloodshed of the revolutionaries, and was jailed. There he wrote *The Age of Reason*, a view of religion which asserted that the universe is a machine with God as its designer. Paine was freed after the end of the Reign of Terror in 1794, and returned to the United States in 1802, where he spent his last years poor, ill, and neglected. He died in 1809.

The Coalition Wars

Two coalitions were formed to fight France during and immediately after the French Revolution:

The First Coalition fought from 1792 to 1799. It consisted of Austria, Britain, the Netherlands, Piedmont, Prussia, and Spain. France, weakened by revolution, was expected to be beaten but French successes forced Prussia, Spain, and Austria to make peace; the Netherlands was conquered.

The Second Coalition was formed in 1799 by Britain – which had remained fighting – Austria, Russia, Portugal, Naples, and the Ottoman Empire. After early defeats the French again scored a series of victories, and by 1802 all the countries had made peace again.

Toussaint L'Ouverture

News of the French Revolution led to a rebellion in 1791 in the French colony of Haiti, in the West Indies. The revolt was by Negro slaves, who had been badly treated. Their leader was Pierre Dominique Toussaint-Bréda (1743–1803), nicknamed 'L'Ouverture' because he found openings (*ouvertures*) in the enemy lines.

The rebellion ended when the French abolished slavery in 1793. Toussaint changed sides and supported France; after a period of civil war he seized power in 1801 and ruled Haiti as its self-proclaimed governor. In 1802 France's new ruler, Napoleon Bonaparte, regained control of Haiti and reimposed slavery. Toussaint was taken to France where he died in captivity. In 1804 the Haitians finally made themselves independent.

1793 In India, Lord Cornwallis, Governor-General, stabilizes revenue system and reorganizes judicial system on British lines.

1794 Dutch republic invaded, and Dutch fleet captured by France (1795).
Execution of Georges Danton and, subsequently, of Robespierre; Reign of Terror draws to an end; Jacobins suppressed in France.
French occupy the Netherlands (until 1795).
Jay's Treaty: commercial and shipping treaty between Britain and United States.
Qajar (Kajar) Dynasty founded in Persia by Aga Mohammed; lasts until 1925.

1795 Batavian Republic set up by France in the Netherlands (until 1806).
Treaty of Basle between France and Prussia; Spain also makes peace with France.
The Directory, a five-man executive set up by the 1795 constitution, rules France.
Third partition: remainder of Poland divided among Russia, Prussia, Austria.
British take Cape of Good Hope from Dutch.
Mungo Park, a Scot, explores Gambia River; reaching Niger River.
Warren Hastings, former Governor-General of India, acquitted by English Parliament of corruption charges.

1796 The Corsican, Napoleon Bonaparte, leads French army and conquers most of Italy (1797).
Paul I, Tsar of Russia (to 1801).
British capture Ceylon from the Dutch.

1797 British navy mutinies at Spithead and Nore.
Battle of Cape St Vincent: British navy defeats Franco-Spanish fleet.
Treaty of Campo Formio: Austria makes peace with France.
Frederick William III, King of Prussia (to 1840).
American ships trade with Japan on behalf of Dutch (until 1809); end of Japanese isolation policy.

1798 Rebellion at Vinegar Hill, Ireland, by the United Irishmen wanting separation.
French occupy Rome; establish Roman Republic.
French invade Switzerland; Helvetic Republic set up.
Bonaparte leads French army on expedition into Egypt (lasts until 1799); battle of the Pyramids: Cairo taken by the French.
Battle of the Nile (Aboukir Bay): British fleet under Horatio Nelson defeats French.

1799 Bonaparte invades Syria.
Coalition of Britain, Austria Russia, Portugal, Naples, and Ottoman Empire against France
Battles of Zurich, Trebbia, Novi: French driven out of Italy.

The Industrial Revolution

The term 'Industrial Revolution' was coined in the 1830s by French historians to describe the change from a world in which farming was the most important occupation, to one dominated by factories and machines.

The Industrial Revolution, which began in the 1700s, developed in Britain first because that country was united and free from wars. This settled state meant that people were generally prosperous, and so had money to buy manufactured goods.

The invention which started the revolution was the flying shuttle, made by John Kay in 1733. This enabled weavers to produce cloth more quickly and in greater widths. Fast spinning machines came 30 years later.

The new machines were too big to drive by hand, so factories were built beside rivers where water-wheels could provide power. By the early 1800s, nearly all spinning and weaving was being done in factories, after having been a home process for thousands of years.

The first steam engines built in the late 1600s to pump water were very inefficient.

James Watt, a Scottish engineer, devised the first satisfactory steam-engine in 1769, and in 1775 with Matthew Boulton he formed a company to make them. This new source of power speeded up production. It meant, too, that factories were located near coal mines, the source of fuel for steam engines – though the rivers were still needed as a water supply and for transport.

In the early 1800s engineers also experimented with mobile steam engines which could replace horses. The first practical modern engine was 'Puffing Billy', built on Tyneside in northern England in 1813; it hauled coal from a mine to riverside loading wharves. The first passenger railway was built in Britain in 1825, and within 10 years railways were operating in North America and continental Europe.

The Industrial Revolution changed the face of the countryside. The new machines were housed in large factories, and towns sprang up around these to provide homes for the workers. Before the revolution, most workers could grow their own food. In the new towns, they lived in cramped conditions with no gardens, depending on their wages for everything.

Right: Before the Industrial Revolution most people worked on the land or in cottages. As towns grew up around the factories, crowded grimy conditions were the mark of the new industrial society.

The demand for factory labour in the Industrial Revolution meant children and women worked long hours in dangerous, dirty conditions.

1799 Bonaparte returns to France; overthrows Directory and sets up a Consulate; headed by Bonaparte, it rules France until 1804.
Tippoo Sahib, last ruler of Mysore, killed in battle with British troops; British control extends over most of southern India.
Combination Laws prohibit trade unions in Britain (second series, 1800).
Discovery of Rosetta Stone enables Egyptian hieroglyphics to be understood.

1800 Battles of Marengo and Hohenlinden: French defeat Austrians.
Pius VII Pope (to 1823).
Italian physicist Alessandro Volta produces first electric battery.

1801 Act of Union formally unites Great Britain and Ireland as the United Kingdom.
Treaty of Lunéville between France and Austria; leads to break-up of Holy Roman Empire; France gains left bank of the Rhine and keeps most of Italy.
Concordat between Bonaparte and Pius VII.
Alexander I, Tsar of Russia (to 1825).

1802 Treaty of Amiens between Britain and France.
Bonaparte is created First Consul for life.
Portuguese explorers begin crossing of Africa from west (Angola) to east; reach Tete, on the Zambezi, in Mozambique in 1811.

1803 War breaks out again between Britain and France.
'Louisiana Purchase': France sells Louisiana to the United States; Ohio becomes the 17th state of the Union.

1804 Bonaparte crowns himself Napoleon I, Emperor of the French.
The First Empire in France (until 1814).
Persia and Russia at war over annexation of Georgia.
Serbian nationalists revolt against Turks in modern Yugoslavia; suppressed 1813.
American explorers Meriwether Lewis and William Clark set out to explore the north-western United States as far as the Pacific Ocean which they reach in November 1805.
Haiti achieves independence from France.
English inventor Richard Trevithick builds first successful steam locomotive.

1804 Third Coalition formed by Britain, Russia, Austria, and Sweden against France.

1805 Battle of Ulm: French defeat Austrians.
Battle of Trafalgar: British navy under Horatio Nelson defeats Franco-Spanish fleet.
Battle of Austerlitz: French defeat Austro-Russian forces.
Mohammed Ali appointed *pasha* (governor) of Egypt by Selim III, Sultan of Turkey.

The Louisiana Purchase

In 1763 France ceded to Spain a huge tract of territory in the heart of North America, lying between the Mississippi River and the Rocky Mountains. It was known as Louisiana. But in 1800 the French, then in a strong position, forced Spain to return Louisiana to them.

France's ruler, Napoleon Bonaparte, then First Consul, planned to create a new French North American empire. But he faced the threat of war with Britain, in which he would not have the resources to develop or defend Louisiana, also threatened by the United States. In April 1803 he offered the whole territory to the United States for $15 million. President Thomas Jefferson at once accepted, though the US Constitution contained no provision for acquiring territory in this way. He said later that he had 'stretched the Constitution until it cracked'. At a stroke he doubled the size of the United States. The purchase money was borrowed from English and Dutch bankers.

The Napoleonic Wars

Following the wars of the First and Second Coalitions against France during and immediately after the French Revolution, a Third Coalition was formed in 1804. The idea of this coalition was to attempt to curb the overweening ambition of France's ruler, Napoleon Bonaparte, who in May 1804 was voted the title of Emperor. Napoleon's actions provoked Britain into war again in 1803, and the following year Britain was joined by Austria, Naples, Russia, and Sweden. Spain was allied with France.

War at Sea: Napoleon massed an invasion fleet to attack England. But in October 1805 a British fleet led by Horatio Nelson destroyed a combined French and Spanish fleet at Trafalgar, ending the invasion threat.

Central Europe: Napoleon switched his armies to attack Austria, which he crushed at the battle of Austerlitz in December 1805. The following year he invaded Prussia and defeated it at the battles of Jena and Auerstadt. In 1807 he defeated the Russians at the battle of Friedland. In 1808 the Austrians resumed the war, but were again defeated and forced to make peace.

The Peninsula: In 1808 Napoleon attacked Spain and Portugal, the countries of the Iberian peninsula, and made his brother Joseph king of Spain. The Spanish people appealed to Britain for aid. British troops landed in Portugal and advanced into Spain. Napoleon forced them to retreat to Corunna, in northern Spain. Arthur Wellesley, later Duke of Wellington, then took command of the British forces in the Peninsular War. In a series of battles Wellesley wore down the French, and forced Napoleon to keep a large army in Spain. Finally in 1814 the British crossed the French frontier and won a resounding victory at Toulouse on April 10.

Russia: Napoleon was determined to crush Russia, and invaded it with 600,000

The Emperor Napoleon I, from a chalk drawing by the Italian artist Andrea Appiani, whom Napoleon made painter to the kingdom of Italy. Napoleon, given command of the French army in 1795, rose to prominence with his Italian and Egyptian campaigns.

men in June 1812. He captured Moscow, which the Russians had set on fire, but found himself short of supplies and in the grip of a Russian winter. He had to retreat, losing almost all his men. Austria, Prussia, and other German states resumed the war, and in October 1813 a combined Russian, Prussian and Austrian force heavily defeated Napoleon at Leipzig. In April 1814 he abdicated and was exiled to Elba.

The Hundred Days: In March 1815 Napoleon escaped from Elba and returned to France. The French king, Louis XVIII, fled, and Napoleon was soon in power again. An allied army was hastily gathered, and under the command of Wellington and the Prussian Marshal Gebhard von Blucher it defeated Napoleon finally at Waterloo, in Belgium in June. Napoleon was exiled to St Helena, in the South Atlantic, where he died in 1821.

Below: Ironworks at Coalbrookdale, England (1805), site of the world's first iron bridge. Factories invaded much of the countryside and farmland in the Industrial Revolution.

1806 Louis Bonaparte, brother of Napoleon, becomes King of Holland.
Napoleon I dissolves Holy Roman Empire; replaces it by Confederation of the Rhine.
Emperor Francis II becomes Francis I of Austria (to 1835).
Battles of Jena and Auerstädt: Prussia defeated by French.
Berlin Decree issued by Napoleon to attempt economic blockade of Britain (the Continental System).
Turkey at war with Russia and Britain (until 1812).

1807 Slave trade abolished in British Empire.
Battle of Friedland: Russian defeat.
Treaties of Tilsit between Tsar Alexander I of Russia and Napoleon.
French invade Portugal; capture Lisbon.

1808 French occupy Spain; Joseph Bonaparte becomes King of Spain. Peninsular War (until 1814): France opposed by British forces and Spanish and Portuguese guerrillas.
Battle of Vimeiro: British victory.
Russia and Sweden at war (until 1809).

1809 Battle of Corunna: British defeated; death of Sir John Moore, British commander-in-chief.

1810 Louis, King of Holland abdicates; France annexes Holland.
British troops in Portugal hold lines of Torres Vedras against the French (until 1811).

1811 French driven out of Portugal.
Luddite riots in England against mechanization in textile industry; repressive legislation introduced (1812).
Mamelukes (ruling family) massacred in Cairo by Mohammed Ali.
Paraguay and Venezuela achieve independence.
George III of England declared insane; Prince of Wales rules as regent.

1812 Britain and United States at war over shipping and territory disputes (until 1814).
Battle of Salamanca: British victory in Spain.
Treaty of St Petersburg between Sweden and Russia.
Treaty of Bucharest ends Russo-Turkish war.
Treaty of Örebro among Britain, Sweden, and Russia.
Napoleon invades Russia with Grand Army; battle of Borodino: French occupy Moscow but are forced to retreat; only 100,000 survive from army of 600,000.

1813 War of Liberation from France begins in Prussia, led by King Frederick William III.
Treaty of Kalisch between Russia and Prussia against France; coalition joined by Britain, Austria, and Sweden.

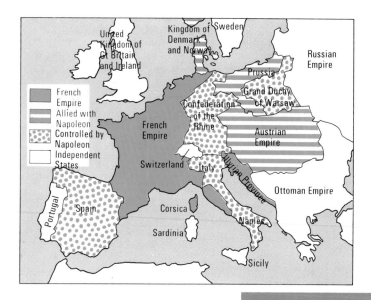

Left: At its height, the empire of Napoleon dominated most of Europe. It was only the disastrous failure of his attempted invasion of Russia in 1812 which marked the end of his grip on Europe. He went into exile after his defeat at Leipzig in 1813 returning only to be defeated again at Waterloo.

The Rise of the Zulus

In the early 1800s the Zulus, a Bantu Negro people of southern Africa, were a small and unimportant tribe of the Nguni people. Around about 1810 a Zulu named Chaka began to organize the neighbouring Mthethwa tribe, and to train *impis* (warrior armies). His soldiers were strictly disciplined. They could travel 40 miles (64 km) in a day, and fought with *assegais* (light spears).

By 1818 Chaka had formed an empire, uniting other tribes of the Nguni, and could command more than a dozen *impis*. He gave the name Zulu to his people, who drove all the other Negro tribes out of their territory which formed the north-eastern part of Natal. Chaka himself was murdered in 1828, but the empire he had built up lived on until it was finally annexed by the British in 1887.

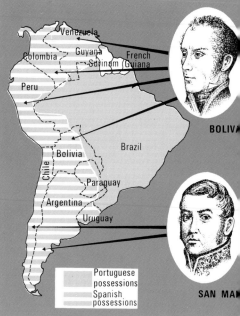

South American Independence

Spain and Portugal between them conquered all South America except the Guianas, and ruled their colonies for nearly 300 years. Isolation from Europe led many colonists to desire complete independence. Their chance came when Napoleon's temporary conquest of Spain left them very much to their own devices.

The wars of independence began in the region of the Rio de la Plata in 1806. The outstanding general of this campaign, José de San Martín, liberated Chile in 1818 with the aid of Bernardo O'Higgins. San Martín went on to invade Peru in 1821. The region then known as Charcas was freed by Simón Bolívar, and it was renamed Bolivia. Bolívar had already helped to liberate Venezuela in 1811. Paraguay and Uruguay had also proclaimed their independence in 1811, while Colombia and Ecuador were liberated by San Martín and Bolívar in 1822. The Mexicans began their campaign for independence in 1808, and finally achieved it in 1821.

Brazil provided a haven for the Portuguese royal family during the Peninsular War. In 1822, faced with Portuguese demands to make Brazil a subordinate state again, the Brazilians proclaimed their independence, with Dom Pedro, son of the Portuguese king, as their first emperor.

Left: South American independence and its architects: Simón Bolívar, liberator of Venezuela, Colombia, Peru, and Bolivia; and José de San Martín, who freed Chile and Argentina from Spanish rule.

1813 Battle of Dresden: French victory.
Battle of Leipzig (Battle of the Nations): French defeated by combined Austrian, Russian, and Prussian forces.
Battle of Vittoria: French entirely driven out of Spain by Wellington.
Allied forces invade France; enter Paris in March 1814.

1814 Napoleon abdicates and is exiled to Elba.
Louis XVIII, brother of Louis XVI, King of France (to 1824).
Treaty of Paris ends Napoleonic Wars.
Congress of Vienna (to 1815): heads of state discuss settlement of post-war Europe.
Treaty of Kiel: Sweden gains Norway.
Treaty of Ghent ends Anglo-American war.

1815 The Hundred Days: Napoleon escapes from Elba and marches on Paris.
Battle of Waterloo: Napoleon defeated and exiled to island of St Helena.
Final Act of Congress of Vienna: Austrian and Prussian monarchies restored; German Confederation replaces Confederation of the Rhine; Kingdom of Netherlands formally unites Belgium and Holland.
Holy Alliance of Russia, Austria, and Prussia.
Second Treaty of Paris: France's boundaries restored to those of 1790.
Quadruple Alliance of Britain, Austria, Prussia, and Russia to maintain Congress System.
English Corn Laws restrict corn imports.
Serbs revolt against Turkey in Balkans; Serb leader Milosh Obrenovich recognized by Turks as Prince of Serbia, 1817.

1818 Congress of Aix-la-Chapelle: France joins the four Great Powers (Quintuple Alliance).
Border between Canada and United States fixed along 49th parallel; both countries occupy Oregon.
Chile becomes independent from Spain.
Zulu Empire founded in southern Africa by Chaka, great military chieftain.

1819 Peterloo Massacre: soldiers fire on political meeting in Manchester, England; several people killed.
Carlsbad Decrees in Germany suppress political activity.
Zollverein (customs union) begins in Germany under influence of Prussia.
Spain cedes Florida to the United States.
Latin American revolutionary, Simón Bolívar, secures independence of Greater Colombia.
Kashmir conquered by Sikh leader, Ranjit Singh.
Singapore founded by British administrator, Sir Stamford Raffles.

Left: The great German composer Ludwig van Beethoven (1770–1827).

Opposite top: Hastings: Deep Sea Fishing *is typical of the light, expansive paintings of the English painter J. M. W. Turner.*

Opposite bottom: Street fighting during the July 1830 uprising in Paris which ended Bourbon rule in France. Nationalist and revolutionary movements typified the 19th century.

The Ramapo, *an American locomotive of the mid-1800s when the railway network began to spread rapidly. The huge smoke stack trapped sparks, and the cowcatcher was essential in the wild, unfenced country.*

Communications

The second quarter of the 19th century saw a revolution in communications. Up to that time travel was by horse or horse-drawn carriage over rough, slow roads, while the only practical way of long-distance signalling was the visual semaphore system.

The electric telegraph was developed in the 1830s, the work of British and American inventors. The most successful was Samuel Morse (1791–1872), who in 1840 patented his invention and the code which bears his name. The telegraph spread rapidly in the next ten years.

Railways developed quickly after the opening of the first all-steam passenger service, the Liverpool and Manchester Railway in northern England, in 1830. It was followed a few months later by the South Carolina Railroad in the United States. Within 15 years railways were in operation in Austria, Canada, France, Germany, Italy, Poland, Spain, Switzerland, and Russia. Steam power was a major advance for shipping, and in the late 1830s the first steamships for the Atlantic crossing were brought into service.

1820 Cato Street conspiracy in England to assassinate cabinet ministers fails.
Liberal revolutions in Spain, Portugal, and Italy.
George IV, King of Britain (to 1830).
Congress of Troppau considers Naples revolt.
Missouri Compromise: admission of several states to the Union, including Missouri (1821) as a slave state.
Egyptian conquest of Sudan (completed 1822).
1821 Congress of Laibach authorizes Austria to put down Neapolitan revolt.
Greek War of Independence against Turkey; succeeds in 1829.
Peru and Mexico proclaim independence.
Persia and Turkey at war (until 1823).
1822 Congress of Verona; breaks down over Britain's refusal to intervene in Spain; ends Congress System.
Brazil achieves independence from Portugal.
Colombia and Ecuador liberated.
Liberia, west Africa, founded as colony for freed America slaves.
1823 Spanish revolution crushed.
United States' President, James Monroe, issues Monroe Doctrine warning European powers not to interfere in American politics.
1824 Combination Acts repealed in England, stimulating trade union movement.
Charles X, brother of Louis XVI and XVIII, King of France (to 1830).
War between British and Ashanti in Gold Coast (Ghana), west Africa (until 1827).
First Anglo-Burmese War (until 1826); Britain begins annexataion of Burma.
Nicholas I, Tsar of Russia (to 1855).
1825 Decembrist rising in Russia against Tsar.
Egyptian forces under Ibrahim, son of Mohammed Ali, invade Greece.
New Republic of Bolivia independent.
1826 Russia and Persia at war (until 1828).
Turks capture Missolonghi from Greeks.
1827 Treaty of London: Britain, Russia, France to guarantee Greek independence.
Battle of Navarino: Egyptian fleet destroyed by French, Russian, and British.
1828 Miguelite Wars in Portugal: regent Dom Miguel overthrows government; finally defeated 1834.
War between Russia and Turkey (to 1829).
1829 Catholic Emancipation Act in Britain; Roman Catholics can hold public office.
Russo-Turkish Treaty of Adrianople.
Greater Colombia divided into Colombia, Venezuela, Ecuador, New Granada.
1830 William IV, King of Britain (to 1837).
July Revolution in Paris; Charles X overthrown.

The Great Trek

Britain took over Cape Colony in southern Africa from the Dutch in 1806, during the Napoleonic Wars. Many of the Dutch settlers, called Boers, resented British rule and complained of inadequate compensation for the abolition of slavery in 1833. From 1835 to 1837 10,000 Boers trekked or travelled northwards to fresh territory, where they settled in Natal and what were to become the independent Boer republics of the Orange Free State, and the Transvaal.

The British annexed Natal in 1843, so the Boers there moved into the Orange Free State and on into the Transvaal.

Below: Plan of a slave-ship. The slave trade served the planters of the hot southern states of America, who grew tobacco, cotton, and sugar. These had to be picked and processed by hand in unpleasant conditions – so huge supplies of cheap labour were needed. European ships went out to West Africa, where local chiefs sold the slaves (often captives from tribal wars). Then they took their tightly packed human cargo to America, where they loaded up with plantation goods to take home. Millions of slaves died on these voyages.

Opposite: A picture of early photography in action. taken by the English pioneer, William Henry Fox Talbot (1800–1877) by the calotype process.

The Alamo

In the 1700s Texas formed part of the Spanish Empire, and after 1821 it came under the rule of the newly independent Mexico. Warfare between American settlers and the Mexicans began in 1830, and flared into open revolt in 1836, when the Texans proclaimed an independent republic.

About the time of the proclamation, a Mexican army of 5000 men led by Antonio de Santa Anna attacked the town of San Antonio. The 150 Texans forming the garrison retreated into the Alamo, a former mission used as a fort. They held out for 11 days, when the Mexicans stormed the fort killing all but six men. Santa Anna had these men put to death and only two women and two children survived the siege. The time gained by the siege enabled the main Texan force to concentrate, and a few weeks later the Texans under General Sam Houston routed the Mexicans at San Jacinto, captured Santa Anna, and forced Mexico to acknowledge their independence. Texas joined the United States in 1845.

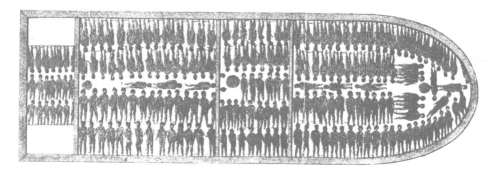

The Irish Famine

During the early 1800s the British Government introduced a series of Corn Laws, which either banned the import of wheat or kept its price high. This was to protect British farmers from foreign competition, but made the price of bread too high for poor people to buy. An Anti-Corn Law League was founded in 1839 in Manchester, led by John Bright, a millowner, and Richard Cobden, a calico printer.

Because of the Corn Laws, about four million poor people in Ireland lived almost entirely on potatoes which they grew. In 1845 a disastrous blight ruined about three-quarters of the potato crop. Worse blight followed in 1846 and relief measures by the British government were too late and too little to provide enough food.

An estimated million Irish died, although the potato crop recovered in 1847. Large-scale emigration to America began and by 1861 about two million Irish had left their native land, bearing a great deal of ill-will towards England. The effects of the famine were instrumental in having the Corn Laws repealed in 1846.

1830 First passenger steam railways open.
Louis Philippe, descendant of Louis XIII, King of France (the Citizen King) (to 1848).
Revolution in Belgium against Dutch rule.
Greece formally declared independent.
Revolution in Poland crushed by Russia (1831).
1831 Gregory XVI, Pope (to 1846).
Uprisings in Modena, Parma, Papal States; put down by Austria.
Italian revolutionary, Giuseppe Mazzini, forms *Young Italy* movement.
Britain and France guarantee Belgian independence; Leopold of Saxe-Coburg becomes Leopold I, King of the Belgians (to 1865).
1832 Reform Act passed in Britain: extends vote to middle class.
War between Egypt and Turkey (until 1833).
Battle of Koniah: Turks defeated.
1833 Factory Act in England forbids employment of children under nine in factories.
Act abolishing slavery in British colonies.
Convention of Kutahia; Mohammed Ali gains Syria.
Treaty of Unkiar Skelessi between Russia and Turkey.
Munchengratz Agreement between Russia and Austria.
1834 'Tolpuddle Martyrs': six Dorset labourers transported for attempt to form a trade union.
Carlist Wars in Spain (until 1839); Pretender Don Carlos attempts to gain Spanish throne.
Quadruple Alliance formed by Britain, France, Spain, and Portugal to safeguard governments in Spain and Portugal.
Beginning of foundation of South Australia (1836) and Victoria (1837).
1835 Ferdinand I, Emperor of Austria (to 1848).
Great Trek (to 1837): Boer (Dutch) settlers in southern Africa found Transvaal.
1836 Chartist movement begins in Britain; demands votes for all adult males; violent support eventually moderates.
Texas wins independence from Mexico; battles of the Alamo and San Jacinto.
1837 Victoria, Queen of Britain (to 1901).
1838 Battle of Blood River: Boers defeat Zulus in Natal, South Africa.
1839 British occupy Aden.
Commissioner Lin destroys foreign Opium.
Opium war between Britain and China (to 1842).
Anti-Corn Law League formed in Britain.
Turks invade Syria.
Battle of Nesib: Turks defeated.
Rebellions in Upper and Lower Canada.
Britain and Afghanistan at war.

The Communist Manifesto

Modern Communism owes its origin to the work of two German philosophers, Karl Marx (1818–1883) and Friedrich Engels (1820–1895). After having his Cologne

A barricade in the Boulevard Montmartre, Paris. Such unrest led to the Revolution of 1848.

newspaper suppressed, and later being expelled from Germany, Marx lived in exile in London, supported by his articles to the *New York Tribune* and by money given to him by Engels, a manufacturer.

In 1848 the two men produced *The Communist Manifesto*, in which they urged a revolution by workers against the ruling classes. It ended with the words: 'The workers have nothing to lose but their chains. They have a world to gain. Workers of the world, unite!'

Marx went on to develop his theories of economics and revolution in *Das Kapital*, a massive work in three volumes (1867–1895), partly edited by Engels after Marx died.

Friedrich Engels (above) and Karl Marx.

Queen Victoria succeeded her uncle, William IV, as Queen of England in 1837 at the age of 18; she reigned for 64 years. This picture was painted in the early years of her reign.

Year of Revolutions

The year 1848 is often called the 'Year of Revolutions', because unrest swept through Europe. Food shortages, trade recessions, and nationalist feelings were the main causes of discontent.

The movement began in France in February; an uprising of citizens drove out King Louis Philippe and set up the Second Republic. In March, a revolt in Austria against the Chancellor, Prince von Metternich, a conservative and autocratic administrator, forced him to flee. The Austrian Emperor, Ferdinand, abdicated in favour of his more democratic nephew Franz Josef.

The Hungarians, then under Austrian rule, won a new constitution for themselves – though it was withdrawn the following year. Riots in Germany and demonstrations in Britain had little lasting effect, but the Danes gained a new constitution, and some Balkan peoples won short-lived concessions from their Turkish rulers.

1840 Treaty of Waitangi: New Zealand becomes a British Crown Colony.
Treaty of London: Britain, Russia, Prussia, and Austria agree to limit Egyptian expansion.
British navy bombards Beirut.
Union Act unites Upper and Lower Canada.
Penny post introduced in Britain.

1841 Convention of Alexandria: Mohammed Ali to be hereditary ruler of Egypt.
Straits Convention among Britain, Austria, Russia, Prussia, and France; Dardanelles and Bosporus to be closed to foreign ships in peacetime.

1842 Webster-Ashburton Treaty settles boundary dispute between Canada and United States.
Boers and British at war; British victorious.
British withdraw from Kabul, Afghanistan.
Treaty of Nanking between Britain and China; Hong Kong ceded to Britain.

1843 Natal becomes a British colony.

1845 Anglo-Sikh Wars in India (to 1848); Britain annexes the Punjab, northwest India.
Texas joins the United States.

1846 Potato famine reaches height in Ireland; about one million die by 1851.
Corn Laws repealed in Britain.
Pius IX, Pope (to 1878).
United States and Mexico at war (until 1848).
War between *Kaffirs* (Bantu) and British in South Africa; Bantu defeated (1847).
First act of segregation in South Africa; Zulu reserves set up in Natal.
Growth of anti-British movement in Ireland.

1848 Year of revolutions in Europe.
Revolution in Paris; Louis Philippe abdicates; Second Republic with Louis Napoleon, nephew of Napoleon I, as president, set up in France.
Revolutions in Milan, Naples, Venice, Rome; most suppressed within a year.
Revolutions in Berlin, Vienna, Prague, Budapest; initially successful.
Prince Metternich resigns; Emperor Ferdinand abdicates.
Franz Josef I, Emperor of Austria (to 1916).
Frankfurt National Assembly meets (to 1849) to discuss unification of Germany.
Uprising in Wallachia (Romania) is suppressed by Russia.
Switzerland introduces federal constitution.
Insurrection in Tipperary, Ireland, is put down.
Treaty of Guadalupe Hidalgo: United States gains California, New Mexico.
Californian gold rush begins.
First Convention of Womens' Rights, New York.
The Communist Manifesto written by German socialists, Karl Marx and Friedrich Engels.

Europe the Overlord

THE PERIOD BETWEEN 1848, the 'Year of Revolutions', and the outbreak of World War I in 1914, was dominated by the countries of Europe. Several European nations had colonial possessions before 1848; Spain, indeed, had won and lost an empire in the Americas. But the real expansion of European colonialism came in the second half of the 19th century. Almost the whole of Africa was colonized, and large parts of Asia were under European influence. The greatest of the empires was the British, on which, it was boasted, the sun never set since its possessions circled the globe.

European expansion was greatly helped by the continent's industry and technology. The factories of Britain, France, and Germany in particular supplied goods and machines to almost all countries of the world, colonial or independent. The world's railways were made in Europe; so were its ships and its telegraph systems. This vast export market, coupled with a supply of cheap food and raw materials from the colonies, made Europe wealthy. In return, the effects of industrial society made themselves gradually felt around the world. French and English became international languages; European systems of parliamentary government, of law, and of commerce, became widespread.

Right: Guglielmo Marconi, inventor of 'wireless telegraphy' or radio, with apparatus like that which he used to send the first wireless signal across the Atlantic – the Morse letter 'S'.

Left: Robert Peary, the American naval officer whose burning ambition to reach the North Pole was realized in 1909, after seven expeditions over 23 years.

EUROPE

1854 Crimean War (to 1856)

1856 Treaty of Paris

1859 France at war with Austria
1861 Unification of Italy
1862 Bismarck becomes Prussian prime minister
1866 Austro-Prussian War
1867 North German Confederation formed by
treaties with Prussia and other states
north of river Main

1870 Franco-Prussian War (to 1871)
1871 German Empire formed:
William I proclaimed Emperor
1872 League of the Three Emperors
1877 Russia at War with Turkey
1878 Treaty of San Stefano
signed by Russia and Turkey

1882 Phoenix Park Murders
Triple Alliance of Germany, Austria, and
Italy (to 1914)
1887 Italy and Ethiopia at war (to 1889)
1888 William II becomes Emperor of Germany
(to 1918)

1890 Bismarck dismissed from office
1895 Italy and Ethiopia at war (to 1896)
1897 Greece and Turkey at war
1898 Social Democratic Party founded in Russia

1902 Anglo-Japanese alliance formed
ending Britain's isolation policy
1904 Outbreak of Russo-Japanese war
1905 General strike and revolution in Russia
1907 Triple Entente
1912 Balkan Wars (to 1913)

ASIA

1850 Revolt in China (to 1864)
1852 Second Burmese War (to 1853)
1854 Commercial treaty between Japan and
United States
1856 Anglo-Chinese War (to 1860)
1857 Indian Mutiny (to 1858)
Treaty of Paris
1858 India Bill: transfers government of India
to British Crown

1862 Cambodia becomes French protectorate
1863 Shimonoseki in China bombarded
by French and American warships
1868 Meiji Period in Japan (to 1912)

1875 Third Anglo-Burmese War
1876 Korea starts trading with Japan
1877 Queen Victoria becomes Empress of India

1894 China and Japan at War
1895 Treaty of Shimonoseki signed
between China and Japan
1896 Anglo-French agreements in Siam
(now Thailand)
1897 Occupation of Kiaochow
1898 Port Arthur ceded to Russia
1900 Boxer Rebellion in China
1901 Manchuria occupied

1904 Russia and Japan at war (to 1905)
Tibet opened for trade
1905 Battle of Tsushima
1906 Liberal revolution in Persia
1910 Japan annexes Korea

AFRICA

1852	Sand River Convention: Britain recognizes independence of Transvaal
1853	David Livingstone crosses Africa (to 1856)
1859	Lake Tanganyika discovered
1868	British expedition sent to Ethiopia
1869	Suez Canal opened
1873	Second Ashanti War (to 1874)
1875	Suez Canal shares bought by Britain from Egypt
1877	Transvaal annexed by Britain
1878	Second Anglo-Afghan War (to 1880)
1879	Zulu War
1880	Boer uprising (to 1881)
1882	Cairo occupied by British troops Anti-Egyptian revolution in Sudan (to 1885)
1884	General Gordon sent by Britain to Khartoum in the Sudan
1885	German East Africa established
1890	Zanzibar becomes a British protectorate
1893	Ivory Coast becomes a French protectorate
1895	Rhodesia founded by Cecil Rhodes
1896	Jameson Raid
1898	Fashoda incident
1899	Second Boer War (to 1902)
1900	Orange Free State annexed by Britain Northern Nigeria invaded and conquered by Britain
1902	Treaty of Vereeniging
1906	Algeciras Conference reaffirms independence of Morocco
1908	Belgian Congo founded
1909	Union of South Africa formed

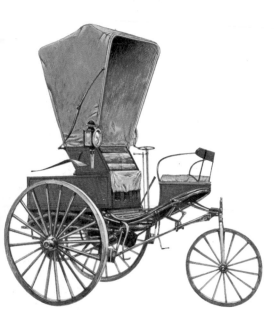

Below: The invention of Karl Benz's 1½-horsepower car of 1888, the world's first standard retail petrol model, marked the beginning of the motor industry.

AMERICAS	ELSEWHERE
	1851 Gold rush in Australia
1860 South Carolina secedes from the United States	
1861 Abraham Lincoln becomes President of United States (to 1865)	1861 Gold rush in New Zealand
American Civil War (to 1865)	
1863 Battle of Gettysburg	
1864 Union Army occupies Georgia	
1865 President Lincoln assassinated	
1867 United States purchases Alaska from Russia	
Dominion of Canada formed	
1868 Ten year war between Cuba and Spain	
1876 Battle of Little Big Horn	
Porfirio Diaz becomes dictator of Mexico	
1881 President James Garfield assassinated	1881 Peace declared between New Zealand settlers and Maoris
1895 Revolution in Cuba (to 1898)	
1898 Spain and United States at War	
	1901 Commonwealth of Australia established
1903 Alaska's boundary determined	
	1907 Dominion of New Zealand established
	1909 American Robert Peary reaches North Pole
	1911 Norwegian Roald Amundsen reaches South Pole
1911 Revolution in Mexico	

The Indian Mutiny

Until the mid-19th century the East India Company controlled British India. The Indians were embittered by British annexations of state after state, and alarmed by a programme of westernization that included abolition of many Indian customs and conversions to Christianity, and threatened the Hindu caste system. Army discipline was slack, administration was inefficient, and Europeans were vastly outnumbered by Indians. Mutiny was finally sparked off by the introduction to the Bengal army of cartridges greased with pig and cow fat, offensive to both Muslims and Hindus.

In May 1857 soldiers at Meerut, near Delhi, killed their officers, captured Delhi, and massacred the British. The mutiny spread to many other regiments in Upper and Central India, who rallied round native princes. The Punjab and Bombay, however, remained loyal. In 1858 reinforcements arrived from Britain and peace was restored in July. A month later the British government took over the rule of India from the East India company.

A scene showing the harsh conditions in which the Crimean War was fought from 1854 to 1856. Most of the 650,000 casualties died from disease, exhaustion, or bad leadership. Below left: Map of the Crimea.

The Crimean War

The Crimean War, from 1854 to 1856, was fought by an alliance of Turkey (the Ottoman Empire), Britain, France, and Sardinia against Russia. It began when Russia invaded Turkish territory in Europe in 1853, demanding free passage for its warships through the Dardanelles Strait – controlled by Turkey – and claiming to protect Christians in Turkish lands.

Britain and France went to Turkey's aid. In September 1854 the allies attacked the Russian naval base of Sevastopol, in the Crimea, intending to immobilize the Russian navy. Within two months they had won three victories, at the Alma River, Balaklava, and Inkerman. The battle of Balaklava is noted for the brave but mistaken charge of the 670 horsemen of the Light Brigade, through confused orders, directly against the Russian artillery. Fighting stopped until spring 1855 when Sardinia joined the allies, and in September the allies captured Sevastopol.

Disease caused more casualties than the fighting; the poor medical care given to British soldiers led the nursing pioneer Florence Nightingale to set up proper hospitals for them.

Under threat of attack from Austria, Russia agreed to peace terms. The Treaty of Paris ended the war in 1856. Under it, Russia had to yield some territory to Turkey, and its warships, together with those of other countries, were banned from the Black Sea. The safety of Turkish Christians was guaranteed by Turkey's allies.

1849 Revolutions in Italy and Hungary crushed. Frankfurt Parliament collapses.

1850 Don Pacifico Affair: British foreign secretary, Lord Palmerston, defends rights of British citizens abroad.
Treaty of Olmütz: German Confederation restored under Austrian leadership.
T'ai P'ing rebellion: revolt in China against Manchu Dynasty (until 1864).

1851 Great Exhibition held in London.

1852 Louis Napoleon sets up Second Empire as Napoleon III, Emperor of the French (to 1870).
Sand River Convention: Britain recognizes independence of the Transvaal.
Second Burmese War (until 1853): British victory.

1853 Turkey declares war on Russia after Franco-Russian disputes over Holy Places in Palestine.
Scottish explorer David Livingstone begins crossing of Africa; discovers Victoria Falls (1855).

1854 The Crimean War (until 1856): Britain, France, and Turkey against Russia.
Battles of Balaclava and Inkerman: Russians defeated
Siege of Sevastopol: Russians besieged for nearly a year.
Liberal revolution in Spain overthrows government.
US naval officer Matthew Perry forces Japan to make commercial treaty with United States.
Orange Free State set up in South Africa.

1855 English nurse Florence Nightingale reforms nursing during Crimean War.
Alexander II, Tsar of Russia (to 1881).

1856 Treaty of Paris ends Crimean War.
Persia captures Herat, Afghanistan; act leads to war with Britain.
Anglo-Chinese war breaks out.

1857 Indian Mutiny (until 1858): rebellion of *sepoys* (native soldiers) in Bengal Army; eventually put down by Britain.
Sepoys take Cawnpore and besiege Lucknow.
Treaty of Paris between Britain and Persia.

1858 Lucknow relieved; Indian mutiny ends.
India Bill: government of India passes to British Crown from East India Company.
Italian nationalist, Felice Orsini, attempts to assassinate Napoleon III.
Secret alliance between Napoleon III and Count Cavour, Premier of Piedmont.
Fenian Society founded in United States by Irish emigrants.
Treaty of Aigun: Russia gains Amur region from China.
Treaties of Tientsin open 11 Chinese ports.

The Afghan Wars

Britain fought two wars in Afghanistan during the 1800s, in order to prevent Russia from gaining control over the country.

In the first, from 1839 to 1842, a British army entered Afghanistan from India, deposed the Emir, Dost Mohammed, who was negotiating with Russia, and restored to the throne Shah Sujah, who had been deposed earlier. In 1841 an Afghan uprising led to the surrender of the Anglo-Indian garrison of Kabul, the capital. During its retreat from Kabul, the garrison was massacred. An avenging British army re-occupied Kabul but later withdrew.

The second war, from 1878 to 1880 occurred when the Emir Sher Ali gained Russian protection. Three Anglo-Indian armies invaded Afghanistan and deposed him. His son, Yakub Khan, agreed to British control, but after a native uprising the British took Kabul, deposed Yakub, and enthroned his more amenable nephew.

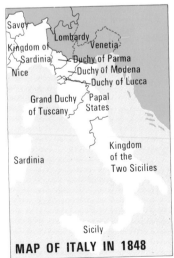

MAP OF ITALY IN 1848

Italy Unified

In 1848, almost all Italy was under Austrian rule or control. The Austrians crushed a rebellion in 1849, but in 1858 the independent kingdom of Piedmont-Sardinia determined to liberate the rest of Italy.

In 1859 Piedmont mobilized its army. Austria demanded that it should disband its troops, so the Piedmontese prime minister, the Conte di Cavour, declared war. With French aid, the Piedmontese won Lombardy; the Austrian states of Parma, Modena, Tuscany, and Romagna voted to join Piedmont. As a price for its help France demanded Nice and Savoy from Piedmont.

In 1860 the Italian patriot Giuseppe Garibaldi overthrew the Kingdom of Naples, allying all southern Italy and Sicily with Piedmont. In 1861 the Kingdom of Italy was proclaimed, and after war in 1866, Austria gave up Venice. The Papal States – lands ruled by the Pope – remained independent under French guarantee; in 1870 these, including Rome, became part of Italy.

Left: Nationalist movements, such as the one in Italy led by the patriot Garibaldi shown here, eroded the old imperial alliances in Europe in the second half of the 1800s. Conscious of their own languages and traditions, Germans, Italians, Magyars, and Slavs of many countries asserted their demands for independent nation states.

The American Civil War

Civil war between North and South ravaged the United States from 1861 to 1865. The South depended on cotton plantations and farms worked by black slaves, the North on industry without slaves. They disputed whether slavery would be extended to new states being settled.

In 1860 Abraham Lincoln, a Republican whose party wanted to limit slavery, was elected president. Afraid of being out-numbered by non-slave states, 11 Southern states separated into a new nation, the Con-federate States of America; they were Alabama, Arkansas, Florida, Georgia, Lou-isiana, Mississippi, North and South Caro-lina, Tennessee, Texas, and Virginia. Lin-coln refused to recognize this secession, and fighting broke out in April 1861.

The Southern General Robert E. Lee won the first battle at Bull Run in July 1861, but eventually the superior manpower of the North began to tell. A turning point came with Union victory at Gettysburg in 1863. The Union navy blockaded Southern ports; General Ulysses S. Grant took Vicksburg, dividing the Confederacy; General Sher-man, after burning down Atlanta, marched through Georgia and the Carolinas.

General Lee finally surrendered in April 1865; 618,000 had died. In 1863 Lincoln had proclaimed all slaves in rebel states free, and despite attempts to rebuild the South's ruined economy without slaves after the war ('Reconstruction'), much bitterness between North and South remained.

1858 British explorers Sir Richard Burton and John Speke discover Lake Tanganyika.

1859 France and Piedmont at war with Austria. Battles of Magenta and Solferino: Austria defeated.
Treaty of Zurich between France and Austria: Piedmont gains Lombardy.

1860 Italian states Parma, Modena, Tuscany, and Romagna unite with Piedmont.
Italian patriot Giuseppe Garibaldi and his 'Thousand Redshirts' conquer Naples and Sicily.
South Carolina withdraws from the Union.
British and French occupy Peking; end of Anglo-Chinese war.

1861 Italy, except for Rome and Venice, united as one kingdom under Victor Emmanuel, King of Piedmont.
William I, King of Prussia (to 1888).
Abraham Lincoln inaugurated president of the United States.
Confederate States of America formed by South Carolina and ten other Southern states.
Civil War in America (until 1865) between Confederates and the Union (Federals); first battle at Bull Run: Confederate victory.
Serfs freed in Russia.
Prince Albert, husband of Queen Victoria, dies.

1862 Otto von Bismarck becomes Prime Minister of Prussia.
French establish protectorate over Cochin-China (western provinces fall in 1867).

1863 Lincoln proclaims abolition of slavery in United States.
Polish insurrection; fails (1864).
Battle of Gettysburg: Confederate defeat.
French occupy Mexico City.
French establish protectorate in Cambodia.

1864 Austria and Prussia take Schleswig-Holstein from Denmark.
United States Union Army controls Georgia.
Expedition of British, Dutch, French and Americans, bombards Shimonoseki, Japan.
Karl Marx founds *First International* in London.

1865 Confederate General Lee surrenders to Union General Grant; American Civil War ends.
President Lincoln assassinated.

1866 Prussia forms alliance with Italy.
Austro-Prussian war over Schleswig-Holstein (Seven Weeks' War).
Battle of Sadowa: Prussian victory.
Battles of Custozza and Lissa: Italy defeated but gains Venice.
Treaty of Prague ends Austro-Prussian war; Austria to withdraw from German affairs.

1867 Second Reform Act passed in England.

The Franco-Prussian War

The main cause of the Franco-Prussian War of 1870–1871 was French resentment of the growing power of Prussia. Relations between the two countries grew worse when Prussia appeared to support the claim of a German prince to the throne of Spain. The final spark occurred when Otto von Bismarck, chief minister of Prussia, made public a telegram from King William which he had altered to appear insulting to the French. Bismarck hoped war with France would unite Germany behind Prussia.

France at once declared war, although not ready to fight. In six weeks its main army, with the Emperor Napoleon III, had surrendered, and in January 1871 Paris capitulated after a 132-day siege.

Under the Treaty of Frankfurt, which ended the war in 1871, France gave Prussia the provinces of Alsace and Lorraine, and paid an indemnity of 5000 million francs. The war had the result Bismarck wanted: a new German *Reich* (empire) was created with William as its first *Kaiser* (emperor).

The Meiji Period

From 1192 Japan was effectively ruled by the *shoguns*, military dictators from a succession of powerful families; the emperor had little real power. In the 1850s the members of the ruling family, the Tokugawa, were weak and incompetent. They angered the people by signing trade treaties with the United States and other countries, ending 300 years of Japanese isolation.

In 1868 a group of nobles persuaded the young Emperor Mutsuhito to overthrow the shogunate. The result was not, as many people hoped, a return to isolation but modernization of Japan on Western lines, with strong central government, a strong army, a parliament, and industrialization.

Mutsuhito took the name of *Meiji*, 'Enlightened Rule', and his reign until his death in 1912 is called the Meiji period.

Opposite: The American poet Walt Whitman (1819–1892). His poems were to set the trend in American literature for a free, informal way of writing. His major work, Leaves of Grass, *shocked many people, and he died in poverty.*

General Ulysses S. Grant, victorious commander-in-chief of the Union forces in the American Civil War, with eight members of his staff. In 1868 Grant was elected 18th United States president and served two terms.

1867 North German Confederation formed under Prussian leadership.
Austro-Hungarian Monarchy: Franz Josef of Austria also king of Hungary.
Russia sells Alaska to United States.
Dominion of Canada established.
France forced to withdraw from Mexico.

1868 Uprising in Spain; Queen Isabella II forced to abdicate.
Ten Years' War (until 1878): Cuba, unsuccessfully, attempts to gain independence from Spain.
British expedition to Ethiopia forces release of British diplomats.
Meiji period in Japan (until 1912).

1869 Disestablishment Act passed; Irish Church ceases to exist, 1871.
The Suez Canal is opened.

1870 Irish Land Act provides compensation for eviction; fails to ease Irish problem.
Franco-Prussian War (until 1871).
French defeated at Sedan; Napoleon III captured; Prussians besiege Paris.
Second French Empire ends.
Third French Republic (until 1914).
Kingdom of Italy annexes Papal States; Rome becomes capital of Italy.

1871 Trade unions legalized in Britain.
German Empire declared with King William I of Prussia as Emperor.
Paris surrenders after gruelling siege.
Paris Commune set up in opposition to national government and peace terms.
Treaty of Frankfurt ends Franco-Prussian war; Alsace-Lorraine ceded to Germany and France forced to pay heavy indemnity.
Government troops crush Paris Commune.

1872 League of the three emperors: William I, Franz Josef, Tsar Alexander II.

1873 First Republic in Spain (to 1874).
Second Ashanti War in West Africa (to 1874): Ashanti defeated by British.

1874 First Impressionist exhibition held in Paris.
Spanish monarchy restored.

1875 British Prime Minister Benjamin Disraeli buys shares in Suez Canal from Egypt.
Insurrection breaks out in Herzegovina and Bosnia (now in Yugoslavia) against Turkey.

1876 Anti-Turkish insurrection in Bulgaria is suppressed; thousands massacred.
Serbia and Montenegro (now in Yugoslavia) declare war on Turkey but are defeated.
Battle of Little Big Horn: Sioux Indians led by Chief Sitting Bull kill General George Custer and his men; last major North American Indian victory.

The Mahdi

The Arabic title *al-Mahdi* means 'the guided one', an Islamic equivalent to the Messiah. Several Muslims have claimed the title, one of the most famous being Mohammed Ahmed of Dongola in the Sudan. In 1882 he roused the people of the Sudan to rebel against the British-influenced Egyptian rule and won several battles.

In the face of a bloodthirsty onslaught Britain sent General Charles Gordon, former governor of Sudan, to oversee the withdrawal of the Egyptian garrisons. The Mahdi besieged Gordon in Khartoum; the city held out 10 months before it fell in January 1885 and Gordon was killed, two days before relief arrived.

The Mahdi died soon after, but his successor ruled the Sudan for the next 13 years.

The paintings of Pissarro (right) are typical of Impressionism. Works by artists like Van Gogh (below) grew away from this style of painting.

Scramble for Africa

Although it lies so close to Europe, Africa remained a largely unknown continent until about a hundred years ago. Trading stations set up along the coasts for the export of such goods as timber, ivory, and slaves had grown into flourishing ports, but by the mid-1800s little of the interior of the continent had been explored or colonized. Portugal held Angola and Mozambique, the British held Cape Colony in South Africa, while the French had established bases in West Africa.

The journeys of explorers such as Livingstone and Stanley in the 1860s and 1870s stimulated interest in the potential riches of the African continent and by the 1880s the European powers had begun an undignified scramble for colonies in Africa. Tension arose as the British and Portuguese became suspicious of French, Belgian, and German ambitions. To ease the tension the German Chancellor, Otto von Bismarck, called the Berlin Conference (November 1884–February 1885). The conference agreed on spheres of influence, and guaranteed freedom of navigation on the Congo (Zaire) and Niger rivers.

Following the conference, Germany occupied Togoland (now Togo) and the Cameroons (now Cameroun) in West Africa, South West Africa (Namibia), and German East Africa (now Tanzania); the Belgian King Leopold II set up a colony in the Congo (now Zaire); France took the Ivory Coast and Madagascar; and Britain established control over Nigeria, Bechuanaland (now Botswana), Rhodesia, Zanzibar, Uganda, and British East Africa (now Kenya). Britain and France jointly dominated the government of Egypt, but clashed over the control of the Sudan, which was a joint British and Egyptian territory. Italy established a protectorate over Ethiopia, but the Ethiopians defeated the Italians and remained independent. By 1902 the only other independent country in Africa was Liberia.

Impressionism

Impressionism was a movement in painting in France in the 1870s and 1880s which later had a great influence. Its followers, who included Paul Cézanne, Edgar Degas, Claude Monet, and Pierre Renoir, aimed to produce a natural effect in their pictures by the precise analysis of colour and light.

The group held an independent exhibition in Paris in 1874 after their work had been rejected by the official *Salon*. A derisive journalist coined the name 'Impressionists' for them from one of Monet's paintings which had the title *Impression, Sunrise*.

Altogether the group held eight exhibitions, the last in 1886. By that time its members were developing their own individual styles and techniques.

1876	Britain and France assume joint control of Egypt's finances.
	Porfirio Diaz becomes dictator of Mexico.
	Korea opened to Japanese trade.
1877	Queen Victoria proclaimed Empress of India.
	Russia and Turkey at war over the Balkans.
	Transvaal annexed by Britain.
	Satsuma rebellion in Japan is crushed.
1878	Treaty of San Stefano between Russia and Turkey: Montenegro, Serbia, Bulgaria, and Romania to be independent.
	Berlin Congress: Great Powers discuss Balkan situation; revise Treaty of San Stefano.
	Second Anglo-Afghan War (until 1880); Britain gains control of Afghan affairs.
1879	Britain and France control Egypt.
	Irish Land League formed by Irish MP Charles Stewart Parnell.
	Alliance between Germany and Austria. Zulu War between British and Zulus; battle of Ulundi: Zulus defeated.
1880	Boer revolt against British in South Africa.
1881	Alexander III, Tsar of Russia (to 1894).
	France establishes protectorate in Tunis.
	US President James Garfield assassinated.
	Battle of Majuba Hill: Boer victory; Treaty of Pretoria; South African Republic (Transvaal) gains virtual independence.
1882	Phoenix Park Murders: Lord Frederick Cavendish, Chief Secretary for Ireland, and Thomas Burke, Under-secretary, murdered, in Dublin.
	Triple Alliance formed by Germany, Austria, and Italy; lasts until 1914.
	British bombard Alexandria and occupy Cairo to suppress nationalists; leads to French withdrawal from Egypt.
	Anti-Egyptian revolt in Sudan (until 1885) led by Muslim leader, Mahdi Mohammed Ahmed.
1883	Sickness insurance introduced in Germany.
1884	Third Reform Act passed in England.
	Berlin Conference: European powers decide on 'spheres of influence' in Africa; partition of Africa virtually complete by 1895.
	Germany occupies Togoland, Cameroons, and South-West Africa.
	British General Charles Gordon sent to the Sudan to rescue Egyptian garrisons; besieged at Khartoum.
1885	New Guinea annexed by Britain and Germany.
	Khartoum taken and Gordon killed by Mahdi.
	Congo Free State set up under Leopold II of Belgium.
	French chemist Louis Pasteur gives first inoculation against rabies.
	France gains protectorates over Annam and Tonkin (Indochina).

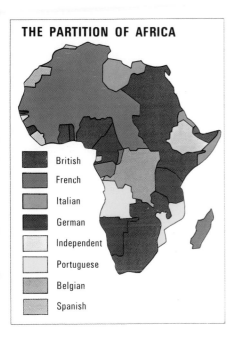

THE PARTITION OF AFRICA

- British
- French
- Italian
- German
- Independent
- Portuguese
- Belgian
- Spanish

Left: An allegory of Socialism (1894) by the English illustrator Walter Crane. With the spread of industry in the late 19th century, Socialism, which aims for a classless society and equal distribution of wealth, gained force in workers' movements, trades unions, and political parties.

The South African Wars

In 1877 Britain annexed the Boer (Dutch) South African Republic, the Transvaal, with Boer agreement. But on December 30, 1880, Paulus Kruger and other Boer leaders proclaimed independence again. Boer forces defeated the British at the battles of Laing's Nek and Majuba Hill. On April 5, 1881, Britain signed the Treaty of Pretoria, restoring Transvaal's independence with Britain supervising foreign affairs.

Gold was discovered in the Transvaal in 1886, and thousands of *Uitlanders* (foreigners) went there to dig for it. Denied civil rights by the Boers, the Uitlanders planned a revolt. Cecil Rhodes, prime minister of the neighbouring British Cape Colony, promised them a small force, led by Dr Leander Starr Jameson.

At the last moment the Uitlanders decided not to revolt, but Jameson, disobeying orders, went ahead with his raid. He had to surrender on January 2, 1896 after only four days. He was jailed; Rhodes resigned.

Further British efforts to persuade the Boers to give rights to Uitlanders led the Boers to declare war in October, 1899. Invading Cape Colony and Natal, they besieged the towns of Mafeking, Ladysmith, and Kimberley, and won several battles. In 1900 Britain sent in many more troops; the Boers reverted to guerilla warfare prolonging the war until surrendering in May 1902.

Britain had annexed the two Boer republics – Transvaal and Orange Free State – but eight years later amalgamated them with Cape Colony and Natal to form the independent dominion of South Africa.

Below: British troops during the South African War (1899–1902).

Louis Pasteur

One of the greatest scientists of the 19th century was the French chemist and biologist Louis Pasteur (1822–1895). In medicine, he proved that microbes carry disease, a discovery which led to the use of antiseptics in operations and the treatment of wounds. He further developed the technique of inoculation – invented in 1796 by the English physician Edward Jenner – to immunize cattle and sheep against anthrax, and chickens against cholera. His most sensational discovery in this field was in 1885, when he developed a successful vaccine against rabies.

In industry, Pasteur developed the process of *pasteurization*, the heat treatment of foodstuffs such as wine, beer, and milk to prevent them from being spoiled by bacterial infection.

The French scientists Pierre and Marie Curie in their laboratory. Marie was born Marja Sklodowska in Warsaw, Poland, in 1867. She met her husband, a physics teacher, in Paris, and married him in 1895. Together they discovered the element radium, and shared the 1903 Nobel Prize for physics with Antoine Henri Becquerel.

1885 Britain establishes protectorates over southern Nigeria and Bechuanaland, south Africa.
German East Africa established.
Third Anglo-Burmese War (until 1886): Britain annexes Upper Burma.

1886 Irish Home Rule Bill, introduced by British Prime Minister William Gladstone, is defeated.
Gold discovered in South Africa.

1887 War between Italy and Ethiopia.

1888 William II, German Emperor (to 1918).

1889 Georges Boulanger, former French war minister, flees after plotting against Third Republic.
Treaty of Uccialli: Italy gains protectorate over Ethiopia.
Brazil becomes a republic.
Cecil Rhodes founds British South Africa Company.
Panama scandal: financial scandal in France caused by collapse of Panama Canal Company; de Lesseps and associates tried for corruption (1892–93); sentences set aside.

1890 German Chancellor Otto von Bismarck dismissed by William II.
Zanzibar Settlement: Britain receives Zanzibar, east Africa; Heligoland goes to Germany.

1893 Gladstone reintroduces Irish Home Rule Bill; defeated by House of Lords.
Independent Labour Party founded in Britain by socialist Keir Hardie.
General strike in Belgium.
French set up protectorate over Ivory Coast, west Africa.

1894 French officer Alfred Dreyfus convicted of treason and deported; becomes major political affair.
Nicholas II, last Tsar of Russia (until 1917).
War between China and Japan over Korea (until 1895).
In China, Sun Yat-sen founds first of several revolutionary societies.

1895 War between Italy and Ethiopia (until 1896).
Armenians massacred in Constantinople.
Revolutionary movement active in Cuba against Spain (to 1898).
Treaty of Shimonoseki; Japan gains Formosa; China recognizes Korea's independence.
Territory of South African Company named Rhodesia after Cecil Rhodes.
Jameson Raid: attack on Boer republic of Transvaal fails (1896).

1896 Anglo-Egyptian forces led by General Kitchener begin reconquest of Sudan.
Battle of Adua: Ethiopian victory.
Final Anglo-Ashanti War; Ashanti defeated.
Treaty of Addis Ababa: Italy recognizes independence of Ethiopia.

The Russo-Japanese War

War between Russia and Japan broke out on February 6, 1904, over their rival ambitions in Korea and Manchuria, where each country wanted to control trade. Although Russia was much larger than Japan it did not have nearly as many troops in the area. After a long siege the Japanese captured the Russian-held Chinese city of Port Arthur, and, following the battle of Mukden, drove the Russians back deep into Manchuria.

Meanwhile a Russian fleet was sent from the Baltic Sea round Africa and across the Indian Ocean. A Japanese fleet met it in the Tsushima Straits between Japan and Korea, and almost annihilated it.

President Theodore Roosevelt of the United States called a peace conference at Portsmouth, New Hampshire. A treaty signed there in September 1905 gave Japan a free hand in Korea and Manchuria. The Russians also had to hand over half of Sakhalin Island, which is just north of Japan.

When the British battleship HMS Dreadnought *was launched in 1906, her armour, speed, and guns made all other battleships obsolete.*

Below: The domineering Tz'u Hsi, Empress-Dowager of China, who was the power behind the throne in the last years of the Ch'ing Dynasty. She acted as regent for her son T'ung Chih, and after his death ruled for her nephew Kuang Hsü. She remained opposed to foreign influence in China until her death in 1908.

1904 Russia and Japan at war (until 1905).
Entente cordiale (friendly understanding) reached between Britain and France.
British explorer Sir Francis Younghusband leads expedition to Tibet; treaty opens Tibet to western trade.

1905 Moroccan crisis between France and Germany.
Union of Sweden and Norway ends. Prince Carl of Denmark, chosen by independent Norway, becomes King Haakon VII (to 1957).
Reforming Liberal government in Britain.
Port Arthur falls to Japan.
Battle of Mukden: Russian defeat; battle of Tsushima: Russian fleet destroyed by Japanese.
Treaty of Portsmouth ends Russo-Japanese war.
'Bloody Sunday': troops fire on workers in St Petersburg, Russia – several killed; general strike and revolution; October Manifesto issued by Tsar Nicholas II grants limited reforms.
Bengal partitioned, arousing strong nationalist feelings in India.

1906 First Labour MPs returned in British general election; Labour Party formed.
French officer Alfred Dreyfus declared innocent of treason on retrial.
Algeciras conference: international meeting to discuss Morocco: French rights recognized.
First Russian *Duma* (representative body) meets, but is dissolved.
Liberal revolution in Persia: Shah Nasir ud-Din grants constitution.
HMS *Dreadnought*, first modern battleship, launched in Britain.
Severe earthquake in San Francisco, USA.

1907 Second Hague Peace Conference: Germany opposes proposed arms limitation.
Second Duma dismissed in Russia; third, more conservative Duma lasts until 1912.
Entente cordiale between Russia and Britain.
Triple *entente* among Britain, France, Russia in opposition to Triple Alliance of Germany, Austria-Hungary, Italy.

1908 Belgium takes over Congo Free State; changes name to Belgian Congo.
Austria annexes Bosnia and Herzegovina.
Revolution in Turkey led by Young Turk movement.
Crete proclaims union with Greece.
Bulgaria declares independence from Turkey.
Successful counter-revolution in Persia, supported by Russia.

1909 Old age pensions introduced in Britain.
Sultan Abdul Hamid II of Turkey overthrown.

Left: This Japanese painting depicts the defeat of the Russian fleet by the Japanese in the Tsushima Straits in 1905.

Europe the Overlord

Right: King George V of England. His reign saw the change from Empire to Commonwealth.

Below: Suffragettes are led away by the police after demonstrating for women's right to vote outside Buckingham Palace in 1904.

The Titanic Disaster

The sinking of the British liner *Titanic* on the night of April 14–15, 1912, was one of the greatest shipping disasters ever. The 46,000-tonne liner was on her maiden voyage from Southampton to New York. She was the largest ship then afloat, and was reputed to be unsinkable. But shortly before midnight she struck an iceberg which ripped a 300-foot (90-m) hole in her side, flooding so many watertight compartments that she went down 2 hours 40 minutes later. Of her 2224 passengers and crew, 1513 were drowned in the icy water.

The *Titanic* did not have enough lifeboat space for everyone on board. As a result of the disaster new international safety rules for ships were drawn up.

Revolution in China

The Manchus, from Manchuria, ruled China from 1644 onwards. But by the early 1900s the Manchu rulers – the Ch'ing Dynasty – had become weak. China was defeated by Japan in 1895, and was increasingly dominated by European countries and the United States, which claimed trading rights. From 1905 revolutionary groups began plotting to overthrow the Manchus.

When the Emperor Kuang Hsü died in 1908 the throne went to his infant nephew P'u Yi. The regency was incompetent and in October 1911 troops near Hangkow mutinied. The revolt spread, and on December 30 the revolutionaries elected Sun Yat-sen as president of a republic. To unite the country, he soon resigned in favour of a veteran Manchu general, Yüan Shih-k'ai. Yüan's efforts to strengthen his own power brought conflict; in 1915 he proclaimed himself emperor, but he died the next year and the republic was restored.

1909 American manufacturer Henry Ford begins 'assembly line' production of cheap motor-cars.
Indian Councils Act: increases elected members on Indian councils.
American explorer Robert Peary reaches North Pole, after seven visits to the Arctic.

1910 George V, King of England (to 1936).
Revolution in Portugal; republic declared.
Union of South Africa becomes independent dominion within British Empire.
Japan annexes Korea.
British suffragette movement becomes increasingly militant.

1911 Parliament Act reduces power of House of Lords in Britain.
British MPs receive salaries for first time.
Agadir Crisis between France and Germany: Germany sends gunboat to Morocco, but withdraws claims.
Italy occupies Tripoli, Libya; war with Turkey.
Revolution in Mexico overthrows President Diaz; period of disorder follows.
Norwegian explorer Roald Amundsen reaches South Pole.
Sun Yat-sen leads revolution in China and overthrows Manchu Dynasty; republic formed (1912).

1912 French protectorate established in Morocco; Spanish zone defined by agreement.
Treaty of Ouchy ends Italo-Turkish war: Tripoli ceded to Italy.
Fourth Russian Duma (to 1916).
Miners' strike in Britain.
British liner *Titanic* sinks with loss of 1513 lives.
First Balkan War: Bulgaria, Greece, Serbia, and Montenegro unite against Turkey.

1913 Third Irish Home Rule Bill passes House of Commons; rejected by House of Lords. Threat of civil war in Ireland; Ulster Volunteers (private Protestant army) formed in opposition to proposed Home Rule Bill.
Young Turks establish dictatorship in Turkey.
Treaty of London ends First Balkan War; Balkan states victorious; new state of Albania created.
Greece officially takes over Crete.
Second Balkan War: Serbia, Greece, Romania, and Turkey unite against Bulgaria; war caused by Serbian claims to Macedonia.
Treaty of Bucharest ends Second Balkan War; Bulgaria defeated; Balkan states again partitioned.
Treaty of Constantinople between Turkey and Bulgaria.

The Modern World

THE OUTBREAK OF World War I in the summer of 1914 marked the end of an era. The stately pace of life in an age used to servants, leisured classes, and horse transport was overwhelmed by the frantic demands of war for men, materials, and machines. Relatively new inventions such as the radio, the aeroplane, and the car rapidly developed; women took over jobs from men who were fighting, and were soon to win recognition of their equal contribution in votes and job opportunities; and the old system of privilege in society broke down before the grisly equality of death in war, which between 1914 and 1918 claimed 40 million lives.

This crumbling of social structure, accompanied by technical advance in industry generally, was greatly accelerated by World War II, after which colonial countries all over the world sought and gained independence. Yet, because of speedy transport and communications, rich and poor countries alike are more than ever interlocked by international trade and finance, all affected by problems of trying to supply expanding populations with a good standard of living. The terrifying increase in the world's population by 76 million births a year in the 1970s has spurred on scientists in their search for more intensive means of food production, and for new power sources to supplement the Earth's dwindling supplies.

Below: Mahatma Gandhi (1869–1948) led a non-violent campaign to free India from British rule.

Above: Tsar Nicholas II of Russia with his family aboard the royal yacht before World War I. During the Revolution in 1917 the family were captured by the Bolsheviks and imprisoned at Ekaterinburg. It is assumed that they were murdered, but their exact fate is still in question.

EUROPE

1914	World War I (to 1918)
1916	Easter Rising in Ireland
1917	Russian Revolution
1918	Revolution in Germany
1919	League of Nations formed
1923	Italy becomes a Fascist state
1925	Locarno Pact
1926	General Strike in Britain
1933	Soviet Communist Party purged
1934	Adolf Hitler becomes *Führer* of Germany (to 1945)
1936	Abdication of Edward VIII
	Spanish Civil War (to 1939)
1938	Germany annexes Austria
	Munich Pact
1939	World War II (to 1945)
	Nazi-Soviet Pact
1940	The Battle of Britain
1941	Germany invades Russia
1944	Normandy Landings (D-Day)
1945	United Nations formed
1946	Nuremberg Trials
1948	North Atlantic Treaty Organization formed
	Soviet Blockade of West Berlin (to 1949)
1955	Warsaw Pact formed in opposition to NATO
1956	Soviet troops crush Hungarian uprising
1957	Treaty of Rome
1961	Berlin Wall built
1963	Nuclear Test Ban Treaty
1965	Fighting breaks out in Cyprus
1967	Military coup in Greece
1968	Soviet troops invade Czechoslovakia
	Crisis in Northern Ireland
1974	Military coup in Portugal
1975	Franco dies; Juan Carlos King of Spain
1980	President Tito of Yugoslavia dies

ASIA

1919	Nationalist movement formed in India
1920	Jewish state of Palestine established
1924	New government in China under Sun Yat-sen
1927	Civil War in China
1931	Japanese occupy Manchuria
1934	Mao Tse-tung's Long March (to 1935)
1935	India Act
1937	Japanese capture Shanghai and Peking
1940	Japan joins Axis
1944	Battle of Leyte Gulf
1945	Atomic bombs dropped on Hiroshima and Nagasaki in Japan
1946	Civil war in Indochina between nationalists and French
1947	Partition of Palestine
1948	War between Arab League and Israel
	Mahatma Gandhi assassinated
1949	Communist regime in China
1950	Korean War (to 1953)
1952	First national election in India
1954	French lose battle of Dien Bien Phu; Vietnam partitioned
	South East Asia Treaty Organization formed
1955	Fighting in Israel
1959	Uprising in Tibet
1965	India and Pakistan at war
	United States sends troops to Vietnam
1966	China's 'Cultural Revolution' (to 1968)
1970	United States invades Cambodia
1971	East Pakistan becomes independent as Bangladesh after civil war
1973	United States withdraws from Vietnam
	Oil crisis follows October War
1975	South Vietnam surrenders to North Vietnam; end of war
1979	Shah is expelled from Iran
	Russian forces move into Afghanistan

The desolation of total war is shown in this view of German positions on the Western Front during World War I. Far right: The changing positions on the Front.

World War I

World War I began after the assassination of Archduke Franz Ferdinand of Austria in June 1914 and ended on November 11, 1918 when an armistice was agreed.

Causes: One of the chief causes of the war was rivalry between groups of European powers over trade, colonies, and naval and military power. Countries formed defensive alliances, which meant an attack on one country automatically involved its allies. The two main alliances were the *Triple Entente* – Britain, France, Russia; and the *Triple Alliance* – Germany, Austria-Hungary, and Italy (which declared neutrality in August 1914).

After the assassination of Franz Ferdinand, Austria-Hungary attacked Serbia, which it blamed for the killing. Russia declared support for Serbia, whereupon Germany declared war on Russia and its ally France. To attack France Germany invaded Belgium, so Britain declared war on Germany in support of Belgium and France. Turkey and Bulgaria later joined Germany, while Japan, Italy, and the United States came to support Britain, France, and Russia (known as the Allies).

The Western Front lay between Germany and France. After initial German successes both sides constructed elaborate trench systems, comparatively easy to defend and difficult to attack. From then on most of the war on the Western Front was a series of costly battles in which millions of men died for the capture of only a few miles of ground. Even the invention of new weapons, particularly poison gas and tanks, failed to break the deadlock. In March 1918 the Germans made a last bid to reach Paris, but were so weakened by the effort that an Allied counter-attack finally broke the German defences.

The Eastern Front stretched 1100 miles (1900 km) from the Baltic to the Black Sea. The Russians made initial advances in Prussia and towards the Balkans, and then retreated, fighting stubbornly. The fighting exhausted Russia more than its enemies, and the Bolshevik government of 1917 was glad to arrange peace.

The Southern Front between Italy and Austria-Hungary lay mostly along the line of the river Isonzo, but in 1917 the Italians had to retreat to the river Piave.

The Middle East: In 1915 British, Australian, and New Zealand troops tried to capture the Dardanelles Strait, held by Turkey, so that reinforcements could be sent to Russia through its Black Sea ports. Bungling by the politicians and higher command caused this Gallipoli expedition to fail. British and Empire troops fought the Turks in Mesopotamia and Palestine, and captured these lands in 1918.

The War at Sea: Germany and Britain

Farthest German advance, Sept. 1914 ⸺
German offensive, Mar. to July 1918 ⸺
Front July 1916 ⸺
Front Nov. 11, 1918 ⸺

both had large battle fleets, but there was only one major battle – off Jutland in 1916. Neither side really won, but the German fleet stayed in harbour after the battle. Germany relied mainly on its huge submarine fleet, sinking merchant ships carrying vital food and war supplies. Britain was close to starvation in 1917 when a convoy system and depth charges brought the submarines under control.

The War in the Air : World War I was the first conflict using aeroplanes as weapons. Initially planes were used for reconnaissance and to support land attacks, but later large-scale bombing of targets behind the battle-lines was introduced. Germany used its Zeppelin airships for bombing, but they proved relatively easy to shoot down.

The Peace Treaties : Five separate peace treaties, known collectively as the Peace of Paris, were signed with the Central Powers (Germany and its allies). The Treaty of Versailles particularly heavily penalized Germany which lost one-seventh of its land and all its overseas territories. It was also made to pay huge sums of money as reparations. In practice Germany was so crippled by the war that it never did pay the vast sums demanded.

1914 June 28 Archduke Franz Ferdinand of Austria assassinated by a Bosnian student.
World War I (until 1918): major Allied Powers – Britain, France, Russia, Italy, United States; Central Powers – Germany, Austria-Hungary, Turkey.
July 28 Austria invades Serbia.
July to Nov. Declarations of war.
Aug. 4 Germans attack Belgium.
Aug. 26 Battle of Tannenburg: Russians defeated by German forces.
Sept. 5 Battle of the Marne, lasts until Sept. 9: Allies halt German advance on Paris.
Sept. 6 Battle of the Masurian Lakes: lasts until Sept. 15, Russians retreat from East Prussia.
Oct. 30 Battle of Ypres, ends Nov. 24: Germans fail to reach Channel ports.
Trench warfare on Western and Eastern Fronts, until end of World War I.
Irish Home Rule Act provides for separate Parliament in Ireland, with some MPs at Westminster. Position of Ulster (Northern Ireland) to be decided after the War.
Panama Canal opened.

1915 Jan. 5 Britain announces naval blockade of Germany.
Gallipoli Campaign (until Mar. 22, 1916): Allied forces land on Gallipoli Peninsula, Turkey, but fail to gain control of Dardanelles Straits.
Feb. 18 Germany begins submarine blockade of Britain.
Apr. 22 Second Battle of Ypres ends May 25: poison gas used for first time by Germans.
May 7 German U-boat sinks British liner *Lusitania*; many civilians including Americans drowned.
May 22 Italy joins Allied Powers.
Sept. Battles of Artois, Champagne, Loos: British and French offensive fails.
Oct. 15 Bulgaria joins Central Powers.
Swiss physicist Albert Einstein publishes his *General Theory of Relativity*.

1916 Feb. 21 Battle of Verdun: German offensive on Western Front February to July; appalling losses; stalemate continues.
Apr. 24 Easter rising in Ireland; suppressed after one week.
May 31 Battle of Jutland: only major naval battle between Britain and Germany.
June 4 Brusilov offensive: Russian attack led by General Alexei Brusilov fails.
July 1 Battle of the Somme: British offensive lasts until Nov. 18; more than one million killed; tanks used for first time by Britain.

The Russian Revolutions

Three revolutions shook Russia during the first years of the 20th century. The first took place in 1905 and was caused by Russia's defeat in the war with Japan. But by early in 1906 the troops of Tsar Nicholas II, the Russian ruler whose power was absolute, had crushed the revolt.

The other revolutions took place in 1917, and one was a consequence of the other. The so-called February Revolution began on March 8 with strikes, riots, and mutinies by the troops in Petrograd (now Leningrad), the capital. The unrest was sparked off by Russian defeats in World War I and bad government, which had led to food shortages. The Tsar abdicated, and a provisional government was formed, first under Prince Georgi Lvov and after a short time under Aleksandr Kerensky.

The new government was moderate in its views, but the Bolsheviks, a radical left-wing party, determined to seize power.

Above: Members of the Bolshevik party in the 1917 Russian revolution.

Their leader, Vladimir Ilyich Lenin, had been in exile in Switzerland, but the Germans allowed him to travel across Europe in a sealed train, hoping (rightly) he would gain power and take Russia out of the war.

The Bolsheviks in Petrograd, under Lenin's colleague Leon Trotsky, had already formed a workers' *Soviet* (council) to control the troops in the city. On the night of November 6 the so-called October Revolution began. Armed Bolshevik workers supported by troops arrested the provisional government, and seized power. The Bolsheviks had a minority in the newly elected Constituent Assembly, so they dispersed it. Soon the new government began to centralize control of land and food production, confiscate Church property, and rule more dictatorially than the Tsar. Lenin also made peace with Germany, and moved the capital from Petrograd to Moscow.

The deposed Tsar and his family, who had been under arrest since the revolution, were executed in 1918.

Trench warfare in World War I: Canadian troops resist an attack at Ypres in 1915. The horrors of this world-wide conflict shocked the world.

The Russian Calendar

The first Russian Revolution of 1917 is called the February Revolution although it happened in March, and the revolution in November 1917 is called the October Revolution, because the Russians were much later than the rest of Europe in adopting the Gregorian Calendar. By 1917, the Russian calendar was 13 days behind that of the rest of the world; the new regime brought it into line, but the old names for the uprisings still persisted.

The Easter Rebellion

For hundreds of years the people of Ireland protested at being ruled from London, and even after the Act of Union of 1801 campaigners demanded home rule. In 1914, after much opposition from the House of Lords at Westminster, a Home Rule Act was passed, but it was declared suspended for the duration of World War I. The Protestants in the north of Ireland opposed home rule because it would leave them in a minority in a Roman Catholic land.

Some of the Roman Catholics did not want to wait for the end of the war; they also wanted complete independence. In 1916 a group called the Irish Republican Brotherhood decided to start a rebellion at Easter. Another Irish patriot, Sir Roger Casement, had gone to Germany to ask for help. Casement landed in Ireland from a German submarine on Good Friday, April 21, and was at once arrested. Despite efforts by some Irish leaders to halt it, the rebellion began on Easter Monday, when armed volunteers seized the General Post Office in Dublin. The British Government quelled the revolt after eight days' fighting. Casement and 15 other rebel leaders were executed.

1917 Mar. 11 British capture Baghdad from Turkey. Revolution in Russia: Nicholas II abdicates; replaced by provisional government.
Apr. 6 United States declares war on Germany.
July 6 British soldier T. E. Lawrence ('Lawrence of Arabia') takes over command of Arab revolt against Turkey (until 1918).
July 31 Third battle of Ypres (Passchendaele): major British offensives on Western Front; initially successful but little gained after German counter-attack.
Oct. 24 Battle of Caporetto: Italians defeated.
Nov. 7 October Revolution: Bolsheviks led by Vladimir Lenin seize power in Russia.
Nov. 8 Balfour Declaration: Britain announces support for Jewish state in Palestine.
Dec. 9 British capture Jerusalem.

1918 Mar. 3 Treaty of Brest-Litovsk between Russia and Germany; Russia withdraws from war.
Women over 30 get vote in Britain.
July 15 Second battle of the Marne: last major German offensive fails on Aug. 2.
July (?) Tsar Nicholas II and family murdered.
Aug. 8 Allies' offensive on Western Front begins; Germans forced to retreat.
Oct. 24 Battle of Vittorio Veneto: Italian victory; Austria-Hungary surrenders.
Nov. 7 Revolution in Germany; William II abdicates; republic declared.
Nov. 11 Germany signs Armistice; World War I ends.
Russia adopts Gregorian calendar.

1919 Jan. Peace conference begins in Paris; founding of League of Nations.
June Treaty of Versailles signed by Germany; Germany to lose Alsace-Lorraine and colonies; also to pay *reparations* (compensation) to Allies.
Sept. Treaty of Saint-Germain signed by Austria; ends Habsburg monarchy; Austria to recognize independence of Czechoslovakia, Poland, Yugoslavia, and Hungary.
Rebellion in Ireland led by Irish nationalist movement, the *Sinn Fein* party.
Weimar Constitution adopted in Germany.
Spartacist (Communist) rising in Berlin crushed; socialist leader Rosa Luxembourg murdered.
Italian nationalist Gabriel d'Annunzio seizes Fiume from Yugoslavia.
Fascist movement founded in Italy by Benito Mussolini.
Indian leader Mohandas Gandhi (Mahatma) begins campaign of passive resistance to Britain. Amritsar massacre: British troops fire on nationalist rioters in India.

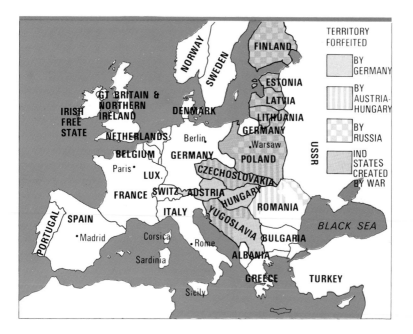

Above: The European powers redrew the map of Europe in the peace treaties which ended World War I. Newly independent countries included Finland, Estonia, Latvia, Lithuania, Poland, Czechoslovakia, and Hungary. Montenegro, Serbia, and part of Austria-Hungary became Yugoslavia. Many frontiers were redrawn, and some of the changes were to lead to new strife and ultimately to World War II.

Prohibition of all alcoholic liquor became law in the United States in 1920. But despite repressive acts like pumping wine into the Los Angeles gutters, below, the law was flouted, and gangsters such as Al Capone flourished because of the demand for illegal liquor. Prohibition ended in 1933. Capone was imprisoned – for income tax evasion!

The League of Nations

At the end of World War I, statesmen from many countries decided to form an international organization designed to keep the peace, and the League of Nations came into existence on January 10, 1920. One of the men most concerned to form it, President Woodrow Wilson of the United States, could not persuade his own country to join, so this weakened the League from the start. Eventually a number of countries withdrew, including Germany, Italy, and Japan.

The League of Nations settled some small disputes in its early years but lacked power to enforce its decisions; by the late 1930s few countries paid it much attention. The League was replaced in 1946 by the United Nations.

Growth of Aviation

The first international airline came into service on August 25, 1919, when a daily service between London and Paris was started. A few weeks before, the first non-stop flight across the Atlantic Ocean had been made by two Britons, Captain John Alcock and Lieutenant Arthur Whitten-Brown, taking just over 16 hours.

The 1920s and 1930s saw steady progress in aviation. The first round-the-world flight, taking 175 days, was made in 1924 by US Army planes. The American Charles Lindbergh made the first solo transatlantic flight in 1927, and the Australian Charles Kingsford Smith made the first transpacific flight a year later.

Americans began the first transatlantic airmail service in 1939, followed by a passenger service. The Germans had earlier operated a transatlantic passenger airship, but stopped it after their giant airship *Hindenburg* was destroyed by fire in 1937.

1920 Civil war in Ireland; situation aggravated by British auxiliaries, the 'Black and Tans'.
Northern Ireland accepts Home Rule Act.
Treaty of Rapallo between Italy and Yugoslavia.
Russia and Poland at war.
League of Nations meets for first time.
Prohibition in United States (until 1933).
Treaty of Sèvres between Allies and Turkey opposed by Turkish nationalists led by Mustafa Kemal (later Ataturk).
Palestine established as Jewish state under British administration.

1921 Irish Free State established; Irish Republican Army (IRA) continues opposition.
Greece attacks Turkey but is finally defeated (1922).
Turkish nationalist government set up at Ankara.
Treaty of Riga ends Russo-Polish war.
Mutiny of Russian sailors at Kronstadt, Finland, is put down.
Washington Conference (to 1922) held to discuss naval armaments: four-power Pacific Treaty among Britain, France, Japan, United States.

1922 Fascists march on Rome; King Victor Emmanuel III invites Benito Mussolini to be prime minister.
Egypt declared independent from British and French influence.
Pius XI, Pope (to 1939).
Union of Soviet Socialist Republics established.
Sultan of Turkey deposed by Mustafa Kemal.

1923 French and Belgian troops occupy Ruhr district, west Germany, after Germany fails to pay reparations.
Virtual dictatorship in Spain under Spanish General Primo de Rivera (until 1930).
Mussolini creates Fascist state in Italy.
Adolf Hitler, founder of the National Socialist (Nazi) Party in Germany, attempts to overthrow Bavarian government but is imprisoned.
Treaty of Lausanne between Greece and Turkey.
Turkey proclaimed a republic; first president, Mustafa Kemal.

1924 First Labour government in Britain.
Dawes Plan settles reparation payments to be made by Germany.
Italian socialist, Giocomo Matteotti, murdered by Fascists.
Death of Vladimir Lenin; Joseph Stalin succeeds him.
Chinese government set up at Canton under Sun Yat-sen; it includes Communist members.

Comedian Charlie Chaplin in the silent film
The Gold Rush *(1925)*.

The Great Depression

A great financial crisis swept the world in the early 1930s, causing appalling unemployment. It was triggered off in October 1929 by the New York stock market 'crash'. Speculators had been buying shares recklessly, forcing the prices up beyond their real value. A reaction set in: people suddenly began to sell their stock, and on 'Black Thursday', October 4, 13 million shares were sold in panic.

The effect of the selling was that many lost all their money, banks and businesses closed, and by the end of 1931 more than 12 million Americans were out of work. The panic spread to Europe; in Britain nearly three million people were jobless, and other countries suffered similarly. Drastic government intervention in the United States helped gradually to restore business confidence, and the world's economies were recovering by the late 1930s.

Statute of Westminster

After the loss in 1776 of the 13 colonies which formed the United States, Britain adopted the *dominion* system of giving its larger overseas territories almost complete independence. Any remaining British influence within the Dominions gradually waned, and at the Imperial Conference of 1926 – a meeting of ministers from Britain and all the Dominions – a report was adopted declaring that Britain and the Dominions were equal in status in every way, bound only by their recognition of the British sovereign as nominal head of state.

This declaration was given the force of law by the Statute of Westminster, 1931. This statute made official the name 'British Commonwealth of Nations', which had been replacing 'British Empire'.

Opposite: Kemal Atatürk (1881–1938) led the movement for reform in his country and was elected first president of the Turkish Republic in 1923.

Below: Fashionable society at the Lido, Venice, enjoying the bright, extravagant 1920s.

The Turkish Revolution

The Ottoman Empire, ruled by Turkey, was at its most powerful in the 1500s. From then it steadily declined, and in the 1800s was known as 'the sick man of Europe'. Sultan Abdul Hamid II became Turkey's ruler in 1876, and governed repressively.

Among groups formed to press for a more liberal government, the chief was the 'Young Turks' many of whose members lived in exile. In 1908 they led a revolt against Abdul Hamid, who gave way and promised to adopt reforms in line with a democratic constitution which had been planned in 1876 but suspended by the Sultan.

In 1909 Abdul Hamid attempted a counter-revolution, seeking to return to dictatorship. He was promptly deposed in favour of his weak brother, Muhammad V. Following Turkey's defeat in World War I, Mustafa Kemal, a successful general, led a new revolt, declared the sultanate abolished, and set up a republic in 1922. He was given the name 'Atatürk' – chief Turk.

1925 Locarno Conference: the great powers agree to put disputes to arbitration.
Arab uprising in Morocco led by Abd-el-Krim; crushed by France and Spain (1926).
1926 General strike in Britain.
Army in Portugal overthrows government.
Germany is admitted to League of Nations.
Canberra becomes the federal capital of Australia.
1927 Chiang Kai-shek, successor to Sun Yat-sen, purges Communists; sets up government at Nanking; civil war begins between Communists and Nationalists.
American pilot Charles Lindbergh makes first solo transatlantic flight.
1928 Kellog-Briand Pact signed in Paris; great powers denounce war.
Scottish scientist Alexander Fleming discovers penicillin.
1929 Young Plan reassesses German reparation payments; replaces Dawes Plan.
United States' stock market collapses, leading to worldwide economic depression.
First major conflict between Jews and Arabs in Palestine.
American explorer Richard Byrd flies over South Pole.
1930 London naval conference: great powers fail to agree on naval limitations.
Treaty of Ankara between Greece and Turkey.
1931 Statute of Westminster clarifies status of Britain and the dominions.
Britain abandons the gold standard.
King Alfonso XIII of Spain flees the country; republic is proclaimed.
Japanese occupy Manchuria; set up puppet state Manchukuo (1932).
1932 Disarmament conference meets at Geneva but achieves nothing.
Imperial conference at Ottawa; Britain gives limited trading preference to Commonwealth.
Portuguese finance minister, Antonio de Oliveira Salazar, becomes dictator of Portugal.
War between Paraguay and Bolivia (until 1935) over the Chaco region.
1933 Adolf Hitler is appointed chancellor by German President Paul von Hindenburg.
Burning of German *Reichstag* (parliament).
International economic conference in London.
Germany withdraws from League of Nations.
National Socialists begin to eliminate all opposition and gain control of Germany.
Communist Party in USSR purged by Stalin.
Anarchist uprisings in Barcelona put down by Spanish Government.
Prohibition ends in United States.

Weimar and Hitler

Germany became a republic in 1919 after the abdication of Kaiser William II and the country's defeat in World War I. The new constitution of the country was drawn up by a national assembly which met at Weimar, a town well away from the capital, Berlin, where there was a danger of intimidation by mobs. For this reason the regime is often called the Weimar Republic.

The first president was a socialist, Friedrich Ebert. When he died in 1925 he was succeeded by Field-Marshal Paul von Hindenburg, who had been Germany's supreme commander during World War I. But Hindenburg's great reputation was largely spurious, and at 78 he was showing signs of senility.

By the time of the presidential elections in 1932 the country was in an economic crisis; the mark was valueless and six million people were unemployed. Hindenburg was re-elected with Adolf Hitler, leader of the National Socialist (*Nazi*) party, as runner-up. Hindenburg, an officer and an aristocrat, despised Hitler, a corporal and a draughtsman.

In the elections of 1932 the Nazi Party secured the largest number of seats in the *Reichstag* (parliament), though not a majority, and Hindenburg was forced to appoint Hitler as Chancellor (prime minister) leading a coalition government. Hitler took office on January 30, 1933. By March 23 he had forced through a bill giving his government absolute powers.

The Nazis quickly tightened their grip on Germany. The Nazi Party was declared the only political party, the power of the German states was curbed, persecution of the Jews began, strikes and lock-outs were forbidden, and concentration camps were set up. In October, Germany withdrew from the League of Nations and disarmament conference.

Adolf Hitler, dictator of Nazi Germany from 1933 to 1945, shown at a mass rally of the Nazi party. His magnetic personality and ruthlessness gave him supreme power, and his ambitions to establish a mighty German Reich (kingdom) to last a thousand years led to World War II.

The *Anschluss*

Many people in Austria and Germany wanted the two countries to unite after World War I. The union was opposed by France and other countries which feared it would make Germany too powerful. German agitation for union – known as *Anschluss* – grew after Adolf Hitler and the Nazi Party came to power in 1933.

An attempted Nazi coup in Austria in 1934 failed, but in 1938 Hitler faced the Austrian chancellor, Kurt von Schuschnigg, with new demands. Schuschnigg wanted a vote on independence, but threatened by Nazi chaos in Austria and German troops on the border, he resigned in favour of the Austrian Nazi leader, Arthur Seyss-Inquart. Seyss-Inquart invited German troops into Austria next day.

The Abyssinian Campaign

In the carve-up of Africa among European countries during the 1800s Italy gained only Eritrea and Italian Somaliland. In 1912 it conquered Libya from the Turks, and had an undefined right to a 'sphere of influence' in Ethiopia (often called Abyssinia). This interest in Ethiopia was not enough for Italy's Fascist dictator, Benito Mussolini.

In 1934 a border clash between Ethiopia and Italian Somaliland gave the Italians a pretext for war. The League of Nations ordered sanctions against Italy but member countries could not agree on how to apply them. In October 1935 Italian troops invaded the country. With the aid of air power and poison gas they conquered the country in seven months and annexed it. It was retaken from Italy in World War II.

The Spanish Civil War

In February 1936 a left-wing Republican government was voted into power in Spain. Supported by socialists and Communists, it opposed the power of the Roman Catholic Church, always dominant in Spanish affairs. The Catholics were supported by right-wing parties and the army.

On July 17, 1936, army leaders in Morocco began a rebellion, which quickly spread to the Spanish mainland. A senior officer, General Francisco Franco, became the leader of the rebels, and was declared 'Chief of State' in October. Bitter civil war followed. The Republicans (also called Loyalists) burned churches, and killed priests and religious people. The rebel Nationalists (also called Falangists or Insurgents) held mass executions.

Intervention by other countries followed appeals for help by both sides. Germany and Italy supported Franco, and used the opportunity to test weapons and men in the field. For this reason, the war is often called the 'opening battle of World War II'. The Republicans were helped by an international brigade of volunteers from 50 countries. After fierce fighting the rebels captured Madrid in March 1939, by which time more than 600,000 people had been killed.

1934 Austrian chancellor Dollfuss killed by Nazis. President Hindenburg dies; Hitler becomes *Führer* (leader) of Germany.
Balkan Pact formed among Turkey, Greece, Romania, and Yugoslavia.
Mao Tse-tung leads Chinese Communists northwards on the Long March from Kiangsi; reach Yenan in 1935.

1935 Hitler renounces Treaty of Versailles; announces policy of rearmament.
Italian forces invade Ethiopia (Abyssinia); League of Nations fails to intervene effectively.
Nuremberg Laws; persecution of Jews begins in Germany.
Monarchy restored in Greece.
Persia officially called Iran.
Government of India Act passed by British Parliament; sets up provincial councils.

1936 Edward VIII, King of England; abdicates after 325 days.
George VI, King of England (to 1952).
Italians take Addis Ababa; annex Ethiopia.
Germany reoccupies Rhineland.
July 17 Military revolt led by General Francisco Franco against Spanish government begins Spanish Civil War (lasts until July 1939); Italy and Germany support rebels; Soviet Union sends aid to Republicans.
Oct. 25 Agreement between Italy and Germany: Rome-Berlin Axis set up.

1937 Apr. 26 German planes bomb Guernica, Spain.
May 28 Coalition government formed in Britain under Neville Chamberlain.
July 7 Japanese invade China; capture Shanghai and Peking.
Sept. Britain adopts policy of appeasement.

1938 Mar. 13 Germany invades and annexes Austria.
Sept. 29 Munich Pact signed by Hitler, Mussolini, Chamberlain, and French premier, Edouard Daladier; Germany to gain Sudetenland in Czechoslovakia.

1939 Jan. 26 Nationalists under General Franco capture Barcelona.
Mar. 10 Germany annexes Czechoslovakia.
Apr. 1 Madrid surrenders; ends Spanish Civil War.
Apr. 7 Italy invades Albania.
Sept. 1 Germany invades Poland; beginning of World War II (until 1945).
Sept. 3 Britain and France declare war on Germany.
Sept. 17 Russia invades Poland
Sept. 29 Nazi-Soviet pact: Poland partitioned between Russia and Germany.
Russo-Finnish war: Finland defeated Nov. 1940.

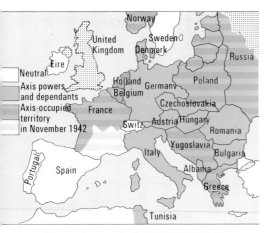

War on the map: the Axis powers and their dependants, and the greatest extent to which Germany overran Europe in 1942.

The Munich Agreement

The Peace of Paris in 1919 created the new country of Czechoslovakia, consisting mainly of Slav-speaking people. But it also included the Sudetenland (bordering Germany in the north-west), whose people mostly spoke German. In 1938 the Nazi government of Germany under Adolf Hitler demanded that the Sudetenland should be German territory, and threatened war. He was supported by Italy's dictator Mussolini.

The Czechs asked for help from Britain and France. Afraid of Germany's threats, the governments of these two countries began negotiations with Germany. The talks ended with an agreement signed at Munich, Germany, in September 1938 by Hitler, Mussolini, and the prime ministers of Britain and France, Neville Chamberlain and Edouard Daladier. It forced Czechoslovakia to give up the Sudetenland in return for a 'guarantee' from Britain and France to uphold the new Czechoslovakian frontiers. The Czechs were not invited to the talks. The Germans occupied the rest of Czechoslovakia unhindered six months later.

World War II

World War II began with the German invasion of Poland on September 1, 1939, and ended with the surrender of Japan on September 2, 1945. The human cost has been estimated at around 50 million dead and 34 million wounded.

Causes: The main cause of the war was the desire of the so-called Axis powers – the three dictatorships of Germany, Italy, and Japan – for more territory. Frontier and economic problems created by severe peace treaties after World War I had added friction and unrest.

The Blitzkrieg Period: Germany began by invading Poland. Britain and France declared war but little happened; Russia invaded Poland to protect its own frontier. Germany occupied Denmark and Norway in April 1940, and in May began its *Blitzkrieg* (lightning war), overrunning Belgium, the Netherlands, and France, against Allied troops, in seven weeks. British forces were evacuated and Germany controlled Europe. Britain survived an air war and bombing blitz, discouraging Hitler's invasion plan. Italy declared war on Britain and France.

The Eastern Front: In the summer of 1941 the Germans attacked Yugoslavia, Greece, and Russia, sweeping forward almost to Moscow. The Russians, aided by their bitter winter weather, put up a stubborn resistance as they retreated. In the summer of 1942 the Germans made further advances, but were halted by the resolute defence of Stalingrad (now Volgograd) in the south, and by the cold of winter. Early in 1943 the German army besieging Stalingrad was destroyed, and a year later the siege of Leningrad was raised.

North Africa: Italian forces in Libya tried to invade Egypt and were thrown back. The Desert War, as it was called, turned on the British victory at El Alamein, in Egypt, in 1942 which started a final retreat by the Italians and German allies.

The Pacific War began without warning on December 7, 1941, when Japanese planes bombed the American naval base at Pearl Harbor, Hawaii. Within five months the Japanese had overrun Burma, Hong Kong, Malaya, the Dutch East Indies, Thailand, and the Philippines, invaded New Guinea and were threatening Australia. But Japanese aggression brought the United States into the war against all the Axis powers.

Invasions: British and American troops invaded French North Africa, then in Axis hands, in November 1942, and by May 1943 had complete control. From Africa the Allies invaded Sicily and mainland Italy, 'the soft underbelly of Europe'. The Italians rejected their Fascist dictator, Benito Mussolini, and joined the Allies; the Germans put up a strong defence in central and northern Italy.

A mushroom cloud rises from the site of an atomic explosion. The atom bomb destroyed Hiroshima and Nagasaki and ended World War II.

1940 Apr. 9 Germany invades Denmark and Norway; on May 10 invades Belgium, the Netherlands, and Luxemburg.
Apr. 30 Japan joins Axis Powers.
May 17 Germany invades France.
May 27 British army evacuated from Dunkirk, in France.
June 10 Italy declares war on Britain and France.
June 14 Germans occupy Paris, France surrenders.
July 10 Battle of Britain: British air victory prevents German invasion (to Oct. 31).
Oct. 28 Italy invades Greece.

1941 June 22 Germany invades Russia.
Sept. 1 Italy and Germany invade Egypt.
Leningrad besieged by German forces; relieved Jan 1944.
Dec. Russian counter-offensive in Ukraine.
Dec. 7 Japan launches air attack on United States' Pacific Fleet in Pearl Harbor, Hawaii.
Dec. 8 United States declares war on Axis.

1942 Jan. Japan captures Manila, Singapore, Rangoon, Mandalay, and the Philippines.
Sept. 6 Battle of Stalingrad: Germans defeated.
Oct. 23 Battle of El Alamein: Germans under General Rommel defeated by Allies in Egypt.
Germans retreat from North Africa; Anglo-American forces take Tripoli and Tunis; end of Axis resistance in North Africa (May 1943).

1943 Jan. 31 German forces at Stalingrad surrender.
July 1 United States begins recapture of Japanese-held islands in the Pacific.
Sept. 3 Italian government surrenders.

1944 June 4 Allies enter Rome.
June 6 Allies land in Normandy, northern France; German forces begin retreat.
July 20 Bomb plot to assassinate Hitler fails.
Sept. 2 Allies liberate Paris and Brussels.
Sept. 8 First V-2 missile lands on England.
Oct. 3 Warsaw resistance crushed by Germans.
Oct. 25 Battle of Leyte Gulf: Japanese navy defeated.

1945 Jan. 17 Warsaw captured by Russians.
Feb. 7 Yalta Conference: meeting of Churchill, Roosevelt, and Stalin to discuss post-war settlements. Mar. 7 Allies invade Germany: Dresden bombed.
Apr. 28 Mussolini assassinated by Italian partisans.
Apr. 30 Adolf Hitler commits suicide.
May 7 Germany surrenders.
San Francisco conference: United Nations charter signed.
First atomic bombs used against Japan; Hiroshima and Nagasaki devastated.
Japan surrenders; World War II ends.

In June 1944 a huge Allied force landed in Normandy, in northern France, from Britain. The Allies liberated Paris in August, and drove the Germans back across the river Rhine early in 1945. At the same time the Russians mounted a new offensive and by the end of 1944 had conquered four countries which supported Germany – Bulgaria, Finland, Hungary, and Romania.

Russian and American troops met on the river Elbe in the heart of Germany in April 1945. Defeated, the German leader Adolf Hitler committed suicide in Berlin on April 30; seven days later the last German forces surrendered.

The Defeat of Japan: Japanese conquest was halted in May and June, 1942, when American fleets defeated Japanese naval forces in the battles of the Coral Sea and Midway, in the Pacific Ocean. A few months later American forces began the slow task of recapturing the scattered Pacific islands which the Japanese held. In a series of bitter battles the Americans captured the Gilbert, Marshall, Caroline, and Mariana islands.

From the Marianas they were able to bomb Japan. In September 1944 they began the invasion of the Philippines. Meanwhile British troops began the reconquest of Burma, while Allied troops fought their way through to China which had been at war with Japan since 1937.

Allied strategy was to invade Japan itself late in 1945. But the development of the atomic bomb, one of the best-kept secrets of the war, made this unnecessary. On August 6, 1945, the first atomic bomb was dropped on the Japanese city of Hiroshima, devastating it. Three days later another bomb wrecked the city of Nagasaki. Faced with this appalling weapon, the Japanese surrendered on August 14.

Results: The countries conquered by Germany and Japan all regained their former status after the war. But Russia increased its influence in Europe, and Communist regimes were established in Poland, Romania, Bulgaria, Hungary, Czechoslovakia, Yugoslavia, and the eastern part of Germany; Berlin stayed under joint control.

War in the desert: Allied tanks and infantry advance through the dust and smoke at the battle of El Alamein in 1942, a turning point in the war.

War in the air: an American B-17 Flying Fortress drops a stick of bombs on Budapest on October 10, 1944 during a strategic raid.

The 1945 Yalta Conference of the 'Big Three'.

The 'Big Three'

Three outstanding statesmen led Britain, the United States, and the Soviet Union for much of World War II.

Winston S. Churchill (1874–1965), soldier, statesman, and author, became Britain's Prime Minister during the darkest days of war in 1940. Defeated in the 1945 elections he held office again from 1951 to 1955. In 1953 he was knighted, and won the Nobel Prize for literature.

Franklin D. Roosevelt (1884–1945), was elected President of the United States in 1932 during the Depression, and re-elected in 1936, 1940, and 1944. His 'New Deal' helped restore his country's economy. He died in office, and was succeeded by Harry S. Truman.

Joseph Stalin (1879–1953) was born Joseph Dzhugashvili, and took the name 'Stalin' (Steel) when he became a Communist revolutionary. He succeeded Vladimir Ilyich Lenin as Soviet Union leader in 1924, and ruthlessly purged all rivals.

1945 Potsdam conference: main Allied powers meet to discuss peace terms and post-war settlements.

1946 League of Nations formally ended.
Norwegian statesman, Trygve Lie, elected secretary-general of United Nations.
Peace conference opens in Paris.
Nuremberg trials: Nazi leaders sentenced for war crimes by international court.
Republic of Hungary proclaimed.
Transjordan (Jordan) gains independence.
Britain and United States agree on economic fusion of British and American zones in Germany.
Civil war in Indochina (until 1954) between Vietnamese nationalists led by Ho Chi Minh, and the French.

1947 Allied peace treaties signed in Paris with Italy, Romania, Hungary, Bulgaria, and Finland.
Four-power conference of foreign ministers on Germany fails to reach agreement.
Marshall Aid: programme of aid for Europe introduced by United States' Secretary of State George Marshall.
Cominform (Communist Information Bureau) is set up with headquarters at Belgrade, Yugoslavia.
Cheribon Agreement between Dutch and Indonesians; United States of Indonesia established.
India gains independence; two dominions created – India (Hindu) and Pakistan (Muslim). Dispute between India and Pakistan over Kashmir; state ceded to India.
Burma gains independence.
Partition of Palestine into Arab and Jewish states agreed by United Nations; Arabs reject proposals.

1948 Communist *coup* (takeover) in Czechoslovakia; People's Republic formed.
State of Israel declared.
War between Israel and Arab League (until 1949).
Indian statesman Mahatma Gandhi assassinated by Hindu extremist.
Soviet Union blockades West Berlin; zone supplied by airlift (until 1949).
Ceylon becomes a self-governing dominion.
China split by conflict between Communists and Nationalists.
Division of Korea into Republic of Korea (South Korea) and People's Republic (North Korea).

1949 South African government adopts *apartheid* (separation of black and white) as official policy.

The United Nations

The United Nations came into being in 1942 during World War II as an alliance of countries fighting against Germany. The leaders of the four great powers on the Allied side, Britain, China, the Soviet Union, and the United States, agreed to establish a new international body as soon as possible.

On April 25, 1945 the four powers called a conference at San Francisco at which the United Nations Organization was formally set up. Fifty-one countries signed the charter on June 26, 1945, and the new body came into operation on October 24. It took over the remaining functions of the League of Nations, which was dissolved in 1946.

Partition of India

Independence movements in India began in the 1860s, almost from the moment when the British government took control of the country from the British East India Company. From the 1890s onwards Britain began to give Indians more power in local government, but the progress to self-rule was not fast enough to suit most Indians.

A further complication was that India contained two major religious communities, one Hindu, the other Muslim. The Muslims were in a minority and would not agree to a form of government which put them under Hindu rule. They demanded partition. In 1946 Britain offered independence to the whole of India, but its leaders could not agree on a form of government, and riots broke out; on consideration the British agreed to partition.

On August 14, 1947, the Muslim parts of India, lying to the east and west, became the independent country of Pakistan. The following day, the Hindu lands became independent as India. Mass migrations of Muslims and Hindus between India and Pakistan were accompanied by massacres.

The Birth of Israel

The establishment of a Jewish national home in Palestine was the result of a British government decision made in 1917. Britain ruled the country under mandate from the League of Nations, but had to curb Jewish immigration under pressure from Arabs in the country. Finally, the British asked the United Nations to make a decision on Palestine's future. The UN decided in 1947 to divide it into two states, one Jewish and one Arab, with Jerusalem as an international city. The Jews agreed, but the Arabs did not.

On May 14, 1948 the British mandate came to an end, and the Jews proclaimed the state of Israel. The same day Arab armies from Egypt, Lebanon, Syria, and Transjordan (now Jordan) attacked Israel. It beat off the invaders, and occupied lands allocated to the Arabs. The United Nations negotiated a cease-fire, and armistice agreements were signed early in 1949.

Communist China

From the 1920s onward, China was torn by sporadic civil war between the Nationalists, led by Chiang Kai-shek, and the Communists, led by Mao Tse-tung. They united to fight Japanese invasion in 1937, but civil war broke out again in 1946.

The Nationalists were ineffective and torn by internal rivalries. They quickly lost popular support, and the Communists won a long series of victories. In 1949 the last Nationalist strongholds were captured, and Chiang Kai-shek with many followers fled to the island of Formosa (Taiwan), where he led his Nationalist regime. The Communists set up a government for mainland China, with its capital at Peking.

Some countries, particularly the United States, did not recognize the Communist regime for many years, and the Nationalist government held China's seat at the United Nations until 1971.

Mao Tse-tung (1893–1976), chairman of China's Communist party, united his country in 1949 and became a hero to his people. Below: An observer of the UN peace-keeping force near the Suez Canal. Egypt.

1949 North Atlantic Treaty Organization (NATO) formed as defensive alliance by Western nations.

Mao Tse-tung establishes Communist regime in China; Chinese Nationalist government escapes to Formosa (Taiwan).

Germany is divided into Federal Republic (West) and German Democratic Republic (East).

Comecon (Council for Mutual Economic Assistance) founded by Soviet Union and Communist states.

France recognizes independent Vietnam and Cambodia.

Russian blockade of Berlin ends.

Arab-Israeli armistice: Jerusalem partitioned.

Russia recognizes newly established People's Republic of China.

1950 Korean war (until 1953) between North Korea supported by China, and South Korea supported by United Nations forces.

Anglo-Egyptian dispute over the Sudan and Suez Canal.

American senator Joseph McCarthy heads inquiry into 'un-American (Communist) activities'.

Agreement between East Germany and Poland fixes Oder and Neisse Rivers as frontier.

1951 West Germany admitted to the Council of Europe.

Egypt withdraws from Anglo-Egyptian agreement on Suez Canal; British troops occupy Canal Zone.

Schuman Plan: France, West Germany, Italy, Belgium, Netherlands, and Luxemburg agree to set up market for coal and steel; becomes effective 1952.

Marshall Plan ends.

Peace treaty signed at San Francisco by Japan, and most of Japan's opponents during World War II.

Chinese Communist forces occupy Tibet.

Colombo plan for economic development of south and south-east Asia comes into effect.

1952 Elizabeth II, Queen of Britain.

Bonn Convention: agreement among Britain, France, United States,. and West Germany ends occupation of West Germany.

Greece and Turkey join NATO.

European Coal and Steel Community holds first meeting at Luxemburg.

China accuses United States of waging germ warfare in Korea.

Mau Mau (secret organization of Kikuyu tribesmen) begins terrorist activities against British in Kenya.

Above: Hillary and Tensing, first to climb the world's highest peak, Mount Everest, in 1953.

The Korean War

At the end of World War II, Russian forces occupied northern Korea and United States troops occupied the southern part of the country. As a result of the influences of the occupying powers, Korea split into two countries, North Korea (Communist) and South Korea (non-Communist) in 1949.

The Korean War broke out on June 25, 1950, when North Korean troops invaded South Korea in a bid to unite the country. The United Nations called on its members to help South Korea. Seventeen nations sent troops, the bulk of them coming from the United States. UN forces arrived only just in time to prevent a complete Communist victory. In a brilliant counter-attack the United Nations and South Korean armies hurled the North Koreans back, invaded North Korea, and by November 24 had at one point reached the Yalu River, the frontier between North Korea and China.

At this point the Chinese sent a huge army into Korea, and drove the UN forces back into South Korea once more. Again the UN armies counter-attacked, and finally a battle line close to the frontier between North and South Korea was established in July 1951. At Russia's suggestion truce talks began almost at once. They dragged on for two years, to the accompaniment of sporadic heavy fighting. Peace was finally restored in July 1953, with the frontier where it had been before the war. Total military casualties were about two and a half million killed and wounded, with about three and a half million civilian deaths.

American troops await an attack in Korea; United Nations-US intervention in 1950 made this one of the first crisis areas in the Cold War period.

French soldiers during the battle of Dien Bien Phu in Vietnam in 1954

The Indochina War

The French gained control of the area known as Indochina – now Cambodia, Laos, and Vietnam – in the 1800s, and continued to rule it until World War II. Japanese invaders then took over. Vietnam proclaimed its independence in 1945, and the French resumed control in 1946, while recognizing Vietnam as a separate state within the French union. In December 1946 Hanoi was attacked by the Communist Viet Minh League under Ho Chi Minh.

The scope of the conflict soon broadened as the League attacked French garrisons. The war dragged on slowly until a Communist government took over in China in 1949, and at once gave massive support to Ho Chi Minh. The climax of the war was the 54-day siege of the French fortress of Dien Bien Phu in north-western Vietnam, in 1954, which the Viet Minh captured. The French finally agreed to withdraw, and Vietnam was partitioned. Civil war continued with American troops supporting South Vietnam until withdrawal in 1973. In 1975 the Communists overran and unified the country.

1952 First national election in India; Jawaharlal Nehru elected prime minister.
1953 New Zealand mountaineer Edmund Hillary and Sherpa Tenzing first to climb highest mountain in the world, Mount Everest in the Himalayas.
Swedish statesman Dag Hammarskjöld replaces Trygve Lie as secretary-general of United Nations.
Stalin dies; Georgi Malenkov becomes Soviet premier.
Bermuda conference of British, American, and French statesmen.
Treaty of Panmunjon ends Korean War.
Military *coup* in Egypt, monarchy ends; republic established.
French forces occupy Dien Bien Phu, North Vietnam; Viet Minh forces invade Laos.
Kenyan politician Jomo Kenyatta imprisoned on charges of Mau Mau involvement.
Yugoslav Communist leader Marshal Tito becomes president of Yugoslavia.
1954 Disturbances in Cyprus and Greece over *enosis* (union of Cyprus and Greece).
French finally defeated by Viet Minh at Dien Bien Phu, North Vietnam.
Geneva conference: Vietnam divided; North Vietnam under Communist government of Ho Chi Minh, South Vietnam supported by Britain and United States; beginning of Communist attempts to take over country.
South-East Asia Treaty Organization (SEATO) formed to prevent spread of Communism in south-east Asia.
1955 Warsaw Pact: eastern European defence treaty signed by Communist nations.
EOKA, Greek Cypriot organization led by Grivas, begins terrorist activities in Cyprus.
Israel raids Egyptian and Syrian borders.
Baghdad Pact signed by Turkey, Iraq, Iran, Pakistan, and Britain.
Bandung Conference: first major meeting of 29 Asian and African nations.
West Germany admitted to NATO.
International conference at Geneva discusses peaceful uses of atomic energy.
Armed rebellion and general strike in Argentina: President Juan Peron goes into exile
1956 Soviet Premier Nikita Khrushchev denounces former premier Joseph Stalin.
Anti-Russian uprising in Hungary crushed by Soviet troops.
Britain withdraws troops from Suez Canal Zone; Colonel Gamal Abdul Nasser elected president of Egypt.
Nasser nationalizes Suez Canal; Israeli forces

The Modern World

African Independence

The scramble for colonies among European powers in the late 1800s led to outside control of Africa. At the start of World War II, only three African countries were independent: Liberia, Egypt, and South Africa. After the war, Africans in all countries demanded self-rule.

Ethiopia, conquered by Italy in 1936, regained its freedom during the war. Libya, an Italian colony, was made independent in 1951 by the United Nations. Then, in the 1950s, in ones and twos, some British and French possessions were given independence – Tunisia, Morocco, Ghana, and Guinea – to be followed by many other colonies in the 1960s – 17 in 1960 alone.

The last colonies to gain independence were those of France, Spain and Portugal in the 1970s. The white rulers of one self-governing British colony, Rhodesia, refused to share power with the black population. In 1965 they declared independence unilaterally. After a great deal of international negotiation and a long guerrilla war, a general election was held in 1980 and a black government took office. Rhodesia became truly independent as Zimbabwe in April 1980.

MAURITANIA — MOROCCO
Tunisia
ALGERIA — LIBYA
Western Sahara
EGYPT
MALI
NIGER
CHAD — SUDAN
SOMALI DEM. REP.
NIGERIA
Central African Rep
ETHIOPIA
Cameroon
GABON — Congo
ZAIRE — Uganda — KENYA
TANZANIA
INDEPENDENT IN 1950
INDEPENDENT AFTER 1950
ANGOLA — ZAMBIA — MOZAMBIQUE
NAMIBIA
Madagascar Rep
REP OF SOUTH AFRICA — ZIMBABWE
BOTSWANA

7 Ivory Co
8 Upper V
9 Ghana
10 Togo
11 Benin
12 Equato Guin
13 Rwand
14 Burund
15 Malaw
16 Lesoth
17 Swazi

1 Senegal
2 Gambia
3 Guinea-Bissau
4 Guinea
5 Sierra Leone
6 Liberia

Below left: General de Gaulle of France and Emperor Haile Selassie of Ethiopia both played very important roles in the move towards African independence.

The Suez Crisis

The Suez Canal in Egypt was constructed by a French company and opened in 1869. The Egyptian government held shares in the company, but sold them to Britain in 1875. Under agreement with Egypt, British soldiers guarded the Canal Zone until withdrawn in June 1956. In July, because Britain refused financial help to Egypt for building the Aswan High Dam, President Gamal Abdul Nasser nationalized the canal.

Britain and France tried to get international control of the canal restored. In October 1956 Israel, following a long series of border incidents, attacked Egypt; Britain and France told Israel and Egypt to stop fighting, or face intervention. Israel agreed, Egypt refused. Britain and France then launched an air and sea attack on Egypt, which was called off under pressure mainly from the United States. A United Nations force took over control of the Canal Zone.

The Common Markets

Six common markets, groups of countries banded together for trade and economic co-operation, were formed during the 1950s and 1960s.

The European Economic Community (*EEC*) was formed by the Treaty of Rome in 1957; it consisted of six countries, Belgium, France, West Germany, Italy, Luxemburg, and the Netherlands. In 1973 Britain, Denmark, and Ireland joined them. Greece joins the EEC in 1981. Spain and Portugal have applied for membership, and may join in 1983.

Comecon (Council for Mutual Economic Assistance) was formed in 1949 by the Soviet Union and six other Communist countries – Albania, Bulgaria, Czechoslovakia, Hungary, Poland, and Romania. Albania later left; East Germany, Mongolia, and Cuba joined.

LAFTA (Latin American Free Trade Association) was founded by the Treaty of Montevideo in 1961. It consists of ten Latin-American countries: Argentina, Brazil, Chile, Colombia, Ecuador, Mexico, Paraguay, Peru, Uruguay, and Venezuela.

Arab Common Market, consisting of Egypt, Iraq, Jordan, and Syria, was formed in 1965.

Central American Common Market – Costa Rica, El Salvador, Guatemala, Honduras, and Nicaragua – was formed in 1960.

European Free Trade Association (*EFTA*) was formed in 1960 by Austria, Britain, Denmark, Norway, Portugal, Sweden, and Switzerland. Britain and Denmark left in 1973 to join the European Economic Community; Iceland joined in 1970. Finland is an associate member.

1956 invade Egypt; Anglo-French forces occupy Suez Canal zone; United Nations calls for cease-fire and sends in emergency forces to enforce it.
France recognizes independence of Morocco and Tunisia.

1957 Guerrilla activity in Cuba begins under leadership of Fidel Castro against dictatorship of Fulgencio Batista.
Treaty of Rome signed by Belgium, France, West Germany, Italy, Luxemburg, Netherlands establishes European Economic Community (the 'Common Market').
Suez Canal re-opened to all shipping.
Soviet Union launches *Sputnik I*, first artificial satellite.

1958 Egypt and Syria form United Arab Republic (UAR); Yemen joins to form United Arab States.
Military revolt in Iraq led by Abdul Kassem; King Faisal II assassinated; republic declared.
United States launches *Explorer I*, its first satellite; space race begins.
Charles de Gaulle elected first president of French Fifth Republic.
Pope John XXIII (to 1963).

1959 Batista government in Cuba overthrown; Communist guerilla leader Fidel Castro becomes premier.
Uprising in Tibet against Chinese rule; Dalai Lama escapes to India; revolt crushed.
Anti-European riots in Léopoldville, capital of Belgian Congo.

1960 Seventeen colonies in Africa gain independence.
In newly independent Congo (Léopoldville) civil war breaks out as Katanga province, under Moise Tshombe, breaks away.
European Free Trade Association (EFTA) and Central American Common Market formed.
United States' reconnaissance aircraft shot down over Soviet territory.
Cyprus becomes independent republic under President Archbishop Makarios.
John Fitzgerald Kennedy becomes youngest, and first Roman Catholic, president of United States (to 1963).
International agreement to reserve Antarctica for scientific research; all territorial claims waived.

1961 East Germany tightens borders: Berlin Wall is built.
Latin American Free Trade Association is formed (LAFTA).
Britain begins application to join European Economic Community.

Cuban Confrontation

Cuba was involved in two international crises in the 1960s. About 100,000 Cubans fled from the Communist regime of Fidel Castro and settled in the United States. In April 1961 a band of these exiles made an armed landing at Bahia de Cochinos (the Bay of Pigs), on Cuba's southern coast, with American backing. They planned to overthrow Castro, but Cuban forces crushed the attack.

The following year the Soviet Union began building missile bases in Cuba which threatened the United States. President John F. Kennedy of the United States ordered a naval blockade of Cuba and demanded that the Russians should remove the missiles. Faced with the threat of war, Russia's Premier Nikita Khrushchev agreed to dismantle the bases. The most tense point of the Cold War had passed.

Opposite: Russian cosmonaut Yuri Gagarin became the first man in space on 12 April 1961. He made a single orbit of the Earth in 89 minutes in his spacecraft Vostok I. He died in a car crash in 1968.

Below: President John Kennedy of America, Fidel Castro of Cuba and Nikita Khruschev of the USSR were the three crucial figures in the Cuba Crisis of 1962.

1961 Death of Patrice Lumumba, president of Congo (Léopoldville).
Soviet cosmonaut Yuri Gagarin becomes first man in space.
Bay of Pigs'; exiles' invasion of Cuba fails.
Dag Hammarskjöld, UN secretary-general, killed in air crash while travelling to talks in the Congo; succeeded by Burmese U Thant.
South Africa becomes a republic and withdraws from the Commonwealth.
1962 Disarmament conference in Geneva.
Confrontation between United States and Soviet Union over Russian missiles and bombers based in Cuba; Soviet Union agrees to withdraw its Cuban bases.
Border clashes between China and India.
Telstar communications satellite launched: first live TV broadcasts between United States and Europe.
Algeria gains independence from France after war lasting eight years.
1963 South Vietnamese government overthrown by military coup.
Organization of African Unity formed by independent African states (OAU).
Paul VI becomes Pope.

Journeys into Space

Man's conquest of space began in October 1957, when the Russian satellite *Sputnik I* was launched. Another *Sputnik* soon followed, and then the USA's first satellite, Explorer 1. Since then hundreds of man-made objects have left Earth. Manned flights began in 1961, when Yuri Gagarin of the USSR orbited Earth; in July 1969 600 million television viewers saw Neil Armstrong of the American Apollo 11 crew become the first person to step on to the Moon.

Small communications and weather-forecasting satellites launched by several nations have perhaps had more effect on our daily lives. The important *Intelsat IV* satellites, now in position in stationary orbits above the Equator, are able to relay signals between the continents and cover virtually the whole of the globe. Unmanned probes have landed on Venus and Mars for tests, and others are sending us spectacular pictures of planets; one has left our solar system – carrying a picture of humans.

France vetoes British application to enter the European Economic Community.
Russian cosmonaut Valentina Tereshkova becomes first woman in space.
Nuclear test ban treaty signed by Britain, Soviet Union, and United States.
President John F. Kennedy of United States assassinated; succeeded by Vice-President Lyndon B. Johnson.
1964 Fighting breaks out between Greeks and Turks in Cyprus; United Nations troops sent in to maintain peace.
War between Indonesia and Malaysia (until 1965).
United States' involvement in Vietnam war increases; support declared for South Vietnam against Communist Viet Cong.
Civil rights Act becomes law in United States.
Soviet premier Nikita Khrushchev falls from power; succeeded by Aleksei Kosygin.
1965 United States undertakes regular bombing raids on North Vietnam.
India and Pakistan go to war over Kashmir; United Nations calls for ceasefire.
First American marines land in South Vietnam.
Death of Sir Winston Churchill.
White government of Rhodesia under premier Ian Smith makes unilateral declaration of independence (UDI) from Britain; British economic pressure fails to halt crisis.

The Israeli Wars

Israel fought two wars in the 1960s and 1970s with surrounding Arab countries.

The Six Day War in 1967 followed a long series of border incidents between Israel, and Syria and Jordan. In May Egypt demanded the removal of a United Nations peace-keeping patrol on its frontier with Israel and barred Israeli ships from the Strait of Tiran, blocking the Israeli port of Elat. Learning that an Egyptian attack was coming the Israelis struck first, against Egypt and Jordan. Arab opposition crumbled by the time a truce was arranged after just six days. Israel captured Jordanian territory on the west bank of the river Jordan, and the rest of Jerusalem; the Gaza strip, on the west coast; and the Egyptian-owned Sinai Peninsula.

The October (Yom Kippur) War in 1973 began on October 6 with Egyptians and Syrians attacking Israel during Yom Kippur, the Jewish holy fast-day. Both sides gained some territory and lost some, suffering severe casualties and losses of weapons, by the time a truce was reached on October 22. The war strengthened Arab positions, and Israel later withdrew from the east bank of the Suez Canal so it could be re-opened.

Israel's defence minister, Moshe Dayan, leads a patrol in Egyptian territory during the Yom Kippur War of October 1973.

Opposite: In July 1969 the race to put a man on the Moon was won by the United States.

Biafra

Civil war broke out in Nigeria in 1967 when the eastern region declared its independence under the name of Biafra. The Ibo people of the region objected to being ruled by people from the north who were of different tribes and cultures. Fighting dragged on until 1970, despite attempts by the United Nations to stop it, and ended with Biafra's collapse.

. The war caused great damage and hardship, but booming revenues from the country's oil wells helped to put it back on its feet quickly. The government kept 250,000 troops in the eastern region to maintain order and prevent further warfare.

Bangladesh

When the British left India in 1947 the land was partitioned into two states: India, whose people were Hindus, and East and West Pakistan – whose people were Muslims – separated by India. West Pakistan had the wealth and the power. East Pakistan, formerly East Bengal, had nothing in common with the West except religion – origins, language, and culture were different.

Although having more people, East Pakistan earned only three-fifths as much as West Pakistan. Dissatisfaction with the central government grew. In 1970 the Awami League, headed by Sheik Mujibur Rahman, won a majority in Pakistan's national assembly, and was pledged to give more independence to the East. President Yahya Khan postponed the assembly and East Pakistanis demonstrated.

The protests were put down by troops, many people were arrested, and civil war broke out in March 1971. In December, India sent troops to aid the East Pakistanis. Fighting ended and East Pakistan became independent as Bangladesh (Bengal state).

The Watergate Scandal

A scandal which drove an American president from office began in June 1972 during the United States presidential election campaign. Five men were found burgling the Democratic Party headquarters at the Watergate building in Washington, D.C. President Richard M. Nixon, a Republican, denied that the White House was involved in any conspiracy against the Democratic Party. But inquiries, confessions, and the trials and convictions of people directly involved culminated in the trial and conviction of five former Nixon aides for conspiracy and obstruction of justice.

Before the final trial Nixon, realizing that his denials were not believed and that he faced possible impeachment, resigned in August 1974, the first American president to do so during office. His successor, President Gerald Ford, at once gave him a full pardon for any crimes he might have committed. This prevented him coming to trial.

1965 Britain abolishes death penalty for murder.
1966 War between Indonesia and Malaysia ends.
South African Prime Minister Dr Verwoerd assassinated; succeeded by John Vorster.
Rhodesian Prime Minister, Ian Smith, rejects British proposals for settlement.
United Nations instructs members to impose economic sanctions on Rhodesia; South Africa and Portugal refuse.
'Cultural Revolution' in China (to 1968); Red Guards formed.
1967 Military *coup* in Greece.
Six Day War (June 5–10) between Arabs and Israelis; Israel occupies Sinai Desert, Jerusalem, west bank of Jordan River; ceasefire arranged by United Nations.
Second British application to enter Common Market vetoed by France.
Civil war in Nigeria (to 1970): Biafra region breaks away from Nigerian Federation.
1968 Civil rights leader Martin Luther King assassinated in United States.
Student demonstrations in Paris lead to clashes with police; universities and factories taken over by workers and students.
Assassination of presidential candidate Robert Kennedy, brother of former American President, John Kennedy.
Soviet troops invade Czechoslovakia to crush liberalism of Czechoslovakian secretary, Alexander Dubcek.
Crisis in Northern Ireland begins; civil rights riots.
Tet Offensive: Vietcong launch major offensive in Vietnam.
1969 Britain sends troops to Northern Ireland.
French President Charles de Gaulle, resigns.
American astronauts Neil Armstrong and 'Buzz' Aldrin land on the Moon.
1970 Biafra surrenders; ends Nigerian civil war.
United States President, Richard Nixon, announces invasion of Cambodia.
Civil war in Jordan between government troops and Palestinian guerillas.
1971 East Pakistan becomes independent as Bangladesh after civil war and intervention by India.
Communist China joins United Nations; Taiwan (Formosa) expelled.
1972 Ceylon becomes republic as Sri Lanka.
Britain takes over direct rule of Northern Ireland.
1973 Britain, Ireland, Denmark join EEC.
United States withdraws troops from Vietnam; peace settlement signed at Paris.
Military *coup* in Chile overthrows Marxist President, Salvador Allende.

The Energy Crisis

The world energy crisis began in 1973 as a result of the Yom Kippur war between Israel and Arab countries. The Arab oil-producing countries cut off supplies of petroleum to the Netherlands and the United States because they had supported Israel, and reduced supplies to other countries by 25 per cent.

The Arab states followed this move by increasing prices sharply, pointing out their need to conserve oil reserves, their main source of income. Oil prices continued to rise in the following years, and industrial countries especially ran up huge international debts to pay for their fuel.

Britain, Norway, and others developed oil fields under the North Sea. By 1980 Britain was self-sufficient in oil. But the crisis has led scientists in all countries to look actively for alternative sources of power, and for alternative sources of oil.

Portugal

More than 40 years of dictatorship in Portugal came to an end in 1974 when a *coup d'état* by left-wing army officers overthrew the government of premier Marcello Caetano. Caetano had become effective dictator after António Salazar, who held office from 1932, retired ill in 1968.

Riots and unrest followed in 1975 and 1976 as the Portuguese tested their newfound political freedom. Some calm returned as free elections were held for a new legislative assembly.

Faced with troubles at home, the new Portuguese rulers freed the country's African territories – Guinea-Bissau, which became independent in 1974, and Angola and Mozambique, which gained independence the following year.

Signing the Rhodesia ceasefire agreement in December 1979. From left to right: Bishop Abel Muzorewa, Lord Carrington, Sir Ian Gilmour, Joshua Nkomo and Robert Mugabe who became the first black Prime Minister in 1980.

Trouble in Ulster

The centuries-old conflict between the Protestant majority and the Roman Catholic minority in Northern Ireland – often called Ulster – flared into open rioting in 1968. Catholics demanded a better deal in elections and a share of power. The government sent troops in to keep order. But rioting continued, with the illegal Irish Republican Army (IRA) setting off bombs in public places.

Ulster's own elected government proved unable to rule, so in March 1972 the United Kingdom government at Westminster took over direct rule of the strife-torn province. By now Protestant gunmen were also shooting and bombing. By 1980 no solution had been found.

China rejoins the World

In the late 1970s China began to move from the isolated position it had held for nearly two decades. This was caused partly by a dramatic drive towards modernization within the country, and partly by a growing hostility between China and its neighbour and former ally the Soviet Union.

In 1978 a treaty of peace and friendship was signed with Japan. At the end of the same year it was announced that normal relations between China and the United States of America would be restored and that the United States would end relations with the Nationalist Chinese government in Taiwan.

Chairman Mao had died in 1976; within two years of his death the Chinese, although acknowledging his great achievements, were admitting that he had not, in fact, been omniscient. They began to demand more genuine democracy and the redress of grievances caused by bureaucracy. China began to open up to the outside world and there was an immediate influx of tourists, trade missions, and other visitors.

1973 October War: Arab states attack Israel; cease-fire imposed after five weeks of fighting.
Arab oil-producing nations restrict oil supplies, resulting in world economic crisis.
1974 Greek-Turkish conflict in Cyprus; Greek military junta resigns; Turks occupy Nicosia.
President Richard Nixon forced to resign after Watergate scandal. Gerald Ford succeeds him.
Coup in Portugal ends dictatorship of President Caetano.
1975 Communist victories in Cambodia; South Vietnam surrenders to North Vietnam; ends Vietnam War.
Spanish dictator Franco dies; Juan Carlos, grandson of last king of Spain, becomes king.
1976 Race riots erupt in South Africa.
1977 President Sadat of Egypt and Prime Minister Begin of Israel exchange visits; negotiations on peace terms begin.
1978 John Paul II is elected as the first non-Italian Pope for over 450 years.
USA agrees to diplomatic relations with China and ends those with Taiwan.
Vietnamese troops invade Cambodia to support the rebels.
1979 The first direct elections to the European Parliament held in all 9 EEC member states.
A peace treaty between Israel and Egypt is signed in Washington.
General Amin flees from Uganda ahead of the Tanzanian and Ugandan forces.
Following riots and political pressure, the Shah of Iran leaves. The exiled religious leader Ayotollah Komeini returns to Iran. An Islamic Republic is declared.
Russian forces move into Afghanistan.
1980 President Tito of Yugoslavia dies.
Rhodesia becomes independent as Zimbabwe with Robert Mugabe as first black Prime Minister.
Polish Solidarity trade union, led by Lech Walesa, confronts Communist government.
War between Iran and Iraq.
1981 Greece becomes 10th member of Common Market.
First flight of US space shuttle.
President Sadat of Egypt assassinated; assassination attempts on President Reagan of the United States and Pope John Paul II fail.
Martial law declared in Poland; many Solidarity members are imprisoned.
1982 Argentines invade Falkland Islands and South Georgia. Diplomatic solutions fail and a British task force reoccupies the Islands.
Israel invades Lebanon and advances on Beirut to drive Palestine Liberation Organization fighters from the country.

Reference Tables

Major Wars

Name	Date	Won by	Against
Abyssinian War	1935–1936	Italy	Abyssinia (Ethiopia)
American War of Independence	1775–1783	Thirteen Colonies	Britain
Austrian Succession, War of the	1740–1748	Austria, Hungary, Britain, Holland	Bavaria, France, Poland, Prussia, Sardinia, Saxony, Spain
Boer (South African) War	1899–1902	Britain	Boer Republics
Chinese-Japanese Wars	1894–1895	Japan	China
	1931–1933	Japan	China
	1937–1945	China	Japan
Civil War, American	1861–1865	23 Northern States (The Union)	11 Southern States (the Confederacy)
Civil War, English	1642–1646	Parliament	Charles I
Civil War, Nigerian	1967–1970	Federal government	Biafra
Civil War, Pakistani	1971	East Pakistan (Bangladesh) and India	West Pakistan
Civil War, Spanish	1936–1939	Junta de Defensa Nacional (Fascists)	Republican government
Crimean War	1853–1856	Britain, France, Sardinia, Turkey	Russia
Franco-Prussian War	1870–1871	Prussia and other German states	France
Hundred Years War	1337–1453	France	England
Korean War	1950–1953	South Korea and United Nations forces	North Korea and Chinese forces
Mexican-American War	1846–1848	United States	Mexico
Napoleonic Wars	1792–1815	Austria, Britain, Prussia, Russia, Spain, Sweden	France
October War	1973	Ceasefire arranged by UN: fought by Israel against Egypt, Syria, Iraq, Jordan, Sudan, Saudi Arabia, Lebanon	
Peloponnesian War	431–404 BC	Peloponnesian League, led by Sparta, Corinth	Delian League, led by Athens
Punic Wars	264–146 BC	Rome	Carthage
Russo-Japanese War	1904–1905	Japan	Russia
Seven Years War	1756–1763	Britain, Prussia, Hanover	Austria, France, Russia, Sweden
Six-Day War	1967	Israel	Egypt, Syria, Jordan, Iraq
Spanish-American War	1898	United States	Spain
Spanish Succession, War of the	1701–1713	England, Austria, Prussia, the Netherlands	France, Bavaria, Cologne, Mantua, Savoy
Thirty Years War	1618–1648	France, Sweden, the German Protestant states	The Holy Roman Empire, Spain
Vietnam War	1957–1975	North Vietnam	South Vietnam, United States
War of 1812	1812–1814	United States	Britain
Wars of the Roses	1455–1485	House of Lancaster	House of York

| World War I | 1914–1918 | Belgium, Britain and Empire, France, Italy, Japan, Russia, Serbia, United States | Austria-Hungary, Bulgaria, Germany, Ottoman Empire |
| World War II | 1939–1945 | Australia, Belgium, Britain, Canada, China, Denmark, France, Greece, Netherlands, New Zealand, Norway, Poland, Russia, South Africa, United States, Yugoslavia | Bulgaria, Finland, Germany, Hungary, Italy, Japan, Romania |

Major Battles

GREEKS AND ROMANS

Marathon 490 BC. Force of 10,000 Athenians and allies defeated 50,000 Persian troops, crushing a Persian invasion attempt and boosting Greek morale.

Salamis 480 BC. Greek fleet of 360 ships under Themistocles defeated Persian fleet of 1000 ships commanded by Xerxes, and Persians had to withdraw from Greece.

Siege of Syracuse 414–413 BC. Athenians besieged city of Syracuse in the Peloponnesian War; siege ended when night attack led by Athenian general Demosthenes was decisively repulsed.

Aegospotami 405 BC. Spartan fleet under Lysander defeated last Athenian fleet, and ended the Peloponnesian War.

Arbela 331 BC. Alexander the Great's Greek army defeated a Persian force twice the size under Darius III, conquering Persia. The battle was fought at Gaugamela, 25 miles (40 km) from Arbela.

Zama 202 BC. Romans under Scipio Africanus defeated the Carthaginians under Hannibal, winning Second Punic War.

Actium 31 BC. Roman fleet of 400 ships under Octavian (later Emperor Augustus) defeated 500 ships, combined fleet of Mark Antony and Cleopatra. The victory made Octavian master of Rome and its empire.

Teutoberg Forest AD 9. German tribesmen under the chief Arminius destroyed three Roman legions, ending Roman plans to invade and conquer their lands.

Adrianople 378. Visigoths under Fridigern defeated and killed the Roman Emperor Valens at Adrianople (now Edirne, Turkey).

Châlons-sur-Marne 451. Romans led by Flavius Aetius and Visigoths led by Theodoric I defeated the Huns under Attila, curbing their threat to the West.

EARLY EUROPE

Tours 732. The Franks under Charles Martel defeated the Saracens (Muslims), halting their advance in western Europe.

Hastings 1066. About 8000 troops under Duke William of Normandy defeated an equal force under Saxon king Harold II. England thereafter came under Norman rule.

Crécy 1346. Invading army of 10,000 English under Edward III defeated 20,000 French men-at-arms. English archers won the day.

Poitiers 1356. Edward the Black Prince of England crushed a French army, capturing the French King John II.

Agincourt 1415. Henry V of England with 10,000 troops defeated 30,000 Frenchmen, and recaptured Normandy.

Siege of Orléans 1428–1429. English troops began siege in October 1428, but in April 1429 Joan of Arc came to the aid of city, and forced the besiegers to withdraw. Victory was a turning point in French campaign to drive the English out of France.

Siege of Constantinople 1453. Ottoman Turkish army of more than 100,000 under Mohammed the Conqueror captured the city, held by 10,000 men led by the last Byzantine emperor, Constantine Paleologus.

WARS OF FAITH & SUCCESSION

Lepanto 1571. Allied Christian fleet of 208 galleys under Don John of Austria defeated Ali Pasha's Turkish fleet of 230 galleys.

Invincible Armada 1588. Spanish invasion fleet led by Duke of Medina Sidonia was defeated by the English under Lord Howard of Effingham.

Naseby 1645. Sir Thomas Fairfax with 14,000 Parliamentary troops defeated Prince Rupert with 10,000 Royalist soldiers, virtually ending Charles I's power.

Boyne 1690. William III of England with 35,000 mixed troops routed his rival, James II, with 21,000 men, ending Stuart hopes of regaining the throne.

Blenheim 1704. A British-Austrian army led by Duke of Marlborough and Prince Eugène defeated the French and Bavarians under Marshal Camille de Tallard during War of the Spanish Succession.

Poltava 1709. The Russians under Peter the Great routed an invading Swedish army led by Charles XII of Sweden, overturning Swedish power in the Baltic.

COLONIAL STRUGGLES

Plassey 1757. Robert Clive with an Anglo-Indian army of 3000 defeated the Nawab of Bengal's army of 60,000 conquering Bengal and setting Britain on the road to domination in India.

Quebec 1759. British troops under James Wolfe made a night attack up the St Lawrence River, climbing the cliffs to the Plains of Abraham overlooking the city. They defeated the French forces under the Marquis de Montcalm; he and Wolfe were killed.

Saratoga 1777. British troops under John Burgoyne surrendered to American colonial forces under Horatio Gates; defeat led France to declare war on Britain.

Yorktown 1781. Charles Cornwallis with 8000 British troops were bottled in, and surrendered to a larger force under George Washington, ending the American War of Independence.

AGE OF NAPOLEON

Valmy 1792. A French Revolutionary army defeated the Prussians in heavy fog. The victory gave new heart to the Revolutionary forces in France.

Nile 1798. Horatio Nelson commanding a British fleet of 15 ships destroyed a 16-ship French fleet under Francis Paul Brueys in Aboukir Bay, cutting off Napoleon Bonaparte's French army in Egypt.

Trafalgar 1805. British fleet of 27 ships under Horatio Nelson shattered Franco-Spanish fleet of 33 ships under Pierre de Villeneuve, ending Napoleon's hopes of invading England. Nelson was killed.

Austerlitz 1805. Emperor Napoleon I with 65,000 French troops defeated an 83,000-strong Austro-Russian army under the Austrian and Russian emperors. The Austrians sued for peace, and the Russians withdrew. Called *Battle of the Three Emperors.*

Jena and Auerstädt 1806. French forces routed the main Prussian armies on the same day (October 14), shattering Prussian power.

Leipzig 1813. Napoleon I with 190,000 French troops was surrounded and crushed by an allied force of 300,000 Austrian, Prussian, Russian, and Swedish troops. This *Battle of the Nations* ended Napoleon's domination of Europe.

Waterloo 1815. A British, Dutch, and Belgian force of 67,000 fought off 74,000 French troops under Napoleon I until the arrival of the Prussian army of Gebhard von Blücher. It ended Napoleon's final bid for power.

FIRST MODERN CONFLICTS

Gettysburg 1863. Federal forces under George Meade defeated Robert E. Lee's Confederate army, a turning point in the American Civil War.

Vicksburg 1863. Federal general Ulysses S. Grant captured Confederate army under John Pemberton, the day after Gettysburg.

Sedan 1870. French army of 100,000 men defeated and surrounded by German force of more than twice the size in decisive battle of Franco-Prussian War.

Tsushima 1905. Japanese fleet destroyed Russian fleet of equal size, bringing victory for Japan in Russo-Japanese War.

WORLD WAR I

Marne 1914. French and British armies halted German forces invading France. From then on war on the Western Front became a trench-based slogging match.

First battle of Ypres 1914. German forces trying to reach Calais lost 150,000 men; British and French armies thwarted attack, losing more than 100,000 men.

Verdun 1916. In a six-month struggle French forces held off a major attack by German armies commanded by Crown Prince William. French losses were 348,000 men, the German losses 328,000.

Jutland 1916. British Grand Fleet led by John Jellicoe fought German High Seas Fleet under Rheinhard Scheer. The Germans never again ventured out to sea.

Somme 1916. In a 141-day battle following Verdun British and French captured 125 sq. miles (320 sq. km) of ground, losing 600,000 men; German defenders lost almost 500,000.

Passchendaele 1917 (also known as third battle

of Ypres). British forces launched eight attacks over 102 days in heavy rain and through thick mud, gaining five miles and losing 400,000 men.

St Mihiel Salient 1918. American victory in World War I: German line broken and salient flattened out. In first major air battle 1480 Allied planes defeated German air force.

WORLD WAR II

Britain 1940. A German air force of 2500 planes launched an attack lasting 114 days to try to win air supremacy over Britain. The smaller Royal Air Force defeated the attack, preventing a German invasion.

Coral Sea 1942. American fleet drove back a Japanese invasion fleet bound for New Guinea in four-day battle in which all the fighting was done by aeroplanes.

Midway 1942. A 100-ship Japanese fleet led by Isoruko Yamamoto aiming to capture Midway Island was defeated by American fleet half the size, under Raymond Spruance.

El Alamein 1942. British Eighth Army under Bernard Montgomery drove back German Afrika Korps under Erwin Rommel, out of Egypt and deep into Libya.

Stalingrad 1942–1943. Twenty-one German divisions tried to capture Stalingrad (Now Volograd), but siege was broken, and Friedrich von Paulus had to surrender with more than 100,000 German troops.

Normandy 1944. Allied forces under Dwight D. Eisenhower invaded German-held northern France in biggest-ever sea-borne attack; after a month of heavy fighting Normandy was cleared and Germans began to retreat.

Leyte Gulf 1944. US 3rd and 7th fleets defeated a Japanese force, ending Japanese naval power in World War II.

Ardennes Bulge 1944–1945. Last German counter-attack in west through Ardennes Forest failed; Germans lost 100,000 casualties and 110,000 prisoners.

POST-WAR CONFLICTS

Inchon 1950. US forces made surprise landing behind North Korean lines in Korean War, leading to major victory over North Korea.

Dien Bien Phu 1954. French surrendered to Vietminh after 8-week siege; end of French influence in Indochina.

Below: The British siege of Quebec in 1759 ended with the successful storming of the French-held Plains of Abraham. Both the British and French commanders, General James Wolfe and the Marquis de Montcalm, died in the battle.

Holy Roman Emperors

FRANKISH KINGS AND EMPERORS (CAROLINGIAN)

	Reigned
Charlemagne	800–814
Louis I, the Pious	814–840
Lothair I	840–855
Louis II	855–875
Charles II, the Bald	875–877
Throne vacant	877–881
Charles III, the Fat	881–887
Throne vacant	887–891
Guido of Spoleto	891–894
Lambert of Spoleto (co-emperor)	892–898
Arnulf (rival)	896–901
Louis III of Provence	901–905
Berengar	905–924
Conrad I of Franconia (rival)	911–918

SAXON KINGS AND EMPERORS

Henry I, the Fowler	918–936
Otto I, the Great	936–973
Otto II	973–983
Otto III	983–1002
Henry II, the Saint	1002–1024

FRANCONIAN EMPERORS (SALIAN)

Conrad II, the Salian	1024–1039
Henry III, the Black	1039–1056
Henry IV	1056–1106
Rudolf of Swabia (rival)	1077–1080
Hermann of Luxemburg (rival)	1081–1093
Conrad of Franconia (rival)	1093–1101
Henry V	1106–1125
Lothair II	1125–1137

HOHENSTAUFEN KINGS AND EMPERORS

Conrad III	1138–1152
Frederick I Barbarossa	1152–1190
Henry VI	1190–1197
Otto IV	1198–1215
Philip of Swabia (rival)	1198–1208
Frederick II	1215–1250
Henry Raspe (rival)	1246–1247
William of Holland (rival)	1247–1256
Conrad IV	1250–1254
The Great Interregnum	1254–1273

RULERS FROM DIFFERENT HOUSES

(Richard of Cornwall (rival)	1257–1272
(Alfonso X of Castile (rival)	1257–1273
Rudolf I, Habsburg	1273–1291
Adolf I of Nassau	1292–1298
Albert I, Habsburg	1298–1308
Henry VII, Luxemburg	1308–1313
Louis IV of Bavaria	1314–1347
Frederick of Habsburg (co-regent)	1314–1325
Charles IV, Luxemburg	1347–1378
Wenceslas of Bohemia	1378–1400
Frederick III of Brunswick	1400
Rupert of the Palatinate	1400–1410
Sigismund, Luxemburg	1410–1437

HABSBURG EMPERORS

Albert II	1438–1439
Frederick III	1440–1493
Maximilian I	1493–1519
Charles V	1519–1558
Ferdinand I	1558–1564
Maximilian II	1564–1576
Rudolf II	1576–1612
Matthias	1612–1619
Ferdinand II	1619–1637
Ferdinand III	1637–1657
Leopold I	1658–1705
Joseph I	1705–1711
Charles VI	1711–1740
Charles VII of Bavaria	1742–1745

HABSBURG-LORRAINE EMPERORS

Francis I of Lorraine	1745–1765
Joseph II	1765–1790
Leopold II	1790–1792
Francis II	1792–1806

A cameo portrait of the first Roman Emperor, Caesar Augustus (27 BC—AD 14).

World Rulers

ROMAN EMPERORS

	Reigned
Augustus (Octavian)	27 BC—AD 14
Tiberius	14—37
Caligula (Gaius)	37—41
Claudius	41—54
Nero	54—68
Galba	68—69
Otho	69
Vitellius	69
Vespasian	69—79
Titus	79—81
Domitian	81—96
Nerva	96—98
Trajan	98—117
Hadrian	117—138
Antoninus Pius	138—161
Marcus Aurelius	161—180
Lucius Aurelius Verus	161—169
Commodus	180—192
Pertinax	193
Didius Julian	193
Septimius Severus	193—211
Caracalla	211—217
Macrinus	217—218
Elagabalus	218—222
Alexander Severus	222—235

Maximinus	235—238
Gordian I	238
Gordian II	238
Pupienus	238
Balbinus	238
Gordian III	238—244
Philip 'the Arab'	244—249
Decius	249—251
Gallus	251—253
Aemilian	253
Valerian	253—259
Gallienus	259—268
Claudius II	268—270
Aurelian	270—275
Tacitus	275—276
Florian	276
Probus	276—282
Carus	282—283
Numerian ⎱	283—284
Carinus ⎰	283—285
Diocletian	284—305
Maximian	286—305
Constantius I	305—306
Galerius	305—311
Constantine I, the Great	311—337
Constantine II	337—340
Constantius II	337—361
Constans	337—350
Julian, the Apostate	361—363
Jovian	363—364
Valentinian I (in the West)	364—375
Valens (in the East)	364—378
Gratian (in the West)	375—383
Valentinian II (in the West)	375—392
Theodosius, the Great (in the East, and after 394, in the West)	379—395
Maximus (in the West)	383—388
Eugenius (in the West)	392—394
Arcadius (in the East)	395—408
Honorius (in the West)	395—423
Constantius III (co-emperor in the West)	421
Theodosius II (in the East)	408—450
Valentinian III (in the West)	425—455
Marcian (in the East)	450—457
Petronius (in the West)	455
Avitus (in the West)	455—456
Majorian (in the West)	457—461
Leo I (in the East)	457—474
Severus (in the West)	461—465
Anthemius (in the West)	467—472
Olybrius (in the West)	472
Glycerius (in the West)	473
Julius Nepos (in the West)	473—475
Leo II (in the East)	473—474
Zeno (in the East)	474—491
Romulus Augustulus (in the West)	475—476

BRITISH RULERS

Rulers of England (to 1603)

Saxons

Egbert	827–839
Ethelwulf	839–858
Ethelbald	858–860
Ethelbert	860–865
Ethelred I	865–871
Alfred the Great	871–899
Edward the Elder	899–924
Athelstan	924–939
Edmund	939–946
Edred	946–955
Edwy	955–959
Edgar	959–975
Edward the Martyr	975–978
Ethelred II the Unready	978–1016
Edmund Ironside	1016

Danes

Canute	1016–1035
Harold I Harefoot	1035–1040
Hardicanute	1040–1042

Saxons

Edward the Confessor	1042–1066
Harold II	1066

House of Normandy

William I the Conqueror	1066–1087
William II	1087–1100
Henry I	1100–1135
Stephen	1135–1154

House of Plantagenet

Henry II	1154–1189
Richard I	1189–1199
John	1199–1216
Henry III	1216–1272
Edward I	1272–1307
Edward II	1307–1327
Edward III	1327–1377
Richard II	1377–1399

House of Lancaster

Henry IV	1399–1413
Henry V	1413–1422
Henry VI	1422–1461

House of York

Edward IV	1461–1483
Edward V	1483
Richard III	1483–1485

House of Tudor

Henry VII	1485–1509
Henry VIII	1509–1547
Edward VI	1547–1553
Mary I	1553–1558
Elizabeth I	1558–1603

Rulers of Scotland (to 1603)

Malcolm II	1005–1034
Duncan I	1034–1040
Macbeth	1040–1057
Malcolm III Canmore	1058–1093
Donald Bane	1093–1094
Duncan II	1094
Donald Bane (restored)	1094–1097
Edgar	1097–1107
Alexander I	1107–1124
David I	1124–1153
Malcolm IV	1153–1165
William the Lion	1165–1214
Alexander II	1214–1249
Alexander III	1249–1286
Margaret of Norway	1286–1290
Interregnum	1290–1292
John Baliol	1292–1296
Interregnum	1296–1306
Robert I (Bruce)	1306–1329
David II	1329–1371

House of Stuart

Robert II	1371–1390
Robert III	1390–1406
James I	1406–1437
James II	1437–1460
James III	1460–1488
James IV	1488–1513
James V	1513–1542
Mary	1542–1567
James VI*	1567–1625

* Became James I of England in 1603.

Rulers of Britain

House of Stuart

James I	1603–1625
Charles I	1625–1649
Commonwealth	1649–1660

House of Stuart (restored)

Charles II	1660–1685
James II	1685–1688
William III } jointly	1689–1702
Mary II }	1689–1694
Anne	1702–1714

House of Hanover

George I	1714–1727
George II	1727–1760
George III	1760–1820
George IV	1820–1830
William IV	1830–1837
Victoria	1837–1901

House of Saxe-Coburg

Edward VII	1901–1910

House of Windsor

George V	1910–1936
Edward VIII	1936
George VI	1936–1952
Elizabeth II	1952–

Right: The official seal of the President of the United States of America.

AMERICAN PRESIDENTS

F = Federalist; DR = Democratic-Republican;
D = Democratic; W = Whig; R = Republican;
U = Union

		Term
1	George Washington (F)	1789–1797
2	John Adams (F)	1797–1801
3	Thomas Jefferson (DR)	1801–1809
4	James Madison (DR)	1809–1817
5	James Monroe (DR)	1817–1825
6	John Quincy Adams (DR)	1825–1829
7	Andrew Jackson (D)	1829–1837
8	Martin Van Buren (D)	1837–1841
9	William H. Harrison* (W)	1841
10	John Tyler (W)	1841–1845
11	James K. Polk (D)	1845–1849
12	Zachary Taylor* (W)	1849–1850
13	Millard Fillmore (W)	1850–1853
14	Franklin Pierce (D)	1853–1857
15	James Buchanan (D)	1857–1861
16	Abraham Lincoln† (R)	1861–1865
17	Andrew Johnson (U)	1865–1869
18	Ulysses S. Grant (R)	1869–1877
19	Rutherford B. Hayes (R)	1877–1881
20	James A. Garfield† (R)	1881
21	Chester A. Arthur (R)	1881–1885
22	Grover Cleveland (D)	1885–1889
23	Benjamin Harrison (R)	1889–1893
24	Grover Cleveland (D)	1893–1897
25	William McKinley† (R)	1897–1901
26	Theodore Roosevelt (R)	1901–1909
27	William H. Taft (R)	1909–1913
28	Woodrow Wilson (D)	1913–1921
29	Warren G. Harding* (R)	1921–1923
30	Calvin Coolidge (R)	1923–1929
31	Herbert C. Hoover (R)	1929–1933
32	Franklin D. Roosevelt* (D)	1933–1945
33	Harry S. Truman (D)	1945–1953
34	Dwight D. Eisenhower (R)	1953–1961
35	John F. Kennedy† (D)	1961–1963
36	Lyndon B. Johnson (D)	1963–1969
37	Richard M. Nixon (R)	1969–1974
38	Gerald R. Ford (R)	1974–1977
39	Jimmy Carter (D)	1977–1980
40	Ronald Reagan (R)	1981–

* Died in office. † Assassinated in office.

RULERS OF FRANCE

Hugh Capet	987–996
Robert II, the Pious	996–1031
Henri I	1031–1060
Philip I	1060–1108
Louis VI, the Fat	1108–1137
Louis VII, the Young	1137–1180
Philip II Augustus	1180–1223
Louis VIII	1223–1226
Louis IX, Saint Louis	1226–1270
Philip III, the Bold	1270–1285
Philip IV, the Fair	1285–1314
Louis X	1314–1316
John I	1316
Philip V	1316–1322
Charles IV	1322–1328
Philip VI	1328–1350
John II	1350–1364
Charles V	1364–1380
Charles VI	1380–1422
Charles VII	1422–1461
Louis XI	1461–1483
Charles VIII	1483–1498
Louis XII	1498–1515
François I	1515–1547
Henri II	1547–1559
François II	1559–1560
Charles IX	1560–1574
Henri III	1574–1589
Henri IV	1589–1610
Louis XIII	1610–1643
Louis XIV	1643–1715
Louis XV	1715–1774
Louis XVI	1774–1792
The First Republic	1792–1804
Napoleon I (Emperor)	1804–1814
Louis XVIII	1814–1824
Charles X	1824–1830
Louis Philippe	1830–1848
The Second Republic	1848–1852
Napoleon III (Emperor)	1852–1870

Index

A

Abdul Hamid II, ruler of Turkey 205
Aboukir Bay, battle of 226
Abraham 13
Abyssinia *see* Ethiopia
Abyssinian War 224
Actium, battle of 225
Act of Settlement 143
Act of Supremacy 108
Act of Union 143
Adrianople, battle of 225
Aegospotami, battle of 225
Aeroplane *189*, 199, *210 see also*
    Aviation
Afghan Wars 180
Africa 85, 184, *185*, *189*, 206, 216, 222
Agincourt, battle of 225
Agrippa I and II 35
Aix-la-Chapelle 146
Akbar the Great, Mughal emperor
    120
Alamo 170
Alaric 41
Alcock, John 203
Alexander III, King of Scotland 83
Alexander V, Pope 91
Alexander the Great 12, 22, 26, *26*
Alfred the Great 54
Allied Powers 198, 212
Alma river, battle of 179
Almoravid dynasty 57
Alp Arslan 66
Alphabet 12
Alsace and Lorraine 182
Amenhotep III 5
American civilizations *106, 107, 107*
American colonies 129, 152, 156
American revolution *see*
    Independence, American War of
Angevin dynasty 74
Angles 54
Anglo-Saxons 54, 59, 230
Angola 222
Anschluss 206
Anti-Corn Law League 171
Anti-popes 91
Apostles 34, 35, 37
Appiani, Andrea *165*
Arab Common Market 217

Arabs 212, 220, 222
Aragon 103, *103*
Arbela, battle of 225
Archaelaus 35
Archimedes 22
Ardennes Bulge 227
Areopagus 22
Argos 23
Aristophanes *22*
Aristotle 22
Armada *98*, 118
Arminius 225
Armstrong, Neil 219
Arouet, François Marie *see* Voltaire
Ashikaga family 77
Asoka 27
Astronomy *120*
Atahualpa, Inca emperor 110
Ataturk, Kemal
Athens 18, *18*, 22, 23
Atomic bomb *209*, 210
Attila the Hun 44
Augsburg, League of 140, *141*
Augsburg, Peace of 111
Augustus, Roman emperor *30*, 32,
    35, 225
Augustus II, king of Poland 147
Augustus III, king of Poland 147
Aurangzeb, Mughal emperor 134,
    134
Austerlitz, battle of 164, 226
Australia 122, 150
Australopithecines 8
Austria
    Anschluss 206
    Habsburgs 80, 173, 180
    World War I 198
Austrian Succession, War of the 146
Aviation 203
Avignon papal court 84, 91
Awami League 220
Axis Powers 208
Aztecs 107, *107*

B

Babar, Mughal emperor 110
Babylon 12, 13
'Babylonian Captivity' 84
Bach, Johann Sebastian 144, *144*
Balaklava, battle of 179
Balliol, John *see* John Balliol, king
    of Scotland
Bangladesh 220
Bannockburn, battle of 83
Bantu people 166
Barbarians 41, 45
Bar-Kockba, Shimeon 41

Battle of Britain 227
Beirut 12
Baroque 132
Bastille *152*, 158
Battles, major 225
Bayeux tapestry *68*
Bay of Pigs 218
Becket, Thomas à *see* Thomas à
    Becket
Belgium 122, *122*, 142, 184, 198, 208
Benedict XI, Pope 84
Benedict XIII, Pope 91
Benedictine 51
Bengal 226
Benz, Karl *176*
Berlin Conference 184
Bernini, Giovanni Lorenzo 132
Biafra 220
Bismarck, Otto von 182, 184
Black Death 88, 137
Bleda the Hun 44
Blenheim, battle of *124*, 142, 226
Blitzkrieg 208
Blücher, Gebhard von 226
Boers 170, 186
Boer War *see* South African Wars
Bolivar, Simón *166*, 167
Bolivia *166*, 167
Bolsheviks 200, *200*
Bonaparte, Napoleon *see* Napoleon
    Bonaparte
Boniface VIII, Pope 84
Borromini, Francesco 132
'Boston Tea Party' 156
Bosworth Field, battle of 101
Botany Bay 150
Bothwell, James Hepburn, Earl of
    119
Boulton, Matthew 162
Boxer Rebellion 188
Boyne, battle of the 226
Brahe, Tycho *120*
Brandywine Creek, battle of 157
Brazil *166*, 167
Brétigny, Treaty of 87
Bright, John 171
British Commonwealth of Nations
    204
Bruce, Robert 83
Brunelleschi 113
Bubonic plague *see* Black Death
Buddha 15, *15*, *42*
Buddhism 15, 27, *42*
Bunker Hill, battle of 157
Burgoyne, John 157, 226
Burgundy 102, 122
Byblos 12

Byzantine empire 41, 44, *52*, 54, 66, *94*, 95
Byzantium 54, 95

C

Cabral, Pedro Alvares 104
Caesar, Julius *30*, 31, 32
Caetano, Marcello 222
Calendar 120
Caliph 57
Calvin, John *108*
Cambodia 215
Cambyses 16
Cape Cod 129
Cape Colony 170, 186
Capet, Hugh, king of France 63
Capetians 63
Capone, Al *202*
Carloman 56
Carmelites 84
Carpini, John of Plano 76, *76*
Carthage 12, 30
Casement, Roger 201
Castile 90, 103, *103*
Castro, Fidel 218, *218*
Catherine de Médicis 118
Catherine of Aragon 103, 108
Cavaliers 133
Cavalli, Francesco 132
Cavour, Conte di 180
Central American Common Market 217
Central Powers 199
Centurion 31
Ceres 36
Cervantes Saavedra, Miguel de *122*
Cesarian *see* Ptolemy XV
Ceuta 93
Chaka, king of the Zulus 166
Chalons-sur-Marne, battle of 41, 225
Chamberlain, Neville 208
Chandragupta I, king of India 27, 42
Chandragupta II, king of India 42
Chaplin, Charlie *204*
Charlemagne 56, *56*
Charles I, king of England 133, *135*, 226
Charles II, king of Spain 142
Charles V, Holy Roman emperor 111, 114
Charles VI, Holy Roman emperor 146
Charles VI, king of France 87
Charles VII, Holy Roman emperor 146
Charles IX, king of France 118
Charles XII, king of Sweden 144, 226

Charles Edward Stuart, the Young Pretender 147
Charles Martel 225
Charles of Austria, archduke 142
Charles the Bold, duke of Burgundy 102
Chaucer, Geoffrey 72, *72*
Ch'eng Tsu, Ming emperor 90
Chiang Kai-shek 212
Children's Crusade 71
China
  art *52*, *62*
  Boxer rebellion 188
  Ching dynasty *191*, 193
  civil war 212
  Ming dynasty 90
  revolution 193
  Shang dynastry 10
  Sung dynasty 62
Chinese-Japanese Wars 224
Ching dynasty *191*, 193
Chivalry 72
Christian IV, king of Denmark 130
Christian Church 66, 108, 113
Christianity *21*, 34, 36, 39, 43, 67
Christians, persecution of 39, 43, 123
Chrysolaras, Manuel 113
Churchill, John *see* Marlborough, John Churchill. duke of
Churchill, Winston S. 211, *211*
Church of England 108
Chu Yuan-chang 90
Cicero, Marcus Tullius *34*
Cistercians *73*
Civil War, American 224, 226
Civil War, English 133
Civil War, Nigerian 220
Civil War, Pakistani 220, 224
Civil War, Spanish *see* Spain, Civil War
Classical World 18–45
Clement V, Pope 84
Clement VII, Pope 91
Cleopatra 32
Clive, Robert 148, 226
Coalition Wars 161, 164
Coal mining 162
Cobden, Richard 171
Cold War 218
Coligny, Gaspard de 118
Columbia 166, 167
Colonialism 167, 174, 184, 189, 216
Columbus, Christopher 104
COMECON *see* Council for Mutual Economic Assistance
Common markets 217
Communications 168, 219

Communism 172, *172*, 210, 212, 214, 215, 218
Confucianism 14
Confucius 14
Conquistadores *107*
Constance, Council of 91
Constantine XI, Byzantine emperor 95
Constantine the Great, Roman emperor 43, 54
Constantinople 43, 54; siege of 74, *94*, 95, 225
Constantius I, Roman emperor 43
Continental Congress 156, 157
Cook, James 150
Copernicus, Nicolaus 128
Coral Sea, battle of the 210, 227
Corinth 23
Corn Laws 171
Cornwallis, Charles 226
Cortés, Hernán *107*
Council for Mutual Economic Assistance 217
Counter-Reformation 108
Crassus, Licinius 32
Crecy, battle of *88*, 225
Crete 9
Crimean War *178*, 179
Cro-Magnons *6*, 8
Crusaders *70*, 71, 72, 74
Cuban crisis 218, *218*
Culloden, battle of 147
Curie, Marie and Pierre *187*
Cyprus 117
Cyrus, king of Persia 16
Czechoslovakia 208

D

Da Gama, Vasco 104
Daladier, Edouard 208
Dalriada 59
Danelaw 54
Danes 54, 58
Dante Alighieri 72, *72*
Danton, Georges *159*
Dardanelles Strait 198
Darius I, king of Persia *17*
Darius III, king of Persia 26
Darnley, Lord 119
David, king of Israel 13
Dayan, Moshe *220*
Declaration of Independence 157
del Cano, Sebastian 105
Democracy 22, 79
Democritus 22
De Montfort, Simon 80
Demosthenes 225

Depression (financial) 204, 211
Descartes, René 128
Dettingen, battle of 146
Dias, Bartolomeu 104
Diaspora 67
Dien Bien Phu 215
Diocletian, Roman emperor 41, 42
Dissolution of monasteries 108
'Divine Right of Kings' 124, 133, *135*
Domesday Survey 68
Dominicans 84
Dominions 204
Dom Pedro, emperor of Brazil 167
Donatello 113
Don Quixote (Cervantes) *122*
Dost Mohammed, emir of
   Afghanistan 180
Drake, Francis 118
Dreadnought, HMS *190*
Dreyfus case 188
Duncan, king of Scots 59
Durer, Albrecht *112*
Dutch *see* Netherlands
Dutch East India Company 134
Dutch East Indies 134
Dutch Wars 139
Dutch West India Company 139

E
Early civilizations 5–21
East Bengal *see* Bangladesh
Eastern Orthodox Church 55
Eastern Roman empire *see*
   Byzantine empire
Easter Rebellion
East India Company 134, 148, 178
East Pakistan *see* Bangladesh
Ebert, Friedrich 206
Ecuador *166*, 167
Edward I, king of England 83
Edward II, king of England 83
Edward III, king of England 87, 90
Edward IV, king of England 101
Edward V, king of England 101
Edward the Black Prince 90, 225
Edward the Confessor, king of
   England 68
EEC *see* European Economic
   Community
EFTA *see* European Free Trade
   Association
Egbert 54
Egypt, ancient 12, 32
   modern 216, 220
Eisenhower, Dwight D. 227
El Alamein 208, 227
Eleanor of Aquitaine 74

Energy crisis 222
Engels, Friedrich 172
England
   Armada *98*, 118
   Civil War 74, 133
   Hundred Years' War 87
   John of Gaunt 90
   Magna Carta 79
   Norman conquest 68
   Parliament 80
   rulers 230
   Saxons and Danes 54
English East India Company 134
Ephesus 14
Epic of Gilgamesh 8
Ericsson, Leif 58
Eritrea 206
Essex, kingdom of 54
Estates-General 158
Ethelbald 54
Ethelred 54
Ethelwulf 54
Ethiopia 184, 206, 216
Etruscans 11, *11*
Euclid 22
Eugène, prince of Savoy 142, *143*, 226
Euphrates, river 8
Euripides *22*
Europe 46, 88, 173, 174
European Economic Community 217
European Free Trade Association
   217
Evans, Arthur 9
Everest, Mount *214*
Evesham, battle of 80
Exploration 93, 104, 219
Explorer I satellite 219

F
Fairfax, Thomas 226
Falangists 207
February Revolution 200, 201
Ferdinand, king of Bohemia 130
Ferdinand, king of Castile and
   Aragon 103
Feudal System 65, 88
Field of Cloth of Gold *98*
Fire of London *136*, 137
Flood, The Great 8
Florence 102
Flying shuttle 162
Ford, Gerald 221
France
   Angevins 74
   Burgundy 102
   Capetians 63
   Coalition Wars 161

   colonialism 148, 161, 163, 184
   Franco-Prussian War 182
   Hundred Years' War 87
   Indochina War 215
   Napoleonic Wars 164
   Revolution 158
   rulers of 81, 136, 231
   St Bartholomew's Day Massacre
     118
Francis I, Holy Roman emperor 146
Franciscans 84
Franco, Francisco 207
Franco-Prussian War 182, 226
Frankfurt, Treaty of 182
Franklin, Benjamin 160
Franks 225
Franz Ferdinand, archduke of
   Austria 198
Frederick, Elector Palatine 130
Frederick the Great, king of Prussia
   148
French East India Company 134
French Revolution 152, *152*, 158, 160
Friars 84, *84*

G
Gagarin, Yuri 218, *218*
Galileo, Galilei *120*, 128
Gama, Vasco da *see* Da Gama,
   Vasco
Garibaldi, Giuseppe 180
Gaul *40*, 44
Genghis Khan 76, *76*
George I, king of Gt Britain 143
Germany
   colonialism 184
   Munich agreement 208
   Weimar Republic 206
   World Wars I and II 198, 210
Gettysburg, battle of 226
Giotto *112*, 113
Girondins 159
Ghana 57, 95
Gods, Roman 36
Goethe, Johann Wolfgang von 157
Gold Coast *see* Ghana
Golden Horde 76
Gordon, Charles 183
Gorgias 22
Gospels 37
Gothic architecture 72, *78*, *81*
Goths 45
Grand Alliance 142
Grant, Ulysses S. 226
Gravitation, theory of 138
Great Britain 143
   ancient Britain *40*, 54

colonialism 178, 180, 184, 186
Crimean War 179
Industrial revolution 162
Munich agreement 208
rulers 230
Suez crisis 216
World Wars I and II 198, 208
Great Charter *see* Magna Carta
Great Northern War 138
Great Schism 91
Great Trek 170
Great Wall of China 90
Greece, ancient 18, *18*, 22, 23, 225
Greenland 58, *58*
Gregorian calendar 120, 201
Gregory VII, Pope 66
Gregory XI, Pope 91
Gregory XII, Pope 91
Guinea-Bissau 222
Gupta dynasty *15*, 42, *42*
Gustavus Adolphus 130, *130*
Gutenberg, Johannes 100, *100*

H
Habsburgs 80, 146, 228
Haiti 161
Hannibal 30
Hanover, house of 230
Hanseatic League 89, *89*
Harappa 10
Harold II, king of England 68
Harold Haardraada, king of Norway 68
Harun al-Raschid 57
Harvey, William 128
Hastings, battle of 68, *68*, 225
Hebrews 13
Hegira 53
Henri, duke of Guise 121
Henri III, king of France 121
Henri IV, king of France 118, 121
Henri of Navarre *see* Henri IV, king of France
Henry I, king of England 74
Henry II, king of England 74
Henry III, king of England 80
Henry IV, Holy Roman emperor 66
Henry IV, king of England 90
Henry IV of Castile 103
Henry V, king of England 87
Henry VI, king of England 101
Henry VII, king of England 90, 101
Henry VIII, king of England *98*, 108
Henry the Navigator 93
Heptarchy 54
Herculaneum 38
Herod dynasty 35

Hero of Alexandria 22
Hillary, Edmund *214*
Hindenburg, Paul von 206
Hindus 212
Hipparchus 22
Hiroshima 210
Hitler, Adolf 206, *207*, 208, 210
Ho Chi Minh 215
Hohenstaufen kings and emperors 228
Holy Land 71
Holy Roman empire 56, 60, *60*, 66, *66*, 80, 130, 228
Homo erectus 8
Homo sapiens 8
Homo sapiens sapiens 8
Houston, Sam 170
Howard of Effingham, Lord 118
Hubertsburg, Treaty of 148
Huguenots 118, 136
Humanism 113
Hundred Years' War 87, *88*, *94*
Hungary 62
Huns 44, 45

I
Ibo people 220
Iceland 58, *58*
Impressionism 185
Incas 107, 110
Inchon, battle of 227
Independence, American War of 152, 156, *156*, 160
India 27, 42, 110, 212
Indian Mutiny 178
Indies 104
Indochina 215
Industrial Revolution 152, 162
Indus Valley civilization 10
Inkerman, battle of 179
Inoculation *160*, 187
Inquisition 103
Intelsat IV satellite 219
'Intolerable Acts' 156
Ireland 171, 201
Irish Republican Army (IRA) 223
Irish Republican Brotherhood 201
Isabella, queen of Castile and Aragon 103
Islam *46*, *52*, 53
Israel 41, 212, 216
Israelites 13
Israeli Wars 220
Istanbul 95
Italy
    Abyssinian campaign 206
    Medici 102

Spanish Civil War 207
    unified 180
    World Wars I and II 198, 208
Ivan V, tsar of Russia 138
Ivan the Terrible, tsar of Russia 114

J
Jacobins 159, *160*
Jacobite Rebellion 147
James I, king of England 143
James II, king of England 147
James V, king of Scotland 119
James VI, king of Scotland *see* James I, king of England
Jameson, Leander Starr 186
Jansz, Willem 122
Japan
    Meiji period 182
    Russo-Japanese War 190
    shoguns 77, *77*, 123
    World Wars I and II 198, 208, 209, 210
Jeanne d'Arc *94*
Jefferson, Thomas 157, 163
Jellicoe, John 226
Jena and Auerstädt, battles of 164, 226
Jenner, Edward *160*
Jerusalem 13, 41, 71
Jesuits 108
Jesus Christ 34, *34*
Jews 35, 41, 67, 103, 212
Joan of Arc *see* Jeanne d'Arc *94*
John XXIII, Pope 91
John, king of England 79
John Balliol, king of Scotland 83, *83*
John of Gaunt 90
John the Apostle 37
Jones, Inigo 132
Jordan 220
Judaea 35
Juan I of Castile 90
Judah 13
Julius Casesar *see* Caesar, Julius
Justinian I, Byzantine emperor 54
Jutes 54
Jutland, battle of 199, 226

K
Ka'aba 53
Kangaroo 150
Kay, John 162
Kaya Maghan Sisse, king of Ghana 57
Kennedy, John F. 218
Kenneth II, king of Scots 59
Kenneth MacAlpine, king of Scots 59

Kent, kingdom of 54
Kepler, Johannes *120*
Kerensky, Aleksandr 200
Khartoum, siege of 183
Khrushchev, Nikita 218, *218*
Kimberley, siege of 186
Knighthood, Orders of 72
Knights Hospitallers 72
Knights Templars 72
Knossos 9, *9*
Koran 53
Korean War 214, 227
Kruger, Paulus 186
Kuang Hsü, emperor of China 193
Kublai Khan 76
Kung Fu-tzu *see* Confucius
Kyoto 123

L

Ladysmith, siege of 186
LAFTA *see* Latin American Free
   Trade Association
Lagash 8
Laing's Neck, battle of 186
Lancaster, house of 101, 230
Laos 215
Lares 36
Latin American Free Trade
   Association 217
Latin League 25
Latins 14
Latium 14, 25
League of Augsburg *see* Augsburg,
   League of
League of Nations 203
Lee, Robert E. 226
Legion 31
Leipzig, battle of 164, 226
Lenin, Vladimir Ilyich 200
Leningrad 200; siege of 208
Leonardo da Vinci 113
Lepanto, battle of *116*, 117, *122*
Lepidus, Marcus *see* Marcus
   Lepidus
Leszczynski, Stanislaus 144, 147
Levant 12, 74
Lewes, battle of 80
Lexington, battle of 156
Leyte Gulf, battle of 227
Liberia 184, 216
Libya 206, 216
Licinius, Roman emperor 39
Lindbergh, Charles 203
Liverpool and Manchester Railway
   168
Locomotive *168*
Lorenzo the Magnificent 102, *102*

Louis IX, king of France 81
Louis XIV, king of France 136, *136*,
   140
Louis XVI, king of France 158
Louisiana Purchase 163
Low Countries 122
Loyola, Ignatius *108*
Luke the Evangelist 37
Luther, Martin 108, *108*
Lützen, battle of 131
Lvov, Georgi 200
Lysander 225

M

Macbeth, king of Scotland 59
Mafeking, siege of 186
Maga dynasty 57
Magellan, Ferdinand 105
Magna Carta 79, *79*
Magyars 62
Mahdi 183
Majuba Hill, battle of 186
Malcolm II, king of Scots 59
Malcolm III, king of Scots 59
Mali empire 85
Malik Shah 66
Malta 116
Man, early 5, *6*, 8
Manchus 193
Mandingo people 85
Mao Tse-tung 212, *213*
Marathon, battle of 225
Marcus Antonius 32, 33, 35
Marcus Lepidus 33
Margaret, Maid of Norway 83
Maria Theresa, empress of Austria
   146
Mark the Evangelist 37
Mark Antony *see* Marcus
   Antonius
Marlborough, John Churchill, duke
   of 142, 226
Marne, battle of 226
Martin V, Pope 91
Marx, Karl 172
Mary, Queen of Scots 119, *119*
Massaccio 113
Massinissa, king of Numidia 30
Matilda, queen of England 74
Matthew the Apostle 37
Maurya empire 27, 42
Maxentius, Roman emperor 43
Maximian, Roman emperor 41
Mayas 61, 107
Mayflower 129
Mecca 53
Media 16

Medici family 102
Medieval period *see* Middle Ages
Medina 53
Meiji period 182
Mendicant orders 84
Menes, king of Upper Egypt 12
Mercia, kingdom of 54
Mercury 36
Messenia 23
Metternich, Prince Klemens von 173
Mexican-American War 224
Mexico 107, 170
Michelangelo *112*, 113
Middle Ages 46–49, *60*
   art and treasure 72, *72*, *73*
   Crusades 71, 72
   feudal system 65, *65*
   Hanseatic league 89
   monks 50, *51*
   Pope v emperor 66
Middle Kingdom 12
Midway, battle of 210, 227
Milvian Bridge, battle of 43
Minamoto family 77
Ming dynasty 90
Minoan civilization 9
Mohammed II, the Conqueror 95
Mohammed Ahmed of Dongola
Mohenjo-Daro 10
Moluccas 104
Monasticism 50, 51, *73*, 84
Mongol empire 76, 90, 95, 110
Montcalm, Marquis de 226
Monte Cassino, monastery of 51
Monteverdi, Claudio 132
Montfort, Simon de *see* De Montfort,
   Simon
Montgomery, Bernard 227
Morse, Samuel 168
Moscow 164
Mossi Kingdom 85
Motion, laws of 138
Motor car *176*
Mozambique 222
Mughal empire 76, 110, *120*, *133*, 134
Muhammad *46*, 53
Mukden, battle of 190
Munich agreement 208
Muslims 71, 85, *85*, 212
Mussolini, Benito 206, 208, 209
Mustafa Kemal *see* Ataturk, Kemal
Mutsuhito, emperor of Japan 182
Mycenae 9

N

Nagasaki 210
Nanda dynasty 27

Napier, John 128
Napoleon Bonaparte 163, 164, *164*, *166*
Napoleonic Wars 164, 226
Naseby, battle of 226
Nasser, Gamal Abdul 216
National Convention of France 158
Nations, battle of the 226
Nazi Party 206, *207*, 208
Neanderthal Man *6*, 8
Nebuchadrezzar 14
Nelson, Horatio 164, 226
Nero, Roman emperor 39
Netherlands 122, *122*, 208
'New Deal' 211
New Kingdom 12
Newton, Isaac 138
New York 139
Nguni people 166
Nicaea 43
Nicholas II, tsar of Russia 200
Nicomedia 41
Nigeria 220
Nightingale, Florence 179
Nile, battle of the 226
Nile Valley civilization 12
Nixon, Richard M. 221
Norman Conquest 68
Normandy invasion 210, 227
Normans 58, 65
North African campaigns 208, 209
Northern Ireland 222
North Korea 214
Northmen *see* Vikings
North Pole *174*
North Sea oil 222
Northumbria, kingdom of 54
Numidia 30
Nystadt, Peace of 144

O

October Revolution 200
October War 220
O'Higgins, Bernardo 167
Oil 222
Old Kingdom 12
Olmecs *21*
Olympia 23
Olympias 26
Opera 132
Oprichniks 114
Orange Free State 170
Oratorio 132
Orléans, siege of 225
Ostrogoths 45
Otto I, the Great, Holy Roman emperor 62

Ottoman empire 95, 114, 116, 117, 179, 205, 225
Ouverture, Toussaint L' 161

P

Pacific War 209
Paine, Thomas 160
Pakistan 212, 220
Palatine hill 14
Palestine 71
Panipat, battle of 110
Papacy 66, 84, 91
Papal States 180
Paraguay *166*, 167
Paris, Peace of (1763) 148; (1919) 199, 208
Paris, Treaty of (1783) 157; (1856) 179
Parliament 80, 133
Passchendaele 226
Pasteur, Louis 187
Patricians 24
Paulus, Friedrich von 227
Pearl Harbor 209
Peary, Robert *174*
Pedro I of Castile 90
Peking, siege of 88
Peloponnesian War 23
Penates 36
Peninsular War 164
Pericles 18, 22
Persian empire 16, *17*, 26
Persis *see* Persian empire
Peru 110
Peter III, tsar of Russia 148
Peter the Great, tsar of Russia 138, 226
Petrarch 72, *72*
Petrograd 200
Pharaoh 12
Pharos of Alexandria 14
Phidias 14
Philip II, king of Macedonia 23, 26
Philip II, king of Spain *98*, 118, 122
Philip of Anjou 142
Philip the Tetrarch 35
Philistines 13
Philosophy 22
Phoenicians 12
Picts 54
Piedmont-Sardinia, kingdom of 180
Pilgrim Fathers 129
Pisa, council of 91
Pi Sheng 100
Pizarro, Francisco 110
Plague *see* Black Death
Plains of Abraham 226

Plantagenets 74, 230
Plato 22
Plebeians 24
Plessey, battle of 226
Plessis, Jean du *see* Richelieu, Cardinal
Plymouth, Mass. 129
Poitiers, battle of 225
Poland 147, 208
Polo, Maffeo, Marco, Nicolò 82, *82*
Pompei *21*, 38
Poltava, battle of 226
Pompey 32
Pope *see* Papacy
Port Arthur 190
Portsmouth Conference 190
Portugal 93, 167, 222
Potato famine 171
Prague *46*
Prestonpans, battle of 147
Pretoria, treaty of 186
Printing 100, *100*
Prohibition *202*
Protagoras 22
Protestantism 108, 111, 118, 121, 122, 130, 223
Prussia 148, 158, 164, 182, 226
Ptolemy XIII 32
Ptolemy XIV 32
Ptolemy XV 32
Punic Wars 30
Puritans 129, 133
P'u Yi, emperor of China 193
Pyramids 12, 14

Q

Quattrocento 113
Quebec, battle of 148, 226

R

Radium *187*
Rahman, Mujibur 220
Railways 162, 168, *168*
Raphael 113
Reformation 108, *108*, 111
'Reign of Terror' 159, *159*
Religious Orders 51, 84
Renaissance 96–105, *112*, 113, *120*
Rhodes, Cecil 186
Rhodesia (Zimbabwe) 216
Richard II, king of England 90
Richard III, king of England 101
Richelieu, Cardinal 130, *131*
Rights of Man (Paine) 160
Rizzio, David 119
Robert II, the Pious, king of France *63*

Robespierre, Maximilien 159, *159*
Roman Catholic Church 108, 119
Romanesque architecture 72
Romantic Movement 146, 152
Rome, ancient 14, 18
  army 31
  battles 225
  classes 24
  decline of 41
  emperors 220
  empire 35
  house *24*
  Latin League 25
  persecution of Christians 39
  Pompeii *21*, 38
  triumverates 32
Rommel, Erwin 227
Romulus and Remus 14, *14*
Romulus Augustus, Roman emperor 41
Roosevelt, Franklin D. 211, *211*
Roses, Wars of the *see* Wars of the Roses
Roundheads 133
Rousseau, Jean-Jacques 146, *146*
Rubens, Peter Paul 132
Rudolf IV, Holy Roman emperor 80, *80*
Runnymede 79
Russia
  Crimean War 179
  Cuban crisis 218
  Korean War 214
  Napoleonic Wars 164
  Peter the Great 138
  revolution 200, *200*, 201
  Russo-Japanese War 190, 224
  World Wars I and II 198, 208, 210
Russ tribe 58
Ryswick, treaty of 140

S
Saguntum 30
St Anthony of Thebes 51
St Bartholomew's Day 118, *118*
St Benedict 51
St Dominic 84
Saint-Chapelle *81*
St Francis of Assisi 84
St Helena 164
St Michael Salient, battle of 227
Sakhalin Island 190
Salamis, battle of 225
Salazar, António 222
Salem witches 141
Samurdragupta 42
Sankore mosque 85

San Martin, José de *166*, 167
Santa Anna, Antonio de 170
Santa Maria 104
Saracens 71, 225
Satellites, man-made 219
Saul of Tarsus 34
Saxons 54, 68, 228
Scheer, Rheinhard 226
Schism *see* Great Schism
Schmalkaldic League 111
Schuschnigg, Kurt von 206
Scipio, Publius Cornelius 30
Scotland
  ancient 59
  Balliol and Bruce 83
  Jacobites 147
  Mary, Queen of 119
  rulers 230
Sedan, battle of 226
Seleucus Nicator 27
Seljuk Turks 66
Semitic people 8, 13
Serbia 198
Serf 65
Settlement, Act of *see* Act of Settlement
Seven Wonders of the World 14
Seven Years' War 148
Seyss-Inquart, Arthur 206
Shah Jahan, Mughal emperor *133*, 134
Shah Sujah, emir of Afghanistan 180
Shang dynasty 10
Sher Ali, emir of Afghanistan 180
Shoguns 77, *77*, 123, 182
Siddhartha Gautama 15
Sidon 12
Silesia 143, 148
Six Day War 220
Sklodowska, Marja *187*
Slavery 161, 170, *170*
Socrates 22
Somme, battle of 226
Soninke tribe 57
Sophia, princess of Hanover 143
Sophists 22
Sophocles *22*
South Africa 186, 216
South African Wars 186
South America *166*, 167
South Korea 214
Space exploration 219
Spain
  Armada *98*, 118
  Civil War 207
  colonialism 110, *166*, 167
  Ferdinand and Isabella 103

Habsburgs 80, 122
Peninsular War 164
Spanish-American War 224
Spanish Netherlands *123*, 142
Spanish succession *124*, 142
Sparta 23
Spice Islands 104
Spice trade 74, 104
Spinning 162
Sputnik satellite 219
Stalin, Joseph 211, *211*
Stalingrad, siege of 208, 227
Stamford Bridge, battle of 68
Statute of Westminster 204
Steam engine 162, 168
Stephen, king of Hungary 62
Stephen of Blois 74
Stuart, house of 143, 147, 226, 230
Stuyvesant, Peter 139, *139*
Sudan 183, 184
Sudetenland 208
Suez Canal 216
Suez crisis 216
Sulaiman, king of Mali 85
Suleiman I, sultan 114, *114*, 116
Sumerians 8
Sung dynasty 62
Sun Ti, Mongol emperor 90
Sun Yat-sen, president of China 193
Sussex, kingdom of 54
Sweden 130, 144, 226
Syracuse, siege of 225
Syria 220
Szigetvár, siege of *114*

T
T'ai Tsu, Ming emperor 62, 90
Taj Mahal *133*
Tallard, Camille de 226
Tamerlane 76, *90*, 95, 110
T'ang dynasty *52*
Tasman, Abel 150
Telegraph 168
Temujin *see* Genghis Khan
Tenochtitlán 107, *107*
Tensing, Sherpa *214*
Terra Australis Incognita 122, 150
Teutoberg Forest, battle of 225
Texas 170
Thales 22
Thebes 23
Themistocles 225
Theodoric 225
Theodosius I, Roman emperor 41
Thirty Years' War *126*, 130, *130*
Thomas à Becket 74, *75*
Three Emperors, battle of the 226

Three Henrys, War of the 121
Tigris, river 8
Timbuktu 85, *85*
Timur the Lame *see* Tamerlane
Titanic 193
Tokugawa family 77, 123, 182
Tokyo 123
Torricelli, Evangelista 128
Tostig 68
Tours, battle of 225
Toussaint L'Ouverture 161
Tower of Babel 8
Trafalgar, battle of 164, 226
Trajan, Roman emperor *40*
Transvaal 170, 186
Trifanum, battle of 25
Triple Alliance 198
Triple Entente 198
Triumverate 32
Trotsky, Leon 200
Tsushima Straits, battle of 190
Tudor, house of 101, 230
Turkey 198, 205
Turkish empire 66, *94*, 95, 116, *116*, 117, 179, 205
Tutankhamun *5*
Two Sicilies, Kingdom of the *66*
Tyre 12
Tz'u Hsi, empress dowager of China *190*

U
Ulster *see* Northern Ireland
Unemployment 204, 206
Union, Act of *see* Act of Union
United Nations 212, *213*, 214, 220
United States of America
    Cuban crisis 218
    Depression 204
    discovery of 104
    independence 156
    Louisiana purchase 163
    Presidents 231
    prohibition *202*
    Watergate scandal 221
    World Wars I and II 198, 209, 210

Urban II, Pope 71
Urban VI, Pope 91
Uruk 8
Utrecht, treaty of 142

V
Vaccination *160*, 187
Valetta 116
Valette, Jean Parisot de la 116
Valmy, battle of 158, 226
Vandals 45
Van Dyck, Anthony 132
Velázquez, Diego 132
Venezuela *166*, 167
Venice 74, 82, 117
Venus 36
Verdun, battle of 226
Versailles, treaty of 199
Vespucci, Amerigo 104
Vesuvius 38
Vicksburg, battle of 226
Victoria, queen of Gt Britain *173*
Viet Minh League 215
Vietnam 215
Vietnam War 215, 224
Vikings 54, 58, *58*
Visigoths 41, 45, 225
Voltaire (François Marie Arouet) 151, *151*

W
Waldeseemüller, Martin 104
Wallace, William 83
War of 1812   224
War of the League of Augsburg 140
Wars, major 224
Wars of the Roses 101
Washington, George 157
Watergate scandal 221
Waterloo, battle of 164, 226
Watt, James 162
Weaving 162
Wedmore, treaty of 54
Weimar Republic 206
Wellesley, Arthur *see* Wellington, Duke of

Wellington, Duke of 164
Wenceslas, king of Bohemia *46*, 51
Wessex, kingdom of 54
West Indies 104, 161
West Pakistan 220
Westphalia, Peace of 130
Whitten-Brown, Arthur 203
William I, the Conqueror, king of England 68
William I, kaiser of Germany 182
William II, kaiser of Germany 206
William III, king of England 226
William the Silent 122
Wilson, Woodrow 203
Windsor, house of 230
Wright, Orville and Wilbur *189*
Writing 8
Witchcraft 141
Wolfe, James 226
World War I 194, 198, *198*, *199*, 202, *202*, 226
World War II 194, 207, 208–211, *208*, 227

X   Y   Z
Xerxes 225
Yakub Khan 180
Yalta conference *211*
Yamamoto, Isoruko 227
'Year of Revolutions' 172
Yin dynasty *see* Shang dynasty
Yom Kippur War *see* October War
York, house of 101, 230
Yorktown, battle of 157, 226
Young Turks 205
Ypres, battle of 226, 227
Yuan dynasty 76
Yüan Shih K'ai, emperor of China 193
Zama, battle of 225
Zeppelin airship 199
Zeus 14
Ziggurat 8
Zola, Emile 188
Zulus 166

ACKNOWLEDGEMENTS

Aldus 148–149; Ashmolean Museum 45; Associated Press 196 (top); Atomic Energy Commission 209; Biblioth que Nationale, Paris 94, 107; Bildarchiv, Berlin 130; Bodleian Library 88 (top); British and Foreign Bible Society 111; British Museum 5, 11, 16 (top), 17, 36, 42, 43, 49, 79, 82 (top), 89, 92, 99, 110, 119, 164, 169 (top), 229; British Tourist Authority 40; Peter Clayton 29; Freer Gallery, Washington 12; French Tourist Office 86; Giraudon 64, 136, 169 (bottom), 184 (right); Sonia Halliday 21 (centre), 23, 32–33, 34, 37, 46 (left), 54–55, 73, 81, 114, 205; Robert Harding 10, 16 (bottom), 28, 52 (left), 70 (top), 85; Michael Holford 4, 15, 42 (bottom), 46 (right), 68, 69, 77, 109, 120, 150; Imperial War Museum 198, 200 (top), 210; Keystone Press 216, 220; Mansell Collection 14, 26, 31, 34, 38, 50, 62, 66, 75, 79, 80, 88 (bottom), 93, 98 (top), 101, 102, 115, 118, 120, 142, 144, 149, 151, 152, 154 (bottom), 156, 158, 159, 160 (right), 162, 163, 165, 168, 170, 172, 174 (left), 178, 180, 182, 183, 187, 191, 192, 194 (right), 204 (bottom), 227; Mauritshuis, Hague 132; Mary Evans Picture Library 63, 82 (centre), 89, 94 (bottom), 100 (bottom), 122, 126 (bottom), 131, 134, 135, 136 (bottom), 138, 139, 143, 144 (top), 146, 157, 160 (left), 186 (bottom), 189; Pat Morris 140; William Morris Museum 186 (top); Musé es de la Ville, Strasbourg 128 (right); National Army Museum 124; National Danish Museum 44; National Maritime Museum 98 (bottom), 116–117; National Gallery 96, 112 (left), 184 (left); National Gallery of the Netherlands 128 (left); National Museum, Stockholm 144; National Museum, Taiwan 76; National Portrait Gallery 106, 137, 154 (top), 173, 192; Novosti 196 (bottom), 200 (left), 219; Paris Match 215; Paul Popper Ltd. 213 (top), 214, 218; Press Association 211; Radio Times Hulton Picture Library 194 (left), 202; Scala, Milan 84, 100 (top); Science Museum 171, 188, 190 (top); Statens Historiska Museum 58–59; Syndication International 222; Topkapi Museum, Istanbul 52 (bottom right); United Nations 213 (bottom); Victoria and Albert Museum 27, 70 (bottom), 190 (bottom); Zefa 21, 56.